ROYAL GARDENS OF THE WORLD

21 Celebrated Gardens from the Alhambra to Highgrove and Beyond

MARK LANE

KYLE BOOKS

An Hachette UK Company
www.hachette.co.uk

First published in the Great Britain in 2020 by Kyle Books, an imprint of
Octopus Publishing Group Limited
Carmelite House
50 Victoria Embankment
London EC4Y 0DZ
www.kylebooks.co.uk

Distributed in the US by
Hachette Book Group
1290 Avenue of the Americas
4th and 5th Floors
New York, NY 10104

Distributed in Canada by
Canadian Manda Group
664 Annette St.
Toronto, Ontario, Canada M6S 2C8

Publisher: Joanna Copestick
Editor: Jenny Dye
Design and Map Illustrations: Robin Rout
Picture Research: Giulia Hetherington
Production Manager: Lisa Pinnell

ISBN 978-0-85783-801-8

A CIP catalogue record for this book is available from the British Library.

Printed and bound in China

10 9 8 7 6 5 4

HALF-TITLE & TITLE PAGES
The Alhambra, Granada, Spain (see page 122)
Fontainebleau Palace, Paris, France (see page 80)

OPPOSITE
The Grand Trianon, Versailles, France (see page 90)

CONTENTS

INTRODUCTION 6

ENGLAND .... HAMPTON COURT PALACE 12

.... HIGHGROVE 24

.... ROYAL BOTANIC GARDENS, KEW 34

SCOTLAND .... CASTLE OF MEY 44

GERMANY .... HERRENHAUSEN 54

.... SCHWERIN CASTLE 68

FRANCE .... FONTAINEBLEAU PALACE 80

.... VERSAILLES 90

ITALY .... ROYAL PALACE OF CASERTA 102

.... LA VENARIA REALE 114

SPAIN .... THE ALHAMBRA 122

AUSTRIA .... SCHÖNBRUNN 132

CZECH REPUBLIC .... PRAGUE CASTLE 142

THE NETHERLANDS .. HET LOO PALACE 152

SWEDEN .... DROTTNINGHOLM PALACE 164

DENMARK .... FREDENSBORG PALACE 174

.... FREDERIKSBORG PALACE 184

RUSSIA .... PETERHOF PALACE 194

INDIA .... TAJ MAHAL 208

BALI .... TIRTA GANGGA 216

JAPAN .... TOKYO IMPERIAL PALACE 224

BIBLIOGRAPHY.. 234

INDEX.. 237

PICTURE CREDITS 239

ACKNOWLEDGEMENTS 240

'GARDENS MAY HAVE BEEN IN CERTAIN PLACES FOR MANY YEARS, BUT,
UNLIKE OLD BUILDINGS, THEY ARE IN A CONSTANT STATE OF CHANGE.'

HRH PRINCE PHILIP

For many years I have thought about creating a 'Grand Tour' book of some of the most iconic royal gardens, as a result of my art history days at University College London and as a former Publishing Director for the Royal Institute of British Architects. Not being of noble descent, I was under no illusion that, as part of my 'artistic, intellectual and sentimental education', I had to visit every royal garden in the world, as many men and some women undertook during the seventeenth and eighteenth centuries. The revival of the European Grand Tour during the nineteenth century became easier, of course, with the advent of the railway. Historically, predominantly men of means travelled for about six months and lived abroad for a further three years as part of their 'coming of age', yet my fascination with gardens and plants and with plant experts started when I was very young and it has remained with me. I have been fortunate in that I have travelled to many countries and it still amazes me how excited I become when visiting a new place or garden or encountering a plant I have never seen before.

Many royal families, rulers, supreme authorities, patrons, head gardeners, landscape designers and plantsmen and women have, over the past 500 years, created remarkable gardens, viewing them as living artforms that have evolved to reflect the changing fashions and preoccupations of the monarchy and the tastes and fashions of their time. I should know, as I have researched some 950 individuals to write this book. But, like any garden, the royal ones are also a reflection of an individual's personality. While there may be similarities in design terms, this sameness pays homage to a myriad of expeditions, Grand Tours and personal trips, as well as the marriages between and political links forged by royal households throughout the world. For some, the garden – its design, its plants and its features – was an all-consuming passion. And 'passion' really is the best word to describe the aspirations, hopes and dreams that are reflected in what I believe to be very personal gardens, very often the fascination of strong-willed, powerful, well-educated noblewomen, from Marie Antoinette to Her Majesty the Queen Mother.

Collectively, there is a rich and varied history behind royal gardens and delving into their past has been exciting, rewarding and sometimes unexpected. It was a challenge to limit myself to 21 royal gardens that I believe have had an impact on garden design and history, and to focus on just a few key dates, aspects and architectural features throughout history. These are renowned spaces that I feel have had an important role in garden design and garden history; they are not a collection of the 'greatest' or the 'best' royal gardens to visit. From medieval hunting parks to mausoleums to water gardens, *Royal Gardens of the World* is a feast for the eyes, and an insight into the theatre of politics, power, personages and personalities. All of the gardens in this book are open to the public, though some have private inner spaces. Public access is important to me, as I want readers to be inspired to visit these magnificent gardens as I have done, to sit in the arbours, walk the avenues and perhaps sail the waters, just as monarchs, emperors and their ennobled entourage down the centuries have done.

It goes without saying that this book champions the royal gardeners, both paid and voluntary. Not every leader or patron was a keen gardener or had an interest in landscape design, but those noble individuals who saw the beauty in nature, whether to train it, overpower it or live alongside the wildness and naturalistic powers and splendour of nature we need to thank. And, during later years, it is the indefatigable work of restorers, conservators and historians who have injected life back into these landscapes.

There are many royal gardens across the world, but my aim here is to showcase the history of each space, with an emphasis on the horticultural feel and style of each garden that the patrons and the gardeners have created. Many more royal gardens are waiting to be visited and researched, each tells its own story. I am simply the interpreter and the messenger. Sometimes, the story focuses on restoration, others follow the lives of the main protagonists and others still simply chart the course of history. It is also worth noting that history is not isolated; these gardens are a response to events occurring throughout history across Europe, Russia, the Far East and elsewhere. And marriages between members of royal households to forge allied territories and create new courts in turn introduced different ideals and creative passions which were reflected in the architecture of their residences and gardens.

As you can imagine, each one of the world's royal gardens could have an entire book written on it, so my intention is to celebrate the glorious 'art of gardening' through some of the world's eminent horticultural jewels. Many argue that gardening is not an art form, but this collection of stunning photographs, plans and insights into some of the world's leading landscape designers clearly support my case that gardening and garden design are artworks and as such bring fulfilment, a sense of wonder and a passion for the living world. Like fine art, gardens and the architecture within them can be experienced in many ways by different people, whether seen in the heat of summer or the cold of winter, on a bright or dull day, from reading the varied written accounts at the time of the creation of the gardens to contemporary interpretations. As such, gardens as art create discussion and critique.

Early Royal Garden Design

Many readers may think of André Le Nôtre, principal gardener and landscape architect to Louis XIV of France (see page 93), as the first to make his mark on the royal gardens scene, but he was preceded by a dynasty of gardeners, the Mollet family, who had already established a French garden style throughout Europe, with the development of the parterre – a geometric ornamental garden – which, as art historian Sir Roy Strong notes:

'evolved during the Renaissance but reached its classic formula in France. The main form it took was known as a parterre de broderie *or embroidered parterre, a symmetrical geometric pattern in clipped green box … set against coloured grounds made of brickdust, gravel, blue cobalt, sand, and even coal dust and ground bones.'*

These ornate gardens, representing man's power over nature, were placed close to the house or created in view from rooms on the first floor. André Mollet's book *Le Jardin de Plaisir* (1651) proved highly influential and was originally translated into Swedish and German (later into English after Mollet's death) and described how the house (or palace) and its garden create 'unity' based on a central axis, often with a large expanse of water or a series of fountains, with radiating avenues with sculpture set within a tree-lined rectangle. At a distance from the house the lands become parkland primarily for hunting, which were later developed into the so-called English landscape movement. Sometimes, the garden close to the property was divided into two mirrored, symmetrical parts with a central axis and *bosquets*, geometrically planted copses, with intricately shaped lawns bordered by low hedges.

The English landscape movement, prefaced by the French style that dominated Europe, ushered in a new, revolutionary style, one that was associated with theology, art, literature and even Newtonian science. The *jardin anglais* bridged the formal geometric layout of the French style and the freer style that hallmarked gardens in the 1750s and 1760s. These gardens were much more economical to maintain; they became places to wander, rather than sights of wonder. With the growth of botany as a subject, botanic gardens – Kew in particular – placed Britain at the forefront of botanical science. Many palaces, royal houses and their gardens were altered and remodelled. Gardens became stage sets, romantic pictures, and by the mid-1850s, pleasure grounds with flower gardens. In the twentieth century, after the destruction of the First World War, garden design embraced Modernist ideas, simplifying garden layouts and planting. By the 1970s and 1980s cottage gardening took hold again with the rise of the ecological movement. As Sir Roy Strong observed:

'We live in a new age of garden history; conservation and restoration are the keynotes of this century [and the twenty-first century]. *The royal gardens are as important as any of the royal palaces* [and other types of building] *and need to be accorded the same degree of sensitive care and consideration… Other royal gardens in Europe, those belonging to now vanished dynasties, are the subject of painstaking restoration to their pristine glory.'*

Tastes, priorities and fashion change, but the central perception of all royal gardens is to leave a living legacy, a natural work of art, which adapts, morphs and reinvents itself.

HAMPTON COURT PALACE

ENGLAND

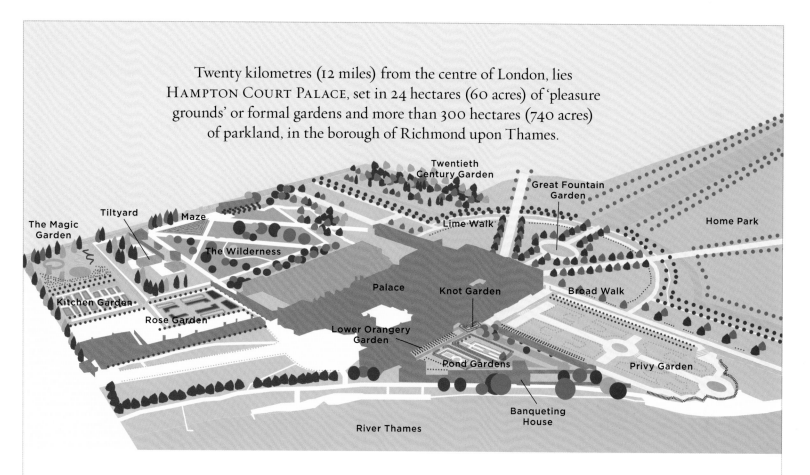

Twenty kilometres (12 miles) from the centre of London, lies HAMPTON COURT PALACE, set in 24 hectares (60 acres) of 'pleasure grounds' or formal gardens and more than 300 hectares (740 acres) of parkland, in the borough of Richmond upon Thames.

The first buildings at Hampton Court belonged to the Order of the Knights Hospitaller of St John of Jerusalem, a religious-military order founded in the eleventh century. The English branch of the Order bought the Manor of Hampton in 1236, a small establishment with land known as a 'camera'. The Grand Prior of the Knights Hospitaller Order constructed a manor house of brick and stone, in c. 1500, and in 1514 the property was leased by Cardinal Thomas Wolsey, Archbishop of York, Lord Chancellor of England and a favourite of Henry VIII (1491–1547); Hampton Court Palace was to be built as Wolsey's private residence. Work started in 1515, with Wolsey himself laying out some of the small knot gardens. However, the cardinal fell from favour between 1528 and 1529 as he was unable to arrange an annulment of Henry's first marriage, to Catherine of Aragon (1485–1536), and Wolsey lost his palace to the king.

More than £62,000 (the equivalent of £18 million today) was spent on rebuilding and extending Hampton Court Palace. Some ten years later, the palace was one of the most modern, sophisticated and magnificent palaces in England. Along with St James's Palace, it is one of only two surviving palaces owned by Henry VIII. Accounts from the time reveal that the king had his privy (private) garden designed in heraldic fashion, and that roses, violets, primroses, 'gilliver-slips, mynts and other sweet flowers', rosemary, and sweet Williams were to be grown.

With the restoration of Charles II (1630–85) in 1660, as a gift from Charles to his new bride, Catherine of Braganza (1638–1705), a canal was dug during the winter of 1661/2 on an east–west alignment, centred on the balcony of the Queen's Lodgings in the middle of the east facade. Known as the Long Water, originally the canal came much closer to the palace. It became an important factor in the subsequent designs both of Sir Christopher Wren's new palace for William and Mary and of William Talman's gardens. The diarist John Evelyn, who visited Hampton Court in 1662, noted, '[The Park] formerly flat, naked piece of ground, now planted with sweete rows of Lime-trees, and the Canale for water now neere perfected.'

PREVIOUS PAGES
Hampton Court Palace from the Privy Garden

OPPOSITE
The Pond Garden with Banqueting House beyond

BAROQUE SPLENDOUR

Built of red brick, Hampton Court is a palace of contrasting yet harmonious architectural styles, influenced by the strong vertical lines of domestic Tudor and perpendicular Gothic, and baroque. William III (1650–1702), popularly known as William of Orange, from 1689 until 1702, was King of England, Ireland and Scotland. He and Queen Mary II (1662–94) moved a large number of plants from their palaces in Holland (Het Loo Palace, see page 152), and, to celebrate the Glorious Revolution (1688), William and Mary commissioned Wren to rebuild Hampton Court Palace and Daniel Marot, a French-born Dutch architect, to create a garden to match its grandeur.

WREN, LE VAU AND MANSART

Wren conceived a modern building as the centrepiece of a vast landscape. His original plan was to demolish the entire Tudor palace, except for the Great Hall; however, neither the time nor money was available, so Wren, together with designer Talman, who worked on the palace interior as well as the gardens, had to be content with rebuilding the king's and queen's main apartments on the south and east sides of the palace, on the site of the old Tudor lodgings. The surviving sketch by Wren of the elevations indicates that the ideas owed much to Louis Le Vau's remodelled Louvre in Paris, France. During William's reign the expansion work on the palace was to rival Versailles (see page 90). Such ambitious plans destroyed much of the original Tudor palace. The Tudor towers and chimneys on the south facades were replaced with the grand and elegant baroque exteriors that dominate the Formal Gardens today. The elevations have a flat, block-like quality that resembles work by Jules Hardouin-Mansart and Louis Le Vau at Versailles.

THE QUEEN'S PASSION FOR PLANTS

The gardens were relandscaped and Dutch gardeners brought to Hampton Court to plant and maintain the gardens, introducing floral varieties from

Holland; it is known that a cargo containing bulbs from Honselaarsdijk arrived at the palace. Mary was passionate about rare plants, and wanted to display her own collection of 'Exoticks', particularly from the Mediterranean, the Canary Islands, the Caribbean, the Americas and Mauritius. With Marot, William and Mary planned flower gardens and a privy garden, located within the south gardens in order to protect tender and exotic species, and bordered on the river side by magnificent gilded wrought-iron screens by Jean Tijou, a master blacksmith. Another feature was some of the earliest greenhouses known in England. Mary's greenhouses, the invention of a Dutch carpenter, Heindrik Floris, incorporated furnaces and flues to maintain the right temperature for delicate plants. Another achievement was the installation of a 'melon ground', where auriculas (also one of Mary's favourites) would grow. Botanist Dr Leonard Plukenet catalogued and detailed more than 2,000 different species and another, Charles Hatton, visited in 1690 and declared having observed 'about 400 rare Indian plants, which were never seen in England'.

Mary died of smallpox in 1694, and the garden designer and writer Stephen Switzer later wrote: 'Upon the death of that illustrious Princess, gardening and all other pleasures were under eclipse with that Prince.' William was deeply affected by the loss of Mary and in 1699 spent £40,000 on new gardening projects. On 16 June 1701 work began on a new Privy Garden, lowering and extending it to afford a view of the Thames from the palace. The earthmoving swept away most traces of the earlier gardens. Work was complete before William's own untimely death in 1702; the king who did more than any other to shape Hampton Court as it is today did not live long enough to enjoy it.

THE INTERNATIONAL STYLE
AND GEORGE I

When George I (1660–1727; formerly Georg Ludwig Elector of Hanover) ascended to the thrones of England, Scotland and Ireland he found Hampton Court very much in the International style, led by France, with a high degree of ornamentation and

ABOVE OPPOSITE
The Broad Walk

BELOW OPPOSITE
The Lime Walk

detail reminiscent of its Dutch origins. George I loved Herrenhausen, the seat of the Hanoverian monarchy in Saxony, which itself has a remarkable baroque garden (see page 54), but spent winters at St James's and summers at Kensington and Hampton Court. He would walk through the gardens with courtiers, six footmen, six Yeomen of the Guard and his mistresses in sedan chairs. He felt comfortable at Hampton Court and liked it just as it was, resulting in very few changes, to the disappointment of the Office of Works and of the Royal Gardens. Sir John Vanbrugh, the Works' Controller, was appointed in 1715 to the newly created post of Surveyor of the Gardens and Waters to several palaces in England, which diminished the position of English gardener and designer Henry Wise who, with George London, had been responsible for many of the alterations at Hampton Court.

FIVE CENTURIES OF GARDENS

Surrounded by parkland and pleasure grounds, the setting for Hampton Court Palace was at once elaborate and extensive. To the north were orchards and to the south the Privy Garden, Pond Garden (the name in reference to the fact that in medieval times this part of the garden was a fish farm) and Mount Garden. On the west side of the palace was Henry VIII's Tiltyard (an enclosed courtyard used for jousting) which, during William III's reign, became the Royal Kitchen Gardens.

Running the length of the Privy Garden is Queen Mary's Bower, which, despite its name, was established in Tudor times, c.1531 rather than during the reign of William III. It is one of the most private and secluded parts of the garden and Queen Mary would often walk beneath the intertwined canopy of trees. One of the most spectacular surviving features of the original Privy Garden is the restored entrance to the Bower of lattice grey-painted iron adorned with gold-leaf symbols of William's four kingdoms. Gardeners have recreated the bower in hornbeam (completed in 1995), all to William's original design.

Near to the Privy Garden is the hedged and terraced Pond Garden designed by Mary II, with a circular pond on its lowest terrace surrounded by formal planting and clipped yews. Adjacent to it, an impressive glasshouse contains what is thought to be the world's oldest and largest grapevine. The vine is a Black Hamburg, an eating variety, planted by Lancelot 'Capability' Brown in 1768; it still bears fruit today. Known as the Great Vine, this plant was a slip (a rooted piece of vine) from another huge vine at Valentines, a manor in the parish of Ilford, Essex, which had been planted in 1758. Twenty years after Hampton Court's Great Vine was planted, it was said to have produced 2,200 bunches of grapes, each weighing an average 450 grams (1 pound).

The Lower Orangery Garden, once home to Mary II's Exoticks, has undergone considerable restoration. Following Mary's death in 1694 the Pond Garden fell into decline and the orange trees, which, during summer, were set out in tubs, were moved to the Orangery Garden. By the 1880s the need for an orange tree garden had been forgotten. However, following restoration in the early 2000s, the garden is back to its original design of c.1700. Steps, previously hidden by years of alteration, have also been restored and delft-ware showcases plants from Mary's Exoticks. William III added the 18-metre (60-foot) wide Broad Walk along the eastern facade. Large expanses of lawn with geometric borders were created by Henry Wise and his apprentice George London.

THE GOOSE FOOT

Radiating east from the palace are three avenues, each aligned with the central portico of Wren's building to the west and with Charles II's canal to the east. The avenues were possibly laid out by London and Wise who were known to admire French gardens. They published a modified translation of a French gardening book *The Retir'd Gard'ner* (1706) and London had met André Le Nôtre in 1698. The three wide gravel avenues take the form common to French formal gardens known as a *patte d'oie* (literally 'goose foot') and are edged with yew and holly. Uniquely, the central avenue does not contain a walk or a drive, however, but Charles II's canal, the original 1.2 kilometre (¾ mile) Long Water possibly designed by André Mollet and executed by Adrian May, Surveyor of the King's Garden. The canal itself was flanked by 738 lime trees and these were replanted between 2003 and 2004.

In addition to the *patte d'oie*, there are further avenues but only a few of those lime trees planted in the seventeenth century remain today. Many were replanted in the eighteenth century and between 1990 and 1994 up to 1,200 were replanted on the Cross Avenue at the eastern end of the Long Water.

To the far north of the palace lies the maze, believed to be the oldest hedge maze in the world, designed by London and Wise in the final years of William III's reign and completed by Wise when he became gardener to Queen Anne (1665–1714). It covers 1,200 square metres (a third of an acre) and is trapezoid shaped. It was created in an area known as the 'Wilderness' as a place for courtiers to wander and take peaceful refuge. The maze was originally planted with hornbeam brought from the Netherlands, but later this was replaced by yew.

THE WILDERNESS AND TILTYARD GARDEN

The Wilderness was created on the site of the Tudor orchard and planted as a *bosquet*, using hornbeams and elms. It is thought to have been designed during the reign of James II (1633–1701) by Guillaume Beaumont, who trained under Le Nôtre at Versailles and became known in England for his work at Levens Hall, a mansion in the Lake District. The present planting in the Wilderness is largely twentieth century.

Separated from the Wilderness by a sixteenth-century wall and lying to the north-west of the palace is Henry VIII's former Tiltyard. The last recorded tournament took place in 1604. It is a rectangular area of about 2.5 hectares (6 acres), which is currently divided by cross-walls and pathways into six separate sections. Today these form the Rose Garden, the Kitchen Garden, the Magic Garden (which opened in 2016 on the site of the former hard tennis court), the Tiltyard and a restaurant area; the final section is laid to tarmac as a carpark. The Kitchen Garden was previously a herbaceous garden and it has been restored to showcase the plants used in the palace.

Charles Bridgeman, Royal Gardener from 1728 until his death in 1738, made a series of surveys of the gardens at Hampton Court. Bridgeman lived at Wilderness House, which still stands west of Lion Gate, as did Capability Brown, appointed as George III's (1738–1820) Master Gardener at Hampton Court from 1764; neither man appears to have made significant changes. A visual record of the gardens at Hampton Court during Brown's tenure is provided by a large collection of watercolours made by his surveyor, John Spyers. It is recorded that Brown refused to sweep away William III's formal layout, 'out of respect to himself and his profession', but possibly he sought to introduce a more naturalistic planting by ending the practice of cutting the topiary into the established formal shapes.

During the eighteenth and early nineteenth centuries Hampton Court became a destination for tourists and a detailed guidebook was printed in 1817. Queen Victoria (1819–1901) opened the gardens to the public in 1838 and the Great Fountain Garden became famous for its floral displays from the 1850s. The gardens retained their popularity despite published criticisms, which indicated that there was no longer an appreciation for 'lawns shaped with mathematical precision and bordered with meagre evergreens, placed at given distances' (Keane 1850). From the mid-nineteenth century the Victorian craze for carpet bedding was evident at Hampton

RIGHT
Black-eyed Susan

OPPOSITE
The Kitchen Garden

Court, where outstanding examples were created. However, carpet bedding declined rapidly in the 1880s and by 1926 the gardens were instead being praised for their herbaceous and mixed borders, notably the Broad Walk, which borders the Great Fountain Garden.

RESTORATION

Both palace and gardens have had their share of disasters in recent memory. On 31 March 1986 fire ravaged Wren's state apartments, including the King's Apartments. They were restored to their original condition and opened to the public on 8 July 1992. Replanting of the lime avenues was undertaken from 1987 and continued after considerable losses during the storms of 1987 and 1990. A programme of works in 1995 to reconstruct William III's 1701 Privy Garden resulted in the palace facade being visible from the river for the first time in 200 years. William's garden had been designed to impress the courtiers and foreign dignitaries who disembarked from barges and proceeded by means of the Watergate (a long building linking the river to the palace) but after his death the trees, once clipped to little over 2 metres (6½ feet), had been allowed to grow freely, obscuring the view.

In the course of the reconstruction of part of William's Privy Garden, significant clearance of the vegetation was followed by excavation which revealed the symmetrical pattern of clipped hedges, topiarized yew paths, lawns and steps, even the position of marble sculptures. Remarkably, trenches dug in the river terrace gravel to introduce good soil, uncovered the original Tudor flower beds formed in a chequerboard design as a 'heraldic' garden. Such a space would have been adorned with painted heraldic beasts on posts and topiarized shrubs. The borders, known as *plates-bandes*, were found to be perfectly preserved, revealing their sharp sides. They were 1.8 metres (6 feet) wide and lined by dwarf hedges of box, in the centre of which were clipped pyramidal yews. Between the *plates-bandes* were areas of cut grass forming elaborate scrolls. Around the outside alternated yews and round-headed hollies, infilled with shrubs such as roses, sweet briar roses, *Syringas*, honeysuckle and lavenders with bulbs on the outer edges.

Today, Hampton Court Palace holds three National Plant Collections – *Heliotropium*, *Lantana* and Queen Mary II's Exoticks. *Heliotropium* first made an appearance at Hampton Court during the nineteenth century for bedding plant displays in the Great Fountain Garden, and *Lantana* appeared in Exotick collections during the seventeenth century. Mary had one of the largest private collections of plants in the world; however, during the First World War, with a lack of labour and attention, the last of the plants died out. Since 1987 the Gardens and Estate team has researched the specimens and the collection of 215 species, including myrtles, palms and aloes, has been recreated in the Lower Orangery and Privy Garden. Acknowledging the legacy of William and Mary, July 2017 marked the start of an exchange of historic plant varieties between Hampton Court Palace and Het Loo Palace in the Netherlands.

OPPOSITE
The Privy Garden

LEFT
The Great Fountain

HIGHGROVE

ENGLAND

Set in the Gloucestershire countryside, south-west of Tetbury,
is HIGHGROVE, the private garden and family residence of
HRH the Prince of Wales and the Duchess of Cornwall.

The original house at 'High Grove' was built for landowner John Paul Paul, who prospered through the cloth trade into the ranks of gentry. Anthony Keck, a local man, was a provincial follower of Robert Adam and he designed the three-storey house in the austere neoclassical style of the late eighteenth century. Built between 1796 and 1798, the house is constructed of ashlar blocks under stone and slate roofs. In his guide to country houses, *Delineations of Gloucestershire* (1824), J. N. Brewer describes the house as: 'entirely free from ostentation ... The situation is fine, and excellent views are obtained from the house and various parts of the attached grounds.'

Highgrove remained in the Paul family until 1860 when it was sold, and resold four years later to a lawyer, William Yatman. However, a fire in 1893 caused the two-storey canted bay (three-sided window) on the west facade to collapse and the new owners rebuilt Highgrove, concealing the roof behind a high, solid parapet decorated with small orbs at a cost of £6,000. Keck's design was lost, leaving the west facades plain and solid.

Highgrove later became the home of Maurice Macmillan, son of former Prime Minister Harold Macmillan, and in 1980 it was purchased by the Duchy of Cornwall. HRH Prince Charles, with his love for architecture, organic gardening and the environment, could see the potential. He asked New Zealand-born painter Felix Kelly to produce an artist's impression of a redesigned Highgrove, adding an airy balustrade, a pediment set within a round window above the main facade and Ionic replacements for Keck's original Egyptian-style pilasters. The Prince was inspired by Kelly's vision based on the model of Stourhead and Chiswick House. Peter Falconer, the architect who had previously carried out alterations for Macmillan, was appointed to oversee the reconstruction, carried out in 1987, based on Kelly's design.

The Prince of Wales has spent four decades transforming the 6 hectares (15 acres) into what have been described as some of the most inspired and innovative gardens in the UK. Highgrove is testament to the individuality of a devoted environmentalist. His Royal Highness's strict adherence to organic and

PREVIOUS PAGES AND OPPOSITE *ABOVE*

The Sundial Garden   The Walled Garden

sustainable methods has helped to create gardens that are unique, personal, magical and intriguing while being environmentally sound. This is quintessentially a country house garden in the English Georgian style, with natural spaces and formal and walled gardens, where plants and wildlife thrive. In contrast to many of the gardens in this book, Highgrove is a young garden and, despite its overall size, it is one that many can relate to and appreciate. Garden buildings and ornaments have been created in the spirit of the eighteenth-century English landscape style.

The garden is one of two halves, which are then further divided into beautifully crafted spaces, making it impossible to reveal all the beauty of the garden at once. The two 'sides' of the garden are separated by a natural divide – the Woodland Garden and the Wildflower Meadow. One side of the garden, which includes the house and several buildings, contains the Sundial Garden (taking its name from the large stone sundial, a gift from the Duke of Beaufort), the Lily Pool Garden, the Dovecote, the Cottage Garden, the Lime Avenue, the Terrace Garden, the Rose Pergola, the Orchard, the Old Carriage Wash, the Thyme Walk, the Orchard Room and the Islamic Carpet Garden. On the other side is the Azalea Walk, the Temple of Worthies, the Arboretum, the Winterbourne Garden with eucalyptus and tree ferns (*Dicksonia antarctica*), the Walled Garden, the Wall of Gifts, the Tree House, the Stumpery, the Sanctuary and Lower Orchard. By combining informality with formality a pleasing balance has been created.

Everything in this garden is meticulously planned, and HRH Prince Charles continues to be involved at every stage. When talking about its reconstruction, HRH Prince Charles described his efforts as representing:

'one very small attempt to heal the appalling short-sighted damage done to the soil, the landscape and our own souls.' Acknowledging that 'Some may not like it, others may scoff that it is not in the "real world" or it is merely an expensive indulgence', the Prince remarks: 'Whatever the case, my enduring hope is that those who visit the garden may find something to inspire, excite, fascinate or soothe them.'

The Wildflower Meadow, created by Dame Miriam Rothschild and His Royal Highness, is one of the most powerful areas of the garden, a tapestry of texture, wildlife and colour, which is constantly evolving. Since the majority of meadows in the UK have been lost, the aim was to recreate an 'old meadow' through the use of 130 species that form the native flora of the Gloucestershire countryside. Meadows take time to establish and it has taken years to achieve the reduction in soil fertility that allows an abundance of wildflowers to proliferate: at Highgrove these include the common spotted orchid (*Dactylorhiza fuchsia*), southern marsh orchid (*D. praetermissa*) and green-winged orchid (*Anacamptis morio*), snakeshead fritillary (*Fritillaria meleagris*) and wild daffodil (*Narcissus pseudonarcissus*). The seasonal cycle of the meadow is natural, from cutting back, grazing by sheep between August and October and treading in the seeds, to germination in the spring.

His Royal Highness believes in working with nature, not against it, and the Arboretum, created in 1992, is a perfect example of his philosophy. It has been designed almost from scratch. In autumn avenues of Japanese maples turn fiery gold, orange and red, followed by carpets of yellow and magenta blooms from winter aconite (*Eranthis hyemalis*) and cyclamens respectively. Several yews in the Arboretum have been topiarized into unique structural shapes. The Arboretum is a very personal space for His Royal Highness, who has said that all he longs to do is plant trees as he gets older.

The Sundial Garden, adjacent to the house, was originally designed by Lady Salisbury, herself a passionate gardener and a friend of His Royal Highness, as a rose garden. Lawn paths, lined with low box hedging, with balls formed in yew on every corner, lead to a circular pattern constructed in brick, with the sundial at its centre. In 1999 it was replanted as a black-and-white garden, striking with black grasses and white peonies and lupins. The flowerheads of dahlias were used indoors for floral displays, allowing their deep purple leaves to enhance the garden's darker tones. Subsequently, the garden has become a scented floral delight of pinks, purples, whites and

ABOVE OPPOSITE
The Arboretum

BELOW OPPOSITE
The Stumpery

lavender. The Prince's love of delphiniums (one shared by his grandmother, HRH Queen Elizabeth The Queen Mother, at the Castle of Mey, see page 44) is noticeable during summer when their blue and purple spires define the Sundial Garden and, with magenta poppies, airy scented clusters of strong pink phlox and late-flowering half-hardy salvias of deep purple, carmine and pink, attract innumerable pollinators. 'Windows' in the clipped hedging that surrounds this garden create niches for busts of HRH The Prince of Wales.

A distinctive element of the garden, one that has been featured in many magazine and newspaper articles internationally, is the Islamic carpet garden – saturated with bright colours and scent. It was designed for the Royal Horticultural Society's Chelsea Flower Show garden in 2001, based on a Turkish carpet found inside Highgrove. The blue and aqua mosaic, perfectly scalloped stone water feature and apricot-pink walls, Italian cypresses, vines, cork oaks (*Quercus suber*) and orange trees have settled into the Gloucestershire countryside yet even on a dull day have the power to transport you to another place.

Pathways connect the majority of the gardens at Highgrove. One, the Thyme Walk, is a patchwork of informally laid stone, interspersed with different, gently scented creeping thymes in pink, purple, white and yellow – planted by His Royal Highness – more recently augmented with golden marjoram, deep blue agapanthus and lavender 'Grosso'. It begins at the French doors of the house, passing an octagonal water feature in the Terrace Garden with its 'salt and pepper pot' pavilions overbrimming with lady's mantle (*Alchemilla mollis*) and cotton lavender (*Santolina chamaecyparissus*), and seasonal planting in large terracotta pots, stretching for 95 metres (more than 300 feet). The walk also provides a vista from the house, the eye following its straight lines. At intervals are golden-yellow yew bushes, reaching 1.8 metres (6 feet) in height, each trained into different shapes and crowns. Behind them stand pleached hornbeams, forming four rectangular shapes, with a further four square shapes in the centre. The dramatic scale of this garden makes it one of the most unique, picturesque and iconic at Highgrove.

There are delights and surprises in what was formerly known as the Woodland Garden, too, where straight lines are nowhere to be seen. It is now called the Stumpery, an area initially started in 1980, designed by His Royal Highness and Julian and Isabel Bannerman. At first sight, a stumpery, a pile of deliberately arranged tree roots and other woody material, might stop you in your tracks. In fact, when HRH the Duke of Edinburgh first saw the one at Highgrove he asked his son: 'When are you going to set fire to this lot?' Despite being manmade, it creates a woodland landscape like no other, and appears as though it has been there for centuries. Stumperies became popular in Victorian Britain, along with a craze for ferns. The first, created in 1856 at Biddulph Grange in Staffordshire, was the inspiration for the one at Highgrove, which is considered the largest stumpery in Britain and which utilizes primarily English oak (*Quercus robur*) and sweet chestnut (*Castanea sativa*) stumps. The aim was to create a habitat for HRH Prince Charles' National Collection of large and broad-leaved hostas, but other woodland plants – ferns, euphorbias and hellebores – also thrive here. The unique topography of the piles of slowly decaying wood makes dozens of pockets with conditions suitable for a community of woodland species – sun-loving, moisture-loving, drought-tolerant and shade-loving plants all find their particular niche. This creation respects the natural carbon cycle as the wood breaks down, returning the organic components to the soil, providing food for its microflora and a haven for other wildlife, such as toads and stag beetles.

A PLANTSMAN'S PARADISE

There are no grandiose statements in this garden. Instead, what is very apparent throughout is the use of trees. HRH Prince Charles is involved with all aspects of tree selection, establishment and management. He has planted 10,000 trees across the garden and wider estate, as well as almost 15 kilometres (9 miles) of hedgerows. Many trees are given as gifts; one, in the Cottage Garden, a gold-leaved Indian bean tree (*Catalpa bignonioides*), which, sadly, has since died, was a present from Sir Elton John CH, OBE. The orchards include several National Fruit Collection apple trees – 'Ashmead's Kernel', 'Golden Knob' and 'Devonshire Buckland' – while the National Collection of *Fagus* (beech) has cultivars such as *F. sylvatica* 'Rohanii', 'Dawyck', 'Pendula' and 'Purpurea Tricolor' (also known as *F. s.* 'Roseomarginata', for its variegated leaves – dark purple edged with pink or rose). When the Dalai Lama visited Highgrove, HRH The Prince of Wales asked him to plant a rare Manchurian ash (*Fraxinus mandschurica*) which HRH already owned. The tree now sits comfortably near the Orchard. In the Arboretum itself are various species of large-leaved rhododendrons, scented azaleas, hydrangeas and Japanese maples (*Acer palmatum*).

Highgrove is inspiring, exciting and fascinating, a garden to feel good in. This can be summed up in Head Gardener Debs Goodenough's own words:

'I know that he [HRH The Prince of Wales] *likes particular light levels in the garden, times where the garden is shown off at its best. Those moments change throughout the year and you can have several of them in one day. His Royal Highness understands the garden well enough to know when to catch that golden light, like when you can see the sun coming through certain tree canopies.'*

In an interview to mark his seventieth birthday, HRH The Prince of Wales told *The Australian Women's Weekly*:

'What the garden means to me now is that, above all, not only has it become a haven for some of the rare and endangered varieties that 40 years ago were being recklessly discarded in a world driven by short-termism, convenience and a rash disregard for nature's place in the scheme of things, but I hope it may also have become a more harmonious place from which to draw inspiration.'

Gardeners are acutely aware of the rhythms and cycles of nature and the changes that occur with the seasons. His Royal Highness has for many years followed these rhythms and cycles while also following organic principles and focusing on sustainability, biodiversity and ecology. Highgrove is a very personal space with a natural pace all of its own.

ABOVE   *OPPOSITE*

HRH The Prince of Wales   The Cottage Garden

ROYAL BOTANIC GARDENS

KEW, ENGLAND

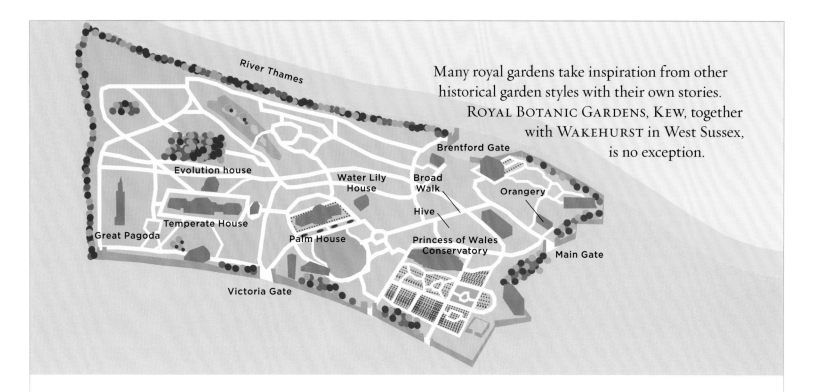

River Thames

Evolution house

Water Lily House

Brentford Gate

Broad Walk

Orangery

Temperate House

Hive

Great Pagoda

Palm House

Princess of Wales Conservatory

Main Gate

Victoria Gate

Many royal gardens take inspiration from other historical garden styles with their own stories. ROYAL BOTANIC GARDENS, KEW, together with WAKEHURST in West Sussex, is no exception.

Yet, Kew differs in that it is not only the gardens within its confines that have evolved throughout the centuries but also gardens throughout the world, through its scientific research and education.

There used to be two estates where Kew now stands, the Kew Estate and the Richmond Estate, set along the south-west side of the meandering Thames at Richmond. The two estates were eventually combined to form the Royal Botanic Gardens. Kew Palace, in the north-east corner, was originally built in 1631 for Samuel Fortrey, a merchant and landowner, and it became a 'domestic retreat' for George II (1638–1760) and George III (1738–1820).

Many internationally renowned landscape architects have been commissioned throughout Kew's history, including Charles Bridgeman, William Kent, Sir William Chambers, Lancelot 'Capability' Brown and William Andrews Nesfield, showcasing and depicting significant periods in garden design from the eighteenth century to the present. The homes of many courtiers and politicians as well as large royal residences sprang up in the Kew and Richmond areas and these greatly influenced the layout, design and architecture of the gardens. Originally created in 1759, the Royal Botanic Gardens were designated in 2003 as a World Heritage Site which, according to UNESCO,

'contributed to the study of plant diversity, plant systematics and economic botany'.

A CHANGE IN GARDEN STYLES

The eastern half of the gardens was formerly Kew Gardens, a chinoiserie-style eighteenth-century landscape. This style is characterized by the use of Chinese motifs and techniques, and, at Kew, strong formal plantings, pathways and trees focus on the Great Pagoda. The western half is more naturalistic and dominated by a woodland. Leading advocates of the English landscape garden style – Bridgeman, Kent and Brown – were involved in its creation in the eighteenth century. The northern part of the site was not included in either garden. Beginning in the 1840s Sir William Hooker, Nesfield and Decimus Burton unified all these areas under one coherent landscape scheme, including the Palm House and its vistas. Their design carries through to today.

KEW'S EARLY YEARS

Many plants came to Britain due to the efforts of plant hunters, botanists and nurserymen and an ever-growing enthusiasm for plants. The Age of Discovery,

PREVIOUS PAGES *OPPOSITE*
The Palm House   The Hive

the period from the fifteenth century up to the eighteenth century, when European nations focused on world exploration, was coming to an end. In the mid- to late eighteenth century the Age of Enlightenment reflected a scientific awakening, that manifested itself especially in the form of plant hunting.

HRH Prince Frederick (1707–51) encouraged gardening, and garden design centred around Kew. The Prince was popular, and wherever he went the Court was sure to follow. After his death in 1751, his widow, Princess Augusta (1719–72), continued the royal patronage, assisted by Lord Bute, a close associate of the Prince. The architect Chambers was commissioned to design a number of buildings from 1757, including the Orangery (started in 1757) and the Great Pagoda of 1761–2. After travels to East Asia he wrote a book on Oriental gardening, in which he observed: 'Their Gardeners are not only Botanists but also Painters and Philosophers', and it was Chambers who introduced the chinoiserie style to Kew.

When the botanic garden was created in 1759 it was only 4 hectares (10 acres) of walled garden, excluding the lawns, groves, woods and walks. When in 1760 George III inherited Richmond Estate he commissioned Capability Brown to create a landscaped park. Scottish-born botanist William Aiton was employed from 1760 to deal with 'plant matters'. He adopted the Linnaean system in which plants are classified according to their structure and characteristics. He produced an extensive description of the collection entitled *Hortus Kewensis* (1789). In 1772, George III also inherited the Kew Estate. With the naturalist and botanist Joseph Banks, a patron of the natural sciences, Kew Gardens flourished and its horticultural influence became international. Plants introduced during the eighteenth century included spotted laurel (*Aucuba japonica*), Portuguese laurel (*Prunus lusitanica*), witch hazel (*Hamamelis virginiana*) and zinnia (*Zinnia elegans*).

Following the death of George III in 1820, over the next twenty years the gardens fell into disrepair. In 1840, Queen Victoria (1819–1901) authorized the establishment as the Royal Botanic Gardens at Kew and bequeathed additional land, bringing the

gardens to over 130 hectares (320 acres). She also appointed Hooker as its first Director in 1841 and he greatly advanced the knowledge of plants through publications such as *British Jungermanniae* (1816), *Genera Filicum* (1838), *Flora Scotica* (1821), *The British Flora* (1830), and *Flora Borealis Americana* (1840).

Hooker had read *Arboretum et Fruticetum Britannicum*, an eight-volume tome by John Claudius Loudon, a Scottish botanist, garden designer and author who also established 'gardenesque' – the Victorian planting design theory, in which indigenous plants are replaced with 'foreign vegetation of a similar character' so that the 'making' of gardens could not be distinguished from 'nature'. Two years after reviewing the book, Hooker started to set out Kew Gardens based on Loudon's principles. The exotic shrubs and trees were planted in naturalistic groups, with great attention to botanical accuracy, showing relationships among the various genera and families of plants. This became known as the Bentham & Hooker classification system, after Hooker and a fellow botanist and friend George Bentham.

PALM HOUSE AND TEMPERATE HOUSE

By the mid-nineteenth century the botanic focus was centred on two large iron-framed glasshouses on the east side of the garden, the Palm House and the Temperate House, which were widely copied in conservatory designs around the world.

The cost of materials was reduced with the abolition of the tax on glass and brick between 1845 and 1850, and in 1847 James Hartley patented an improved method for producing clearer, larger panes of sheet glass. Around the same time new techniques for glazing bars, either cast iron or wood, were being developed. The Palm House, designed by Burton and Turner and built between 1844 and 1848, provides an excellent example of these innovations. It is a full 110.5 metres (362 feet) in length and its curved profile maximizes daylight. The climate is controlled to provide protection for the plants within.

At the same time the Palm House was built, one of the most prolific of Victorian garden designers,

Nesfield, remodelled the surrounding gardens, and created the areas of parterres and a formal pond beside the Palm House. Nesfield's use of a triangular layout made up of vistas (Syon Vista, Cedar Vista and Pagoda Vista) spatially and functionally reunited the former separation of Richmond and Kew Gardens into a coherent configuration (known as a 'pictorial' arrangement), in which architecture and landscape are united.

The late garden historian Christopher Thacker described the Palm House as having 'the purity of form and singleness of purpose of an igloo and the size of a cathedral.' While the Palm House provided the right conditions for many exotic plants, specimens from temperate parts of Africa, Asia, Australia and New Zealand started to die. This prompted the building of a second glasshouse. The Temperate House, originally designed by Burton, took nearly 40 years to complete, opening in 1863. It is twice the size of the Palm House and it was (and still is) seen as a marvel of Victorian engineering. Burton adorned his Temperate House with decorative motifs, among them *Acanthus*-leaf capitals, swags of tropical fruits and flowers.

Thacker continued, '*the Water Lily House (1852) has, more or less, the same functional qualities* [as the Palm House], *but the Temperate House ..., has returned to an architecture of human as well as botanic concern. It is certainly beautiful, but it is the beauty of a fairy palace, not of a home for plants.*' Despite Thacker's comments, plants from temperate zones had a place in which to flourish.

The Temperate House is built on a raised terrace, using gravel and sand excavated from Kew's lake during the first stage of construction. When it opened to the public, only the towering centre and two adjacent octagons had been built. It was another 40 years before enough funds were raised to construct the south (opened 1897) and the north (opened 1899) wings, Himalaya House and Mexican House, respectively. In 1925 a teak annex was added to the west side of the north octagon to house Chinese and Himalayan rhododendrons.

The Water Lily House, completed in 1852, designed by Burton and later built by Turner, is the hottest of Kew's glass houses. Originally, its purpose was to showcase the giant Amazon water lily (*Victoria amazonica*). Today it also accommodates the world's smallest water lily and other tropical aquatic plants. Its pond is 10 metres (33 feet) in diameter but only 65 centimetres (little more than 2 feet) deep at its centre.

RECENT WORK

To the north of the Palm House is the most technologically advanced glasshouse, the Princess of Wales Conservatory, designed by Gordon Wilson, and named after George III's mother, Princess Augusta. Construction began in 1982 and in 1985 Sir David Attenborough filled a time capsule with seeds of endangered species, which was buried in the foundations of the glasshouse. In 1986 planting started, and the building was opened by Princess Diana, the then Princess of Wales, in 1987. Inside the glasshouse are ten climatic zones from cool desert to tropical rainforest, all monitored and run by an advanced computer system. Most of the space is below ground level, with the hottest zone in the centre of the conservatory. But it is not only plants that can be found here. There are also fish and five Chinese water dragons. The biggest tree is a Venezuelan species, *Brownea grandiceps*, also called the scarlet flame bean for its spectacular red flowers. However, not all the flowers in the conservatory have an attractive scent: the titan arum, *Amorphophallus titanum*, which is known only from Sumatra, smells of rotting flesh. To the east of the Princess of Wales Conservatory is the Davies Alpine House designed by Wilkinson Eyre as two back-to-back arches. It opened in 2006 and has a unique shade system to help regulate the environment for the alpine plants within. The fan-shaped shade is reminiscent of a peacock's tail.

In August 2013 the Temperate House closed for the largest restoration project in its history. Layers of paint were painstakingly removed, 5,280 litres (more than 1,000 gallons) of fresh paint were applied, and 15,000 panes of glass were replaced. The number of cleaned, repaired or replaced elements totalled more than 69,000, including the restoration of 116 urns that sat

OPPOSITE
The Great Pagoda

on top of each column, and which had to be carefully lifted off the building by crane. At the start of the restoration, 500 plants were removed and nurtured and propagated until they could be returned. A further 150 plant species were grown from seeds stored in the Millennium Seed Bank at Wakehurst in West Sussex. The full restoration took 1,731 days to complete, using 400 staff members and contractors to return the glasshouse to its original design of Victorian splendour, albeit using twenty-first-century materials and cutting-edge engineering.

Gardens, even Royal Botanic Gardens, never stand still. Stretching for some 320 metres (more than 1,000 feet) are the Great Broad Walk Borders that link the Palm House to the Orangery. Originally, during the 1840s, the Broad Walk would have served as a formal promenade, its borders filled with a formal planting scheme by Nesfield. New double herbaceous borders have been designed by Richard Wildford, Kew's Manager of Garden Design, to emphasize the perspective, with over 30,000 plants providing a great diversity of texture and colour during the summer flowering season, with a single row on each side of pyramid-shaped topiarized yews along the path's edge to accentuate its length. A series of circles bisect the path, inspired by the tropical vine with the largest seed pod in the legume family, *Entada gigas* (monkey-ladder or sea bean). New double herbaceous borders are viewed from all sides. Some beds are based on a single plant family or group, such as Lamiaceae (the mint family) and Compositae (the daisy family).

Another important modern addition to Kew is the Hive, a 17-metre (56-foot) tall permanent installation by British artist Wolfgang Buttress. Twisting out of the ground the shape is suggestive of a swarm of bees and is a visual symbol of the pollinators' vital role in sustaining the crops on which humanity relies and the challenges facing bees today. A wildflower meadow leads up to the Hive, and once inside, thousands of flickering LED lights, bring this 40-tonne lattice structure to life. Bees hum to the key of 'C', and the use

of a musical accompaniment in the form of vocals and cello enhances the overall experience. As energy levels in a nearby beehive fluctuate, so do the sound and light levels within the space.

DIVERSITY OF PLANTS

The diversity of plants at Kew is remarkable with 30,000 different species. The Palm House has bananas, plantains, gingers and palms, orchids and spice and nut species. It also contains what has been dubbed 'the oldest pot plant in the world', a huge Eastern Cape giant cycad (*Encephalartos altensteinii*), which was brought back to Kew in 1775 by its first plant hunter, Francis Masson, from South Africa's Eastern Cape. Inside the Temperate House are specimens of feather-leaved banksia (*Banksia brownii*) and silky eremophilia (*Eremophila nivea*) from Australia, the bush lily (*Clivia miniata*) and red-hot poker (*Kniphofia pauciflora*) from Africa, Kakhetian bellflower (*Campanula kachethica*) from Asia, and Cayman sage (*Salvia caymanensis*), once thought to be extinct, from the Cayman Islands. The Arboretum is a unique collection of some of the rarest as well as ancient species. They include what are known as Kew's heritage trees, planted in the eighteenth century, among them the Japanese pagoda tree (*Styphnolobium japonicum*), lucombe oak (*Quercus x hispanica* 'Lucombeana') and the black locust tree (*Robinia pseudoacacia*). In the Redwood Grove there is a mix of Coastal and Giant Redwoods (*Sequoia sempervirens* and *Sequoiadendron giganteum*, respectively).

Once a royal retreat and pleasure garden, the modern institution that is Kew combines science, garden history, conservation and beauty. As part of its work to protect biodiversity its remit includes the management of the botanic gardens of Wakehurst in West Sussex, the location of the Millennium Seed Bank, which opened in 2000.

OPPOSITE

Protea cynaroides

CASTLE OF MEY

SCOTLAND

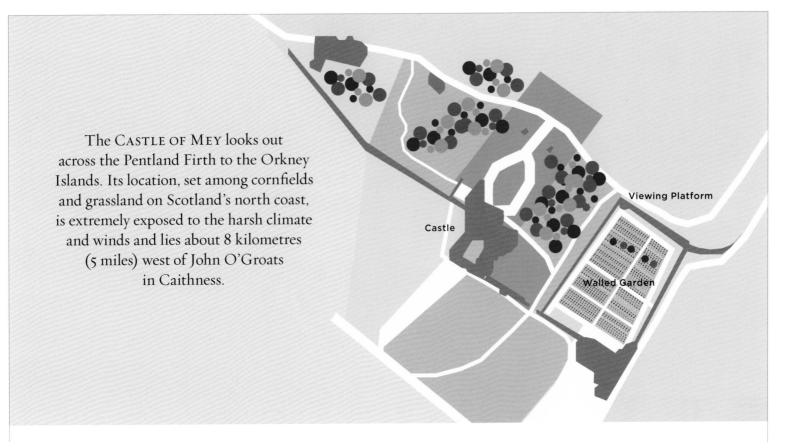

The CASTLE OF MEY looks out across the Pentland Firth to the Orkney Islands. Its location, set among cornfields and grassland on Scotland's north coast, is extremely exposed to the harsh climate and winds and lies about 8 kilometres (5 miles) west of John O'Groats in Caithness.

The castle was the private holiday residence of the late Her Majesty Queen Elizabeth The Queen Mother (1900-2002). It stands barely 460 metres (1,500 feet) from the shoreline, and appears almost to have risen from the bedrock itself. Not exactly the perfect spot for a garden, but thanks to Her Majesty Queen Elizabeth The Queen Mother's energy, passion for plants and gardens, and perseverance it is now one of Britain's most iconic gardens.

A BLOODY TALE

As described in *House and Garden*, from the archive: 'The Castle of Mey, the Queen Mother's Scottish retreat', 1959, by Loelia, Duchess of Westminster:

'The early history of Mey is a bloody tale of family feuding and betrayal. The castle was built by the 4th Earl of Caithness [1527–1582] *for his son, William Sinclair,* [the 1st Laird of Mey 1544–1573]. *In 1573 William visited the family seat at Castle Girnigoe, near Wick, where his elder brother John* [Garrow Sinclair, Master of Caithness, 1543–1576] *was being held prisoner by the Earl.*

William discovered that John was planning an escape, and told the Earl. John killed William in revenge, but John himself was then killed, and the new castle at Mey eventually passed to the Earl's 3rd son, George [1555–1616, 2nd Mey Chancellor of Caithness].

In 1819 the 12th Earl [James Sinclair, 1766–1823] *called in architect William Burn (1789–1870) to transform the 16th-century castle into a comfortable mansion'.*

Small reminders, including the initials of the 4th Earl, George Sinclair, and his wife Lady Elizabeth Graham are left throughout the castle. The main entrance had always faced the sea, but Burn and the 12th Earl wanted to change this, by creating a new gatehouse that stuck out on the landward side, and adding a dining room. His son, Alexander Campbell Sinclair (1790–1855), erected a monument known as Lady Fanny's seat, which was a tribute to Viscount Charles John Canning, who later became the Viceroy of India when the Crown of Queen Victoria took control from the East India Company.

Tragically, the 15th Earl, George (1858–89), who never married and had no children, died aged 30. The castle was therefore bequeathed to his friend

PREVIOUS PAGES
The Castle of Mey from the Walled Garden

OPPOSITE
The Shell Garden

F. G. Heathcote, a Scottish zoologist, in 1889. A condition of taking over the castle was that he legally changed his name to Frederick Granville Sinclair (which he did). Later, his widow sold it to Captain Frederic Bouhier Imbert-Terry. During the Second World War the house was requisitioned as a coastal-defence billet for a company of the Black Watch.

THE ARRIVAL OF HER MAJESTY QUEEN ELIZABETH THE QUEEN MOTHER

Months after the death of her husband, Bertie, King George VI (1895–1952), Her Majesty was visiting friends in Caithness. On a journey along the coast road towards John o' Groats, Her Majesty spotted 'this romantic-looking castle down by the sea'.

The castle was in a bad shape after the war and had been damaged by a more recent storm. Her Majesty later wrote to a friend: 'The next day we discovered it was going to be pulled down, and I thought this would be a terrible pity.'

Her Majesty wrote to her treasurer Sir Arthur Penn:

'When I was staying up in Caithness I passed a dear little castle down by the sea and when I visited it I discovered it was going to be sold for nothing, just the value of the lead on the roof.

This seemed so sad that I thought I would buy it and escape there occasionally when life becomes hideous.

The old man who has lived there a long time was very anxious to give it to me but I resisted the kind gesture and he has now offered it to me for £100.

It might be rather fun to have a small house so far away – the air is lovely, and one looks at Orkney from the drawing room.

The only sad thing is that part of the roof was blown off in the great gale last January and I shall have to put in electric light of course.'

Her Majesty was attracted to the castle, despite its poor condition, and purchased it, with restoration work starting almost immediately. Her Majesty then turned her attention to the 12 hectares (30 acres) of gardens and grounds, or as they are sometimes called *policies*. By 1955 most of the restoration work had

been completed and Her Majesty restored the Castle's name, formerly Barrogil Castle, to the Castle of Mey (not Mey Castle).

Her Majesty spent three weeks in August at the castle, returning for about ten days in October each year. For three days a year the gardens were opened for Scotland's Gardens Scheme, the Scottish equivalent to England's National Gardens Scheme, a tradition continued to this day by the trustees. As William Shawcross wrote in the official biography (2009):

'She loved the fresh air and the open space that the castle offered, with the ever-changing view of clouds and sea and the shadows on Orkney beyond.

She loved being in Caithness because it was Scotland, to which she was devoted, and yet a part of Scotland which had no memories of happier days.'

THE FORMATION OF A GARDEN

To provide shelter from coastal winds and salt, the Great Wall of Mey was built. It is 5 metres (16 feet) tall at its highest, and extends eastward to meet the East Garden and Woodland and westward to create one side of a 0.8-hectare (2-acre) Walled Garden. The overall design of the gardens remains much as it was in Her Majesty Queen Elizabeth The Queen Mother's time.

Her Majesty The Queen Mother was a passionate and experienced gardener. Her green fingers ensured that the garden at the Castle of Mey prospered, overseeing the development of two of the gardens. Her love for gardening started in 1936 when, as Duchess of York, she helped restore the Royal Lodge garden in Windsor Great Park and later helped to shape Sandringham and Buckingham Palace gardens.

THE EAST AND WEST GARDENS: 'GREENFACED GARDENS'

The East Garden, enclosed on the north and east sides, was, according to Historic Environment Scotland, created by the 14th Earl (James Sinclair, 1821–81), with a glasshouse that was a reproduction of the exhibition hall (Crystal Palace) of the 1851 Great Exhibition.

ABOVE AND BELOW OPPOSITE
The Walled Garden

An article written in the early 1850s describes the glasshouse being filled with purple *Cineraria* and red and white camellias, with a vine growing over the inner walls. Unfortunately, it was derelict by the 1950s and replaced by a bed of primulas. Today, the East Garden, which forms a long shady strip, is planted with hostas, hellebores, the Himalayan blue poppy (*Meconopsis*, which features in many Scottish gardens), ferns and primulas, with height coming from the deciduous shrub *Weigela* 'Bristol Ruby'. At the far end of the East Garden there are walks through sycamore-filled woodlands where cow parsley grows freely.

The West Garden is considered to be the older of the two. It is enclosed on all sides by walls, with a turret in the north-west corner. It is thought that this was the area that traveller and writer William Lithgow described in 1628 as 'greenfaced gardens'. Deep borders along the southern side of the north wall are packed full of delphiniums, salvias, valerians, hostas, buddleias, *Agapanthus* 'Castle of Mey' and white daisies.

The West Garden is the main cultivated garden and is divided into eight by neatly pruned wildlife-friendly hedges of berberis, elder, privet and hawthorn underplanted with yellow Tibetan cowslips (*Primula florindae*). The south-facing greenhouses – one a lean-to against the wall, the other free-standing – are used for propagation and more tender plants. Peaches and tomatoes can be found growing in the free-standing one, while the warmth from the stone wall is perfect for pots containing pineapple lilies (*Eucomis* spp.), bird of paradise (*Strelitzia*), lobelias, geraniums and petunias. Another feature in the greenhouses is an extensive collection of old scented-leaved pelargoniums, selected by Her Majesty. Cuttings are taken annually, and new introductions are made, ensuring the garden remains fresh without altering its essential personal character. A screen of wooden posts and wire from the corner of the lean-to greenhouse is covered with the glorious yellow flowers of *Clematis tangutica* during the summer months.

In the shelter of the northern wall is the Shell Garden, a personal favourite of Her Majesty, where crushed shells form pathways around organic-shaped beds of roses. Here Her Majesty even managed to nurture her favourite scented old roses, *Rosa* 'Albertine' and *R.* 'London Pride'. The garden is also full of marigolds, pansies and dahlias. This was a place where Her Majesty The Queen Mother would sit with her corgi dogs in the afternoons surrounded by nasturtiums – orange 'Tom Thumb' and scarlet 'Empress of India'. A green-painted doorway in the stone wall opens up to views of the sea beyond.

The gardens at Castle of Mey, like those at Highgrove (see page 24) are very personal, and although large compared to those of many households, the divisions create smaller garden 'rooms' that people can easily relate to. Plants like *Alchemilla* spp. spill over the pathways and climbers cascade over the salt-sprayed walls. From ground level the hedges and subdivisions mean that sightlines are obscured, creating surprises around each corner, except along the main border paths.

HRH Prince Charles The Prince of Wales takes great interest in the development of the gardens and enjoys staying here in August, when the best of the grown produce is saved for the royal table. He also assists the trustees with their plans. Produce and flowers are still used by the castle today, and any surplus sold at the plant stall.

In 2012 a new Rose Garden was opened to commemorate the tenth anniversary of the death of Her Majesty Queen Elizabeth The Queen Mother. The flowers for the new Rose Garden were all chosen by HRH Prince Charles.

PARKLAND AND WOODLAND

To the south of the castle are the parkland and woodland, originally planted by Captain Imbert-Terry, although part of the shelterbelt was replanted in 1939. Twisted and wind blown, the trees are reminiscent of ones drawn in story books. Sycamore, ash, horse chestnut, copper beech and wild cherry can be found in both the parkland as well as the woodland. Like many deciduous woodlands, during springtime, before the canopies are covered with leaves blocking direct sunlight, the ground is covered with daffodils,

ABOVE OPPOSITE
The Castle of Mey from the Walled Garden

BELOW OPPOSITE
A view of the castle with the island of Stroma in the distance

bluebells, primroses, aconites and celandines. During the summer, cool temperatures and dappled shade provide the perfect growing conditions for lichens and cow parsley. Leading from the parkland towards the castle the naturalistic landscape gives way to formal lawns with cannons.

PLANTS AND CONDITIONS

Both natural and manmade microclimates allow for a wide range of plants to be grown at the Castle of Mey. This part of Scotland has cool summers and high rainfall. The air is especially clean, albeit with salt-laden winds, but the stone walls provide the needed shelter. Although the solid wall deflects the wind up and over, the internal hedging reduces the impact of strong winds by acting as a filter. Salt causes leaf burn and defoliation, so the hardy mixed hedging proves invaluable.

Homemade compost and crushed shells help to loosen the structure of the soil. Annual sweet peas now thrive in this free-draining, enriched soil. Grown from seed in the greenhouse, these sweet-scented flowers were picked for Her Majesty The Queen Mother's bedside table. In front of the sweet peas, companion planting of orange calendula and blue cornflowers create a dazzling display.

Around the perimeter of the West Garden, different planting schemes create different effects, with warm colours to lift the mood on the east and cooler colours to calm on the west.

Protected by the walls, statuesque delphiniums stand tall. These were a favourite of Her Majesty the Queen Mother. Other borders are a mix of reds and greys from red masterwort (*Astrantia*), the maroon of brook thistle (*Cirsium*) and the leaves of *Heuchera*, rich yellow of Dyer's chamomile (*Anthemis tinctoria*) and the silver-grey foliage of the butterfly bush (*Buddleia*), with a shot of bright blue from sea holly (*Eryngium*).

During the Second World War the entire walled garden was used for vegetables. Today the garden is planted in neat rows, with lettuces, beetroots, onions and brassicas rotated very four years to reduce pests and diseases, and using seaweed as a mulch. Growing alongside staple vegetables are artichokes (a gift from a French garden) and heritage dark-skinned Shetland and Pink Fir Apple potatoes. The use of different colours and textures is deliberate to make the garden visually stunning and more interesting. To continue the displays the head gardener will cut a cabbage head and make a cross in the top of the remaining stalk, which then produces four buds and in turn mini cabbages, filling an otherwise blank space.

Much of the hedging produces an edible crop, including raspberries, black-, red- and white-currants, but more can be found in the fruit cage. Her Majesty planted blackcurrants for the blackbirds and, over the years, these bushes have self-seeded.

Her Majesty The Queen Mother contributed greatly to many royal gardens, but none more so than the Castle of Mey which remains truly her own. It is remarkable that her gardens are born out of willpower against the elements. Her foresight and energy clearly show that a garden can be created in the most improbable of locations with the most difficult of conditions. The Castle of Mey is a very personal 'pleasure' garden, romantic in feel, enclosed by the walls and the hedges and in stark contrast to the pasture land surrounding it. Yet the woodland and parkland blend seamlessly into the wider landscape, making it a truly Scottish garden.

Her Majesty's blue Wellingtons and raincoat hang in the front hall; her homely sitting room is still as it would have been if she were present today. A more humorous side to the castle can be found in the form of tacky trinkets, such as Nessie statues and other cheap gifts, provided by many of her younger guests as a 'thank you' for their time at the castle with the Queen Mother.

HERRENHAUSEN

GERMANY

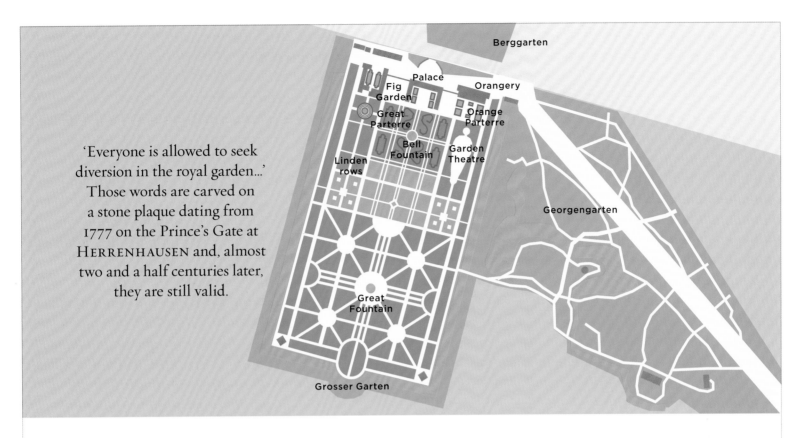

Berggarten

Palace

Fig Garden

Orangery

Great Parterre

Orange Parterre

Bell Fountain

Garden Theatre

Linden rows

Georgengarten

Great Fountain

Grosser Garten

'Everyone is allowed to seek diversion in the royal garden...' Those words are carved on a stone plaque dating from 1777 on the Prince's Gate at HERRENHAUSEN and, almost two and a half centuries later, they are still valid.

Herrenhausen is one of the most important historical gardens in Europe and has been the scene of politics, science, art and love for more than three centuries. It comprises the Grosser Garten (Great Garden) in the baroque style, Georgengarten and Welfengarten in the English landscape style, and Berggarten (Mountain Garden) botanic garden. The palace is a former summer residence of the House of Hanover in the Herrenhausen district of the north-west German city of Hanover. The residence itself is relatively modest, but the gardens are extensive: 130 hectares (more than 320 acres) – a horticultural delight on a grand scale – and here it is possible to trace garden design from 1680 to the present day.

Herrenhausen was originally built as a summer residence for the noble Welf dynasty. Their principal residence, Welfenschloss, a white Deister sandstone castle east of Herrenhausen, subsequently became the building for the University and Welfengarten its park.

In 1679–80 Duke Ernest Augustus (1629–98) and his wife, the Electress Sophie (1630–1714), moved to Hanover from Osnabrück. Electress Sophie's mother was Elizabeth Stuart (1596–1662), the only sister of Charles I of England (1600–49). Under the duke

and Electress Sophie, the court became one of the most magnificent in Germany, known for its Venetian masquerades, gondola festivals and illuminations.

ELECTRESS SOPHIE AND HERRENHAUSEN

Inspired by the French palaces of Vaux-le-Vicomte and Versailles (see page 90) and Het Loo Palace, in the Netherlands (see page 152), where she had spent her childhood and youth, Electress Sophie wanted to extend the gardens at Herrenhausen. In 1682 she commissioned the French gardener Martin Charbonnier whom she had previously employed in Osnabrück. Electress Sophie was at the centre of all ideas and, with Charbonnier, she spent the next 30 years shaping the Grosser Garten – her 'little paradise', framed by the Graft canal – which she doubled in size to 50 hectares (more than 123 acres). Wishing to be seen as modern and forward-thinking, Sophie introduced rare plants from all over the world and commissioned works from leading master sculptors to bring her garden alive. She said: 'The great garden at Herrenhausen is the only thing with which we can show off.' Her passion was summed up in a comment

PREVIOUS PAGES AND OPPOSITE

The Grosser Garten

to her niece 'Lieselotte' (Princess Elisabeth Charlotte, Duchess of Orleans), the sister-in-law of the French king Louis XIV (1638–1715): 'the garden is my life.'

Sophie, who almost became Queen of England, was both creative and intellectual, having been tutored in art, law, mathematics, theology, philosophy, history and several languages. She travelled widely in Europe and hosted the wealthy and famous. As if to anticipate the Enlightenment, the court invited architects and poets, the composer and musician George Frederick Handel and the philosopher Gottfried Wilhelm Leibniz, who became adviser to the Electress. She and Leibniz would discuss philosophy on many occasions and spent much time together. Leibniz wrote:

'here one finds scarcely anyone with whom to talk; or rather, in this region a courtier is not supposed to speak of learned matters, and without the Electress [Sophie] they would be spoken of even less.'

Their discussions would invariably return to the design of the garden. At the age of 80, Sophie wrote:

'I am sitting in my cabinet, right in the sun, like the melons in the hothouse, I have twelve canaries that make a noise as if I were in a thicket. I must thank God for my good constitution, that I can still make the grand tour around the Herrenhausen garden without effort because I very much like to go walking in these beautiful pergolas.'

She died on 8 June 1714, from heart failure, while walking in her garden. A statue of this remarkable woman stands as a monument to her life's work. After her death, the court moved to London in 1714 and Herrenhausen remained dormant, which had the effect of preserving its uniqueness, because it did not succumb to tastes of the time. The King of England George I (1660–1727), formerly Georg Ludwig, Elector of Hannover, enjoyed the extended vistas afforded by the flat terrain and the Thames at Hampton Court, and continued to have a particular attachment to the gardens at Herrenhausen where he abandoned the palace building project and concentrated on adding water features, in particular its Great Fountain, planned during Sophie's time. In a bid to outdo Versailles and Het Loo, he asked Leibniz to devise a water system that would create the tallest jet of water in Europe.

George II (1683–1760) revisited a plan for a new palace at Herrenhausen, more in proportion with the Grosser Garten, but never realized it, as he wanted to rotate the entire palace 180 degrees, to be more in the manner of Versailles. Over the course of a century, the palace fell into disrepair and even faced demolition. The Kingdom of Hanover was established in 1814; however, Hanover was increasingly seen as a reminder of the past by the English and in 1837 the personal union with England came to an end when Queen Victoria ascended to the throne. With Hanover's independence, interest in the garden was reawakened, but the independence ended in 1866 when Hanover was made a province of Prussia. The last Hanoverian king, George V (1819–78) went into exile in Austria.

THE GROSSER GARTEN AND ORANGERY

The Grosser Garten is indeed a great garden, covering 36 hectares (almost 90 acres), and epitomizes an early baroque garden. It is laid out precisely 2.8 degrees askew, a displacement that is intended to fool the eye and produce an unconscious tension. Leibniz remarked that 'the eye is able to detect an irregularity only from 3 degrees onward.' The Grosser Garten is very much an artificial one, celebrating the beauty of nature shaped by humans. It contrasts the adjoining Berggarten and Georgengarten, which are laid out according to English landscape design principles.

The current Orangery was built in 1720 with a half-timber extension added in 1819 by Georg Ludwig Friedrich Laves who later became the court master builder. The Orangery houses the garden's oldest plant – a pomegranate tree brought to Hanover from Venice in 1653. Other species include hibiscus, cypress and palms such as the Chinese windmill palm (*Trachycarpus fortunei*) and the European fan palm (*Chamaerops humilis*). In 1965 garden director Karl H. Meyer updated the Orange Parterre layout as a series of chessboards using coloured marble gravel and low ornamental box hedging. As a direct response to the architecture of the nearby Orangery, orange trees are brought outside in the summer months in large terracotta pots and set out in the manner of chess

ABOVE OPPOSITE
The Grosser Garten

BELOW OPPOSITE
The Blumengarten in the Grosser Garten

pieces. Other plants, belonging to the nightshade family of plants, such as *Brugmansia*, are brought out in wooden containers.

From the Orange Parterre the famous Golden Gate opens onto the Grosser Garten. To the west of the long Grand Galerie, which was originally designed as the Orangery, and is now filled with beautiful stuccoes, and west of the Orange Parterre is the former privy garden, which was redesigned by the Swiss landscape architect Guido Hager as a flower garden. This intimate space contains 36 long, narrow beds echoing the long glass foyer designed by the Danish architect Arne Jacobsen, which on the garden side melds beautifully with the ornate ironwork arches. The narrow beds represent simple carpet patterns found in the palace. The grid pattern is permanent, but every year slight changes are made to the planting, with five colour variations. On the remaining three sides of this flower garden is a *bosquet* of clipped lime trees standing in a sea of evergreen *Bergenia* (elephant's ears) and *Epimedium*. Under the trees, which are trimmed each winter to maintain their cube-like appearance on clear trunks, the shade provides perfect cover from the sun.

On the opposite side of the lime trees in Hager's flower garden is the garden's oldest structure, the Great Cascade by Marinus Cadart from Denmark. It dates from the 1670s and water still falls over its lead shell and mineral decorations. The shells are arranged one above the other in six levels, with 24 curtains of water falling from level to level. Above the cascade are sculptures of Hermes, Luna, Ares, Pallas Athena, Zeus, Hephaestus and Heracles. A second cascade, the Little Cascade, creates a sound that can be heard throughout the garden. When the fountain operates, the increased water pressure in the pipes causes excess air to escape, through the horns of Titans, creating the sound.

Separated by what is now the Herrenhausen Palace Museum and its simple four rectangles of grass with single-species flower borders on either side, was the Fig Garden and pit hothouses for peaches and apricots. Fresh produce, including exotic fruit, was expected by the royal household all year round. In order to keep the hothouses warm inside, layers of horse manure were piled up against the external walls. This proved so effective that the first fruits could be harvested in April. Today, once again, Herrenhausen has a Kitchen Garden and a Fig Garden.

On the opposite side of the Fig Garden is another very popular element of a formal baroque garden: a grotto. Records show that it was designed by Michael Riggus from Augsburg in 1676. Although no drawings or plans survive to show how the grotto once looked, researchers and restorers believe that internally it was probably decorated with crystals, minerals, shells and glass. Starting afresh, in 1996 French-American artist Niki de Saint Phalle started creating a modern art piece to delight the senses. She interpreted a new vision of an artificial dripstone cave, transforming the rooms in the grotto into a walk-through work of art with her use of coloured pebbles and mirror-glass mosaic. The work was completed within two years and opened on 29 March 2003.

THE GREAT PARTERRE AND UNNATURAL PRECISION

The Great Parterre is a vast expanse of pure artificial decoration laid out on a level substrate, linked by means of pathways and neatly trimmed lawns in a larger chequerboard formation with a central axis. It was designed by Henri Perronet between 1674 and 1678 as a main focal point. The circular Bell Fountain (Glockenfontäne) is in the centre of eight highly decorated motif rectangular beds. The Great Parterre and the rest of the Grosser Garten are a spatial expression of order, values and identity. To claim it is purely created in the French formal garden style would be misleading. The Dutch style, and in particular Het Loo, had a strong influence, and in order to create a sense of identity Electress Sophie and George I developed gardening as an art form with a true identity, which is more akin to the German term *landschaft*. The Bell Fountain has 164 jets of water that meet in the middle, creating a dome of water. The perspective of the wide longitudinal pathways, like those at Versailles and Het Loo, emphasizes the length of the parterre and creates a sense of infinity and continuity as it passes through the *bosquets* and ends at the Vollmond, a circular seating area. The entire garden has been designed with remarkable regularity and symmetry. All of the plants are cut and trimmed as ornament, as a geometric element. The planting beds are edged with ornamental box and in summer may contain more than 30,000 flowering plants.

A creative and effective element within the garden is provided by the dazzling white Deister sandstone sculptures, which stand out among the dark surroundings. In fact, in its natural state the sandstone is grey-brown in colour, so previously the gardener Jens Petersen was in charge of painting the sculptures white. Today, every three to four years the sculptures are cleaned with a water jet before an open-pored chalky paint is applied. Statues of the four continents known at the time, the seasons, the elements, mythological figures and creatures and gods, along with decorative vases on pedestals lead the eye around the garden. To the east is the Garden Theatre (dating from 1689–92), the oldest in Germany. Behind the stage forming a half-circle and in front as two rows are box-shaped lime trees which are trimmed regularly, strengthening the impression of 'unnatural precision'. Also in front of the stage are two rows of gilded-lead statues, equally spaced while narrowing to a point before reaching the Little Cascade of 1892, reinforcing the regular formality and fooling the eye into believing the area is longer than it actually is. The entire theatre space is enclosed with tall hornbeam hedging, creating a separate outdoor room. To the west is a viewing terrace providing a panoramic view of the garden. This embankment is symmetrical to the theatre and was raised in 1937 so that the geometry of the Great Parterre could be fully appreciated from above. On the opposite side of the viewing terrace is an octagonal labyrinth with orbiting circles containing a decorative vase on a pedestal and a bench – somewhere quiet to sit. In the centre of the labyrinth is a small wooden temple, and half a kilometre (a third of a mile) of hornbeam hedging creates a border to the labyrinth. What is seen today is a reconstruction from old plans dating from between 1936 and 1937.

Running along the far end (south) of the Great Parterre are eight theme gardens which depict the notion of *landschaft*, creating separate outdoor rooms that embrace the history of garden art with spaces designed in the Italian Renaissance style through to the late baroque style. While some inspiration came from France, and in particular André Le Nôtre's Vaux-le-Vicomte, Hortus Platinus (a baroque garden at Heidelberg Palace in south-west Germany) was also a creative stimulus.

To either side of the theme gardens are the *bosquets*. Hornbeam hedges have been trained into precise geometric shapes, forming green corridors with private niches. Along the outer, longer lengths of the Grosser Garten are dense parallel groupings of limes. In summer their canopies provide much-needed shade. However, the parallel grouping to the west of the Grosser Garten has an additional row of trees, highlighting the 2.8-degree discrepancy.

The Nouveau Jardin lies to the south of the Grosser Garten. Over a ten-year period, starting in 1699, the area was divided into four and then each quarter subdivided into eight triangles. Pathways and lawns dissect the area at the centre of which is the Great Fountain. Originally it was planted with hornbeam hedges and fruit trees as an orchard. At the two southernmost corners are two pavilions by Charles Louis Remy de la Fosse. When first built in c.1706 they were both constructed of wood; however, in 1754 the one in the south-western corner burned down and was rebuilt of stone. At the end of the central axis is the Vollmond, from which the palace and the two pavilions can be viewed through the corridors of lime and hornbeam trees.

THE GREAT FOUNTAIN

Like French gardens of the period, in order to demonstrate unimaginable wealth and power, there are 30 cascades and fountains within the Grosser Garten. The Great Fountain has been in place since 1720, with water diverted from a spring on the Benther ridge above Hanover via a network of 15 kilometres (more than 9 miles) of pipes made of 1,400 hollowed pine

trunks; however, at the time the water pressure was not powerful enough to produce a great fountain. It was George I of England who sent English technicians, including William Benson, to Herrenhausen with the task of producing a watering pump system that would create a great fountain. In 1721 they succeeded with a 35-metre (more than 110 feet) jet directly up into the air. Water was forced through a 4-millimetre (⅛-inch) slit at an incredible speed of 140 kilometres per hour (87 miles per hour). It eclipsed the fountain at Peterhof Palace (see page 198) which reached only 21 metres (69 feet). This spectacle was described by garden writer Christian Cay Lorenz Hirschfeld:

'It is perhaps the only fountain that one looks at because of its height with a delight that approaches a feeling of sublime. Meanwhile the proud column froths upwards, and glistening diamonds drop away, fall and disappear, like the crown jewels on the heads of monarchs.'

The Great Fountain was alleged to be the tallest in Europe at the time. In 1956, fitted with an electric pump, its jet achieved a height of 72 metres (236 feet). The 2-kilometre (more than a mile) long canal was constructed between 1696 and 1701, requiring 100,000 cubic metres (3.5 million cubic feet) of earth to be excavated by hand. Although intended for flood defence, the canal was used for pleasure: to ride on a Venetian gondola. The boathouse and gondolas were built by gondolier Pierre Madonetto, who was brought from Venice especially.

BERGGARTEN, GEORGEN-GARTEN AND WELFENGARTEN

Within the Berggarten, to the north of the palace, there is no lofty peak, but there is a plethora of plants. Today, 11,000 different plant species can be found here.

The first mention of gardeners tending the Berggarten dates back to c.1700. In 1726, two identical parallel avenues of double-rowed lime trees were planted in the Georgengarten and the Berggarten to connect the summer residence with the city of Hanover. The rows of trees in the Berggarten extend the central axis of the Grosser Garten when viewed from above and end at the Welf family mausoleum. The rows in the Georgengarten of Herrenhauser *allée*, heading in an easterly direction, reached 2 kilometres (more than a mile) in length, and were completely renewed between 1972 and 1974.

In 1666 Duke John Frederick, the older brother of Ernest Augustus, commissioned the gardens at Herrenhausen, turning the area of land to the north of the palace into a productive kitchen garden, but it was Electress Sophie who, in 1668, built the first glasshouse at Herrenhausen to grow coffee and cocoa. However, the climate of north-west Germany was not conducive for many exotic plants, and towards the end of the seventeenth century a more hardy option – a mulberry plantation complete with silk worms – was introduced (and lasted for about a century).

Friedrich Ehrhart, a pupil of the great Swedish botanist Carl von Linné, was working at the Berggarten when a pineapple house was built in 1734; pineapples were the treat of nobility. In 1790 Ehrhart compiled a plant catalogue using the Linnaean taxonomy. His task:

'To correct and expand the knowledge on everything concerning foreign plants existing in Herrenhausen, and to procure everything it was

lacking, to draw everything unknown and unfamiliar into the light, to define everything indefinite and to make known everything useful.'

With the desire to grow more exotic plants, towards the end of the eighteenth century Berggarten became a botanic garden filled with plants from around the world, including rhododendrons and azaleas. This garden, reminiscent of a park landscape and more natural compared to the formal rigid

OPPOSITE

Berggarten greenhouses

LEFT

Pomegranate

structure of the Grosser Garten, was set out with expanses of lawn with grouped plantings of trees and areas dedicated to certain species. Johann Christoph Wendland was appointed as master gardener in 1795 and subsequently became garden inspector. Three generations of the Wendland family cared for the Berggarten. Johann's son Heinrich Ludolph took over in 1829. New greenhouses were built under Heinrich Ludolph, and it was he who brought the first 21 palm trees to the Berggarten in 1834, expanding the collection over the next 20 years to 224. In 1815 Heinrich Ludolph was an intern at Kew Botanic Garden (see page 34) and he enlisted the help of others at Kew to restore the losses incurred in Hanover during the Napoleonic occupation.

To the east of the Grosser Garten is the Georgengarten, which covers 50 hectares (124 acres). It was named after George V, King of Hanover (1819–78). The garden was laid out from 1835 by Christian Schaumburg in the new English landscape style and is one of the few mature landscape gardens in Germany. The Welfengarten, now a city park, is earlier still, dating from 1720, and also in the style of English landscape gardens with beech, oak, chestnut, maple, ash and plane trees arching over vast expanses of lawn.

Following in the tradition of his father and grandfather, Hermann Wendland was appointed court gardener in 1859. He travelled widely, reaching Central America and Costa Rica. He introduced the African violet (*Saintpaulia*) and the antirrhinum to Europe. The mid-nineteenth century was the 'golden age of palms' and Wendland became the continent's expert. He named 129 species of palm and grew at Herrenhausen the tallest palm in Europe: an Australian fan palm (*Livistona australis*), which when measured in 1826–7 had reached 32 metres (more than 100 feet) in height. Unfortunately, it was cut down in 1920.

During the Second World War areas of Hanover, like many other European cities, were destroyed by bombing, and Herrenhausen did not escape damage. Plants were uprooted or wrecked, the gardens and palace suffered badly: all that remained of the palace were the outdoor steps that form the Herrenhausen Balcony. Its greenhouses were razed, except one. Years of restoration work and dedicated staff and volunteers restored its fortunes. In 1903 Herrenhausen had the largest orchid collection in Europe. In 1948 the Orchid House (Orchideenschauhaus) and the Canarian House (Kanarenhaus) were erected; the latter displays the Dragon tree (*Dracaena draco*) and Canary laurels (*Laurus novocanariensis* and *Apollonias barbujana*). In 1958 a Tropical House (Tropenschauhaus) was added, measuring 300 square metres (3,300 square feet). It displays tropical plants including bromeliads, cocoa, coffee and the Amazon water lily (*Victoria amazonica),* also found at Kew (see page 41). The Cactus House (Kakteenschauhaus) displays 2,400 different cacti and 1,000 succulents. Remarkably, the tallest cactus, *Cereus forbesii*, which currently stands at 7 metres (23 feet), survived the bombings.

Immediately behind the Tropical House is the iris, stone and pergola garden based on the work of the internationally renowned plantsman Karl Foerster. It gradually blends into the rocky steppe garden and the prairie garden, both created in 1996. This area of the Berggarten is a mass of colour and texture, coming into its own in the autumn with helenium, rudbeckia, ornamental grasses and *Origanum laevigatum* 'Herrenhausen' (a German nursery introduction, named after the palace). Together these areas cover about 0.9 hectare (a little more than 2 acres). Where the Great Palm House once stood is the Rainforest House (Regenwaldhaus), opened in 2000. It is the work of architects Gordon Wilson and Ray Hole, who also designed the Princess of Wales Conservatory at Kew. Beneath the building's 15-metre (50-foot) glass dome is a Sealife Aquarium, opened in 2007.

Herrenhausen and the gardens that surround it are truly a diversion from modern life. The gardens have become an art form, bringing a sense of identity and shaping horticultural, social and political values. Inspiration may have come from French, Dutch and English formal gardens, but the vision of Electress Sophie means that Herrenhausen has remained unchanged, as a German baroque garden.

OPPOSITE

Berggarten exterior

SCHWERIN CASTLE

GERMANY

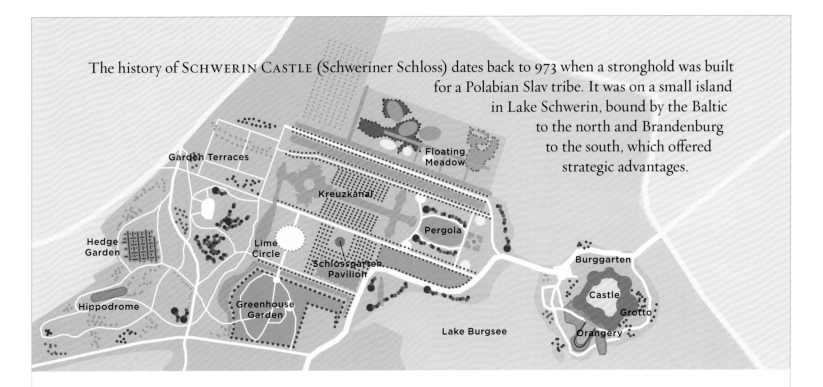

The history of SCHWERIN CASTLE (Schweriner Schloss) dates back to 973 when a stronghold was built for a Polabian Slav tribe. It was on a small island in Lake Schwerin, bound by the Baltic to the north and Brandenburg to the south, which offered strategic advantages.

Garden Terraces

Floating Meadow

Kreuzkanal

Pergola

Hedge Garden

Lime Circle

Schlossgarten Pavilion

Burggarten

Castle

Grotto

Hippodrome

Greenhouse Garden

Lake Burgsee

Orangery

Schwerin Castle now stands on the same site, 100 kilometres (60 miles) east of Hamburg. During the twelfth century Germanic territories were under threat from Henry 'the Lion' van Beieren (1129–95), Duke of Saxony and Bavaria, and the stronghold was destroyed in 1160 by the Obotrites under Niklot (1090–1160). The Slavic Obotrites opposed Saxon rule and after many years of revolt and destruction Henry the Lion made Privislav, Niklot's son, Prince of Mecklenburg. This marked the formation of a ducal dynasty, the House of Mecklenburg, and from 1358 Schwerin became the seat of the Duchy of Mecklenburg until 1918. The fortified castle itself, constructed in c.1500, was one of the main residences.

During the Renaissance, architecture across the North German states was transformed when John Albert I (1525–76), Duke of Mecklenburg, sponsored the introduction of terracotta from Lübeck, a city renowned for its brick Gothic architecture. Several cathedrals, including Schwerin, were constructed of brick, and the castle itself was gradually altered from stronghold to palace, using brick for ornamentation. However, in 1612 the architect Ghert Evert Piloot was commissioned by the Mecklenburgs to redesign the castle entirely differently. Work started in 1617 but was interrupted by the Thirty Year's War (1618–48) and

was realized only in part between 1635 and 1643 when Dutch Renaissance-style inspired facades were added. Most of the castle as it appears today dates from the early nineteenth century.

NEO-RENAISSANCE AND HISTORICISM

Schwerin Castle's transformation into one of Europe's leading examples of the neo-Renaissance style with baroque gardens began under the patronage of Frederick Francis I (1756–1837), Grand Duke of Mecklenburg-Schwerin, then Paul Frederick (1800–42). But Frederick Francis II (1823–83) oversaw its reconstruction and completion between 1843 and 1857. Rekindling a form of Romanticism, following the historicism style, the castle morphed into its current five-wing form with ornamental gables. Responsible for this work were leading builders of the time: master builder Karl Friedrich Schinkel, Friedrich August Stüler and Georg Adolf Demmler.

Demmler, however, was more of a 'modern' architect and could not please the Grand Duke with his designs. After travels across Europe, Demmler finally based his third design for Schwerin Castle on Château de Chambord, a Renaissance-style hunting lodge in the Loire Valley belonging to the king of France

PREVIOUS PAGES

Schwerin Castle

OPPOSITE

The Burggarten

Francis I (1494–1547). Schwerin is the archetypal fairy-tale castle, resplendent with towers and turrets, set on a small island within a lake, and surrounded by magnificent gardens.

FREDERICK FRANCIS II, GRAND DUKE OF MECKLENBURG-SCHWERIN

Frederick Francis II was born at Ludwigslust Palace on 28 February 1823, the eldest son of Paul Frederick and Princess Alexandrine of Prussia (1830–92). In 1842 Frederick Francis II became Grand Duke of Mecklenburg-Schwerin. He married three times and reigned for 41 years, during which he oversaw numerous legal, health and religious reforms throughout the Grand Duchy. On his death in 1883 an equestrian statue by Ludwig Brunow was commissioned by his son, which stands at the entrance to the main gardens at Schwerin Castle. In 1920 a museum was established in the Grand Duke's quarters and since 1990 the *Landtag* (the parliamentary assembly of Mecklenburg-Vorpommern) has resided here.

THE GARDENS

Today, the gardens and parks of Schwerin Castle cover 25 hectares (over 60 acres) comprised of thirteen main areas. On the small island itself is the Burggarten, which is where Schwerin Castle, the Orangery and the Grotto are located. There are also three bastions, north, west and south (the Orangery and Grotto lie to the east). From the Burggarten, a bridge connects the castle to the Schlossgarten, the main gardens and parkland, and the Schlossgarten Pavilion. The Schlossgarten is composed of regularly spaced trees, avenues, flower borders, large lawns and arcades, with clusters of trees, all of which emphasize the views of the castle, the city, the lake and surrounding countryside. Particular features of the Schlossgarten include two pergola walks, a contemporary 'floating meadow', the canal, a circular grove of lime trees, Alexandrine's Greenhouse Garden as well as the Hedge Garden, garden terraces and the Hippodrome.

The formal water gardens of the cross-shaped canal (Kreuzkanal) are assigned to the French architect Jean Laurent Le Geay, commissioned during the reign of Christian Ludwig II (1683–1756). Le Geay designed the double-armed cross channel along the gardens' central axis, surrounded by sculptures from a famous Saxony sculptor Balthasar Permoser, who trained under Giovanni Battista Foggini and Gian Lorenzo Bernini. The gardens and park were originally constructed as a secluded French-style *château de plaisance* in 1748 with shady walks, statuary and ornamental water features.

Peter Joseph Lenné, a Prussian gardener and landscape architect, expanded the Schlossgarten during the nineteenth century and, altering Le Geay's design for a kitchen garden, created new baroque gardens and parks, which helped to shape the development of nineteenth-century German garden design. Lenné introduced the principles of the English landscape garden to some areas, including Alexandrine's Greenhouse Garden and the Hippodrome, which contrast the baroque gardens and parkland.

THEODOR KLETT, COURT GARDENER

The court gardener throughout this period was Theodor Klett, who was responsible for the Grand Ducal Palace Gardens in Ludwigslust and Schwerin Castle. In 1843 he adopted Lenné's plans for the English landscape castle garden, covering the 1.8 hectares (4½ acres) that forms the Burggarten. It is a deliberately landscaped set of gardens on three sides of the island with curved pathways lined with rare trees and planting that extends to the lake shore, terminating with the small granite Grotto.

Klett had horticultural and creative skills and believed that 'not only the castle island but the whole environment of the castle must correspond to the grandeur and beauty of the castle.' Directly under the castle's main tower, a semi-circular colonnade encloses a symmetrical carpet of trimmed box, shrubs and colourful flowers, including agapanthus, fuchsias and *Brugmansia*. Numerous potted plants – bananas,

ABOVE OPPOSITE
The Burggarten Grotto

BELOW OPPOSITE
The Burggarten Orangery

oleanders and tree ferns – figures and tiles as well as a central shell fountain complement the space.

Around 1840, Klett moved to a property, Wickedesche Büdnerei, on the edge of the lake, where he reworked the plans by Demmler and Lenné. Christine Rehberg-Credé writes in her 2010 book *Theodor Klett: '... einer der vorzüglichsten Gärtner'* [one of the most exquisite gardeners]:

'Garden fence and pergola frame the house of the court gardener and later garden director on a drawing from this period. Years later, a barn planned by court architect Demmler was built behind it. The Grand Duke personally inspected the site and approved the design. From Klett's records it is known that the official residence not only served him and his family as a dwelling, but also a drawing and writing office.'

THE ORANGERY

Following the Industrial Revolution cast-iron became a relatively cheap material for construction and from the mid-nineteenth century it became a prominent structural and decorative feature of many buildings. The delicate ironwork of the Orangery at the heart of the castle garden is an outstanding example of craftsmanship. The Orangery itself was inspired by Roman terraced villas. Plans from 1857 clearly show that every design element – the separate garden areas and roof terraces, the fountain, the stone steps, the sculptures and the flower beds – is consciously placed. It was painstakingly restored to the original plan between 1995 and 2001 and the result provides a true sense of humans' power over nature, beautifully contrasting the landscaped gardens. On top of the Orangery (and the Grotto) is a garden terrace that offers views of the surrounding lakes and shores.

KREUZKANAL AND SURROUNDING AREAS

The castle and gardens at Schwerin are low-lying and waters of Lake Burgsee dominate the landscape. Water features play a major part in the design of the gardens, in the form of channels, fountains, small cascades and the impressive Kreuzkanal. This cross-shaped canal is the perfectly symmetrical central feature of the baroque Schlossgarten, its waters reflecting the castle's Renaissance-style towers. Originally, the plans for the baroque axis led the eye straight to open sky, representing the Grand Duke's power into infinity, with an impressive water cascade on the hillside, but this was never implemented. Instead, the ducal axis was breached, in the nineteenth century, with the construction of a villa and the erection of Brunow's equestrian statue of Frederick Francis II. In 1861 hornbeams were planted around the canal to form two pergola walks (Laubengänge). Despite the geometric formality, there is a simplicity and lightness to the garden.

A lawn terrace designed by Le Geay, at the end of the canal, is known as Ostorfer Berg. In 1766, the Irish travel writer Thomas Nugent wrote of it:

'At the very end of the garden is one
Hill to which a staircase leads up from the lawn!
From the top of this hill you have a lovely
View to the whole surrounding area.'

In 1812 another writer, Stephan Schultz, added:

'The Schwerin Castle Garden extends through the many armed Gartenparthien; one strolls from bridge to bridge via channels to a high terrace on lawn steps from there to the lawn seats, from where the view of the Castle [is the reward]*'*

Further redesigns and additions were made in the nineteenth century, including the hexagonal Schlossgarten Pavilion (now a cafe), set among a rigid grid layout of lime trees, which open up different views across the castle garden and the circle of lime trees (Lindenrondell), and the Greenhouse Garden, which is reached by a low-arched footbridge crossing a straight smaller canal parallel to the Kreuzkanal, where a large open area of lawn leads off to meandering pathways below canopies of trees and a flowing tributary from the Kreuzkanal.

Another feature is the grinding mill on Lake Burgsee, which, from 1706, produced tan from oak tree bark for tanning leather, milled barley up until the 1750s and turned to producing wool from 1862 until 1904. Klett commented in 1853:

'The grinding mill has a historical value for Mecklenburg, and for centuries it has produced art treasures that have been preserved as sanctuaries in many of the highest courts in Europe…. Likewise, the mill as such is an ornament of the castle garden, it brings life into the landscape.'

THE FLOATING MEADOW

To the east side of Lake Burgsee, on an island connected by small bridges is the Floating Meadow (Schwimmende Wiese), covering 6 hectares (almost 15 acres). This is a truly contemporary garden, designed for the Federal Garden Show in 2009. It is approached through a series of white colonnades, 7 metres (23 feet) in height. The 'floating' illusion is achieved by 84 half-moon segment-shaped beds planted with herbaceous perennials, ornamental grasses, bulbs and heathers, with wave-like benches and stretches of green-dyed asphalt, designed by landscape architects Breimann & Bruun (now Bruun & Möllers) at a cost of €18,000,000. One hundred and seventy golden false acacias were planted in a rigid grid-like pattern and pathways formed using the finely crushed glass of hundreds of thousands of wine bottles.

RESTORATION WORK

In order to preserve the magnificent work of 'garden art' (*Gartenkunstwerk*) created by Klett, Lenné and Demmler, as well as the stunning architecture of Schwerin Castle, the Staatliches Museum Schwerin was initiated in 1984. A separate department for parkland and gardens was founded in 1986, which established a set of renovation plans for the future, as well as long-term professional goals. In the 1990s further work focused on the Orangery and the reconstruction of Klett's ornamental beds and plantings in the courtyards. The main goal was always to safeguard the smooth transition from the castle to the garden, Lake Schwerin and the surrounding landscape. This was achieved between 2001 and 2008 following a detailed reconstruction of the castle garden complex. One example, which is of special architectural significance, is the classical round wooden pavilion in the southern area of the Schlossgarten, built originally in 1822 by Johann Georg Barca. It was destroyed by a storm in 1836 and rebuilt the following year, then replaced by a pavilion known as the Youth Temple in *c.*1870. This was demolished in 1964, by which time it was in very poor condition. In 2014 a new Youth Temple was built according to the original plans of 1821. The latest wooden construction is reinforced with steel and sits on a concrete foundation paved in sandstone.

ABOVE AND OPPOSITE
The Schlossgarten

TREES AND HEDGES, OLD AND NEW

On the approach to the castle garden via the bridge on Lennéstrasse there is a large 'hanging' hedge formed of weeping beech, ginkgo and yew. Under the large canopy of a magnificent plane tree, radial rose beds create a formal garden restored to Klett's plans. In the formal area of the geometric baroque garden of the Schlossgarten itself the wide central axis is flanked by two avenues, which are lined with newly planted lime trees. The *bosquets* either side of the Kreuzkanal were replanted between 2006 and 2007 for the Federal Garden Show, and still follow eighteenth-century plans – eight rows of twenty-five trees. The two avenues along the canal parallel to the Kreuzkanal were formerly intended for lords and ladies to stroll separately, resulting in their respective names: Herrenallee and Damenallee. The tree-lined avenues, *bosquets*, pergolas of hornbeam and large expanses of lawn emphasize the length and perspective of this remarkable garden.

Lost over the years, and now marked with a white marble statue of the Grand Duchess Alexandrine, is the Alexandrine Greenhouse Garden (Grunhausgarten mit Alexandrine). A summer house (the Greenhouse), a gift from her husband Paul Frederick, was built between 1835 and 1840, along with a cavalier's house, connected to the Greenhouse by a metal bridge. The buildings still exist today, although the Greenhouse is now a kindergarten, the oldest in Mecklenburg. The Greenhouse was erected on the site of an old palm house mentioned in 1760

and redesigned by Lenné in the early part of the nineteenth century. It was once surrounded by a large winter garden where the Grand Duchess would stroll. Nothing remains of the winter garden; today the area is dominated on two sides by brick walls with roses, bedding plants, lawns, nut trees, planes, gingkos and, close to the water, swamp or bald cypresses, which are perfectly adapted to marshy conditions with their fascinating air roots (known as 'knees', because that is what they resemble) above ground.

The Heckengarten was designed as a garden art installation for the Federal Garden Show in 2009. It is a hedge garden based on the idea of a traditional maze but with a contemporary twist. The hedges create separate rooms and, unlike traditional mazes, all the hedges are different. There are 32 different deciduous and 18 coniferous trees, all of various heights, including yew, hornbeam, crabapple, ornamental cherry and berberis, with flower beds containing campanulas, tulips, saxifrages and Japanese anemones. Seen from above the garden resembles a Mondrian painting, with strong vertical and horizontal lines in shades of green, red and yellow.

Schwerin Castle maintains its sense of history with formal avenues and water features, majestic trees and open spaces. It may not have the expensive gold statues, large areas of intricate parterres or towering glasshouses of many other royal gardens, but its 'simplicity' lends the garden a connectedness to the larger environment and is a nod to a once forgotten past, revived.

Trees and hedges in the Schlossgarten

FONTAINEBLEAU PALACE

FRANCE

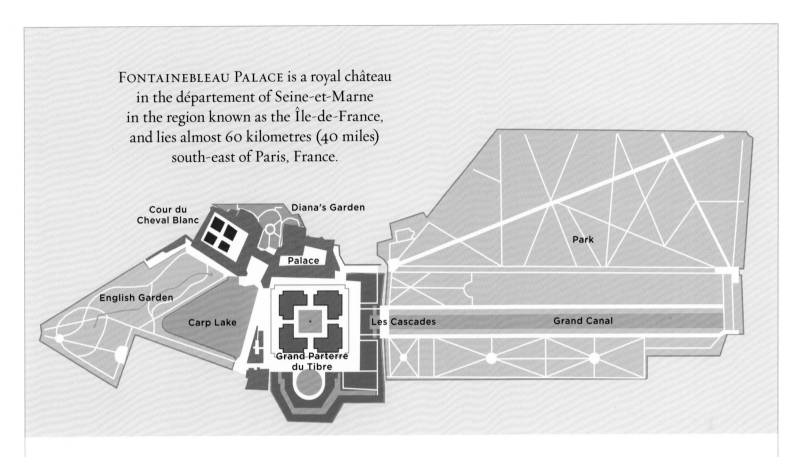

FONTAINEBLEAU PALACE is a royal château in the département of Seine-et-Marne in the region known as the Île-de-France, and lies almost 60 kilometres (40 miles) south-east of Paris, France.

It is situated in the Forest of Fontainebleau, an area of over 17,000 hectares (42,000 acres), which, for centuries, attracted French sovereigns wishing to hunt in the deciduous woodland. Although the palace was built on the site of an earlier royal residence dating back to the twelfth century, what we see today is a masterpiece of French Renaissance architecture, commissioned by Francis I (1494–1547). Fontainebleau has long been overshadowed by its more famous counterpart, Versailles (see page 90), south-west of Paris, yet Fontainebleau predates Versailles by five centuries. Unlike other palaces, it has been continuously occupied for 700 years and has served as a residency for no fewer than 34 French monarchs and 2 emperors, from Louis VII (1120–80) to Napoleon III (1808–73). Napoleon Bonaparte (1769–1821) fondly referred to the château as *La Maison des Siècles*, the House of the Centuries.

MEDIEVAL ORIGINS

It is reported that as early as the twelfth century a manor was built where the château now stands beside a natural spring which gave it the name 'the Blue Fountain' or Fontainebleau. In 1259 a monastery was established by Louis IX (1214–70), for the Trinitarian monks who ran a hospital for the local residents. It remained to the west of the present château until the French Revolution. The palace was also enlarged by Louis IX. Every autumn the king would spend up to two months at the château to enjoy hunting and the peace and quiet away from court. The surrounding park and gardens cover 147 hectares (363 acres), with four main courtyards and three gardens.

BEAUTY AND ELEGANCE

Fontainebleau remained a royal hunting lodge until the reign of Francis I, who was king of France from 1515 to 1547. He has been referred to as France's original Renaissance monarch and was a major patron of the arts. In 1520 Francis I tore down the original building, leaving only the *donjon* (tower). He sought a departure from Gothic architecture in favour of a place of beauty and elegance. Architect and master mason Gilles Le Breton was commissioned to supervise

PREVIOUS PAGES
Fontainebleau Palace

OPPOSITE
The forest

and build the château in the new Renaissance style. Fontainebleau quickly became Francis I's favourite residence. Le Breton was inspired by the Ducal Palace in Urbino in central Italy, adding a refined Oval Court and a series of verdant gardens set out using a strict geometric structure. Other Italian features borrowed and adapted, include open loggias and Corinthian colonnades.

The topography at Fontainebleau was not particularly favourable. The area did not drain freely, and an insufficient slope meant that the water would stagnate in what was the current gardens and castle grounds. However, the excess water was removed by an elaborate system of channels, ditches and a hydraulic system, turning the marshy valley into productive and beautiful gardens.

MANNERISM AND THE SCHOOL OF FONTAINEBLEAU

The main entrance to the palace, to the south, was a mix of new and old styles and introduced Mannerist architecture to France, the style in which artistic invention and imagination were valued, with the use of cartouches, grotesques, scrolls and stucco figures in high relief. Le Breton built a monumental Renaissance internal stairway and a portico called the Serlio Portico (taking its name from one of the Italian architects), to give access to the royal apartments on the north side of the Oval Court. This court was, for centuries, the château's real *cour d'honneur* (court of honour).

Architectural decoration and ornamentation was created by Italian artists, notably the Florentine painter Giovanni Battista di Jacopo (known as Rosso Fiorentino), Francesco Primaticcio, the Italian Mannerist architects Sebastiano Serlio and Giacomo Barozzi da Vignola, as well as French and Flemish artists from 1528 to 1558. The style became known as the School of Fontainebleau, and informed French art and architecture until the end of the sixteenth century, and influenced Flemish Mannerism and architecture in England, Germany and the Netherlands.

The Palace of Fontainebleau was surrounded by a new park in the style of the Italian Renaissance garden, with pavilions and the first grotto in France. Francis I instigated the King's Garden (formerly the privy garden of the queen and therefore also referred to as the Queen's Garden), known today as Jardin de Diane (Diana's Garden), the Jardin des Pins (Pine Garden, which later became the English Garden) and, to the south-east of the castle, the Grand Parterre. Unlike the King's Garden, which had no water feature, until the reign of Henry IV (1553–1610) the Pine Garden, created in 1535, contained a fountain (Belle Eau), which is the spring that inspired the name Fontainebleau. It feeds the artificial river in the Jardin Anglais (English Garden).

HENRY IV: A LOVE AFFAIR WITH FONTAINEBLEAU

After Francis I's death, his son, Henry II (1519–59), and Henry's wife, Catherine de Medici (1519–89), further expanded the palace. But the creation of the gardens owes most to Henry IV, who especially loved Fontainebleau. By the time he settled in Fontainebleau it had become an abandoned château. A Venetian ambassador wrote in 1577: 'Now everything is falling apart: the beautiful lake at the foot of the gallery is almost closed and the gardens themselves are quite messy.' Henry IV set out to enrich both palace and gardens while respecting the achievements of his forebears.

The Renaissance gardens created for Francis I and Henry IV were based on a series of water features and canals that lead to the Grand Canal. One of these water features is the 4-hectare (almost 10-acre) Carp Lake adjacent to the palace, which was used for boating parties by members of the court, and as a source of fish for the kitchen. Below ground, throughout the entire estate, a huge network of drainage channels links all the water features, lakes, canals and fountains, turning this once waterlogged site into a useable pleasure garden.

In 1599, Francis I's small parterre was altered and enlarged by Henry IV to create an enclosed courtyard, the King's Garden. The statue of Diana the Huntress from Francis I's reign remained its main focus and the fountain was built in 1602, embellished with bronze

stag heads and seated hounds that, through clever hydraulic engineering, are made to pee continually into the water. Parterres edged with box and elevated terraces rim the perimeter. Originally it was the king's privy garden, designed in the classic Italian and French styles. An aviary to the north was soon to become an Orangery. Four regular flower beds, copies of ancient bronze sculptures and sweet and bitter orange trees (*Citrus* x *sinensis* and *C.* x *aurantium*) filled the space.

FOUNTAINS AND PARTERRES

The estate's fountains were entrusted to two Tuscan engineers, Tommaso and Alessandro Francini. Henry IV created the Jardin de l'Étang (Island Garden) in the Carp Lake in front of the Cour de la Fontaine. The garden was originally laid out in 1595 as a *parterre de broderie* but it was destroyed in 1713 then restored between 1807 and 1811. Louis IV laid out the Grand Parterre du Tibre, in reference to the colossal sculpture of Father Tiber reclining on a rock in the centre. At the corners of this parterre there were other fountains, arranged in pairs.

Along the axis of the Grand Parterre, on the site of the garden of Francis I, Henry IV built a Grand Canal reminiscent of one at the nearby château of Fleury-en-Bière. It stretched 1,200 metres long (almost 4,000 feet) and 40 metres (more than 130 feet) wide eastwards from the Grand Jardin of the Valois (Great Royal Garden) and was created purely as 'theatre'.

Hunting was one of the favourite sports of the French aristocracy but another was *jeu de paume* 'the game of kings, the king of games', the forerunner of tennis. Originally the *jeu de paume* hall at Fontainebleau was built under Henry IV's reign, then rebuilt in 1732, having been destroyed by a fire in 1702. It was restored in 1812 and still retains almost all of its original features, including its limestone flags.

The magnificent horseshoe-shaped double staircase in the Cour du Cheval Blanc was designed by French architect Jean Androuet du Cerceau. The Cour du Cheval Blanc was named after a plaster cast (untraced) of the horse from a statue of Emperor Marcus Aurelius in Rome.

LOUIS XIV, LE NÔTRE AND LE VAU

Louis XIV (1638–1715) came to the throne in 1643, and although Fontainebleau was by far the finest of his palaces, he was more interested in Versailles. During his reign, his greatest architectural achievement at Fontainebleau was the Grand Parterre, which, at 11 hectares (27 acres) was the biggest formal garden in Europe. It was created between 1660 and 1664 by Louis XIV's principal gardener André Le Nôtre and baroque architect Louis Le Vau. The four symmetrical areas were defined by geometric patterns, topiarized yew and paths edged with box and the borders filled with colourful herbs and flowers. Although the French formal box hedge 'embroidery' style disappeared under Louis XIV's successor, his great-grandson Louis XV, today the Grand Parterre is filled with up to 45,000 flowering plants during summer. In this area are two basins, a square one known as the Boiling Pot and, just to the south, a round one known as Romulus, with the statue of Father Tiber at its centre. A viewing terrace was introduced, better to appreciate the arabesque decoration. The Grand Parterre provides the perfect spot to look back at the sprawling palace, its linked buildings and overall sense of grandeur.

Le Nôtre also added a basin to the north-east of the Grand Parterre, called Les Cascades (it is decorated with fountains), at the head of the Grand Canal, planted hornbeams parallel to the canal for shade, and formed a wide path. Le Nôtre's use of the 'art of perspective' leads the eye across the canal.

In the northern area of the Grand Canal, already largely shaped during Henry IV's reign, 60,000 trees were planted in an area described as a 'small Boccage filled with [five] bright sources of water'. This was later called La Grande Prairie (the Great Meadow) and it departed from the rigid geometry of the formal gardens to represent the wider landscape beyond the estate. The expanse of meadows was scattered with pines, *Sorbus* and willows – nature in all its glory. Running the length of the landscape-style park Le Nôtre established a decorative trellis on a high terrace on which Chasselas vines grew. At their peak, the vines produced 2,700–3,000 kilograms (6,000–7,000

ABOVE OPPOSITE   *BELOW OPPOSITE*

The Grand Canal   The Grand Parterre du Tibre

pounds) of grapes. Le Nôtre also installed five pools and fountains in the park area. By the time of Louis XIV's death in 1715 there was very little left of the gardens created by his grandfather Henry IV.

NAPOLEON BONAPARTE AND MAXIMILIEN-JOSEPH HURTAULT

Perhaps no other royal favoured Fontainebleau as much as the first emperor of France, Napoleon Bonaparte, who restored the palace at a cost of 12,000,000 francs. He also commissioned the architect Maximilien-Joseph Hurtault between 1810 and 1812 to remodel the gardens to the south into a Jardin Anglais (English Garden), following the fashion of the picturesque garden – even though the style was not one that Napoleon himself favoured – and to restore the Jardin de Diane. The English Garden contains the first Renaissance-style grotto of Francis I, a rustic stone structure decorated with four statues of Atlas. It also features two seventeenth-century bronze copies of ancient Roman originals, the Borghese Gladiator and the Dying Gladiator. The English Garden was an entirely artificial environment with a river, boulders, plants, groves and sinuous pathways, designed for gentle recreation and pleasant pursuits. Avenues were created with a remarkable collection of exotic trees, including white fir (*Abies concolor*), red horse chestnut (*Aesculus x carnea*), catalpa (*Catalpa bignonioides*), Judas tree (*Cercis siliquastrum*), purple beech (*Fagus sylvatica* f. *purpurea*), black walnut (*Juglans nigra*), tulip tree (*Liriodendron tulipifera*), Corsican pine (*Pinus maritima*), Scots pine (*P. sylvestris*), oriental plane (*Platanus orientalis*), Italian poplar (*Populus x canadensis* var. *serotina*), Canadian poplar (*P. x canadensis*), white acacia (*Robinia pseudoacacia*), Japanese pagoda tree (*Styphnolobium japonicum*) and bald or swamp cypress (*Taxodium distichum*). Hurtault radically changed the palace gardens yet left the Grand Parterre and the park practically unchanged.

During the period 1852 to 1870, Fontainebleau once again became an imperial château with the return of the empire under Napoleon III.

UNUSUAL PLANTS

In *Description générale du Château de Fontainebleau* (1842), Claude-François F. Denecourt listed the following plants:

Bugle ivette (*Ajuga chamaepitys*), Buglose officinale (*Anchusa officinalis*), Euphraise officinale (*Euphrasia rostkoviana*), Laser à feuilles larges (*Laserpitium latifolium*), Molène officinale (*Verbascum thapsus*), Ornithogale jaune (*Gagea lutea*), Ornithogale des Pyrénées (*Ornithogalum pyrenaicum*), Potentille ou quinte-feuille (*Potentilla reptans*), Rosier églantier (*Rosa canina*), Spirée filipendule (*Filipendula ulmaria*) and Véronique officinale (*Veronica officinalis*).

Such plants were not common in royal gardens but represented Le Nôtre's desire to use 'wilder' species to tie the manmade landscape to the natural world. *Sorbus latifolia* (broad-leaved whitebeam, or the service tree of Fontainebleau) occurs widely in the English Garden and the palace hunting woods. It is a hybrid, a cross between *S. torminalis* (the wild service tree) and trees of the whitebeam subgenus, but – unlike many hybrids – it can grow true from seed. These vigorous, glossy-leaved trees are endemic to the area around Fontainebleau, but rare elsewhere. Until the 1950s, their edible orange-brown little fruit were sold at the market in Fontainebleau.

RESTORATION

During the Franco-Prussian War (1870–71), Fontainebleau was occupied by Prussian troops, then during the Second World War the palace was again occupied – by German troops. After liberation in 1944 it became a Western Allied headquarters from 1945 to 1966. The palace was falling into disrepair until, under Charles de Gaulle's presidency, restoration work began.

Fontainebleau now has a twelve-year restoration plan, from 2014 to 2026, aided by €115,000,000 of funding. Versailles, which embarked on its own €350,000,000, seventeen-year overhaul in 2003, is the only other royal residence in France to have received public funding of a similar largesse.

VERSAILLES

FRANCE

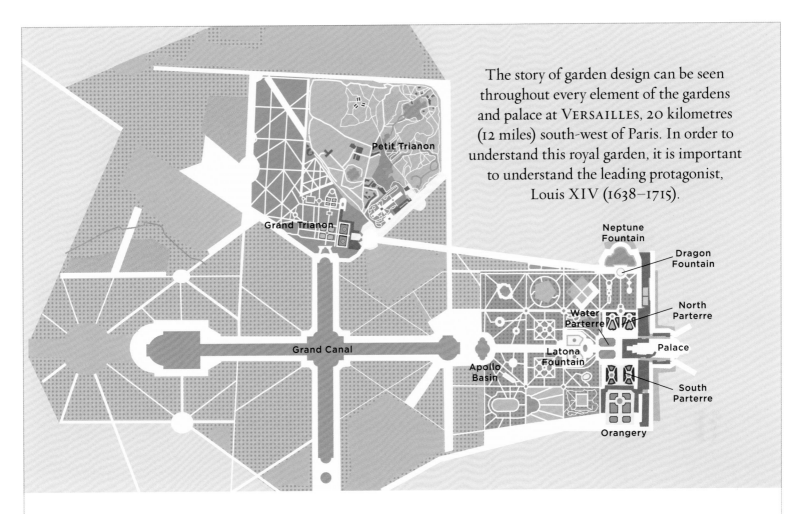

The story of garden design can be seen throughout every element of the gardens and palace at VERSAILLES, 20 kilometres (12 miles) south-west of Paris. In order to understand this royal garden, it is important to understand the leading protagonist, Louis XIV (1638–1715).

His reign is often referred to as *le grand siècle* (the great century), for he was seen as a strong, absolute monarch. Born on 5 September 1638, at the age of four he became king when his father, Louis XIII (1601–43), died. His mother, Anne of Austria (1601–66), served as regent with chief minister Cardinal Mazarin, who also tutored and was godfather to the young king. Upon Cardinal Richelieu's death on 4 December 1642, Mazarin continued the work of Richelieu to establish France's supremacy within Europe and cripple the domestic opposition to the power of the monarchy.

Louis XIV's early years as king were marked by a series of rebellions and revolts known as the Fronde, which arose from discontent over new taxes being imposed upon leading Parisians. The events of the Fronde and being fearful for his life in Paris meant Louis spent more time at Versailles. The Fronde came to an end in 1653, and Louis XIV was crowned the following year. In 1660 he married the daughter of Philip IV of Spain (1605–65), Maria Theresa (1638–83),

the Spanish Infanta. When Mazarin died in 1661, Louis decided to rule without a chief minister, believing his power to be divine. He carefully fashioned this image and took the sun as his emblem, aligning himself with Apollo, (Greek god of peace, light and the arts) as his emblem – hence his title 'Sun King' – and he controlled everything, from court ceremonies to portraiture.

THE START OF VERSAILLES

Versailles was originally a small château used as a hunting lodge by Louis XIII with grounds that extended to 800 hectares (almost 2,000 acres). Formal gardens were laid out and records show that they were designed during the 1630s by Claude Mollet and Hilaire Masson and remained little altered until the 1660s. An early layout, known as the Du Bus Plan of c.1662, shows a north–south and east–west set of axes.

The year 1661 marked the beginning of the opulent palace and gardens that is Versailles, and it became

PREVIOUS PAGES

The Orangery

OPPOSITE

The Apollo Fountain

the political centre of France, when the government moved there in 1682. Louis XIV and his courtiers alternated between the Louvre Palace, then the Tuileries, the châteaux of Saint-Germain-en-Laye (where he was born), Vincennes, Fontainebleau (see page 80) and the fast-growing Versailles. Leading artists of the day surrounded the king and he greatly enjoyed hunting, promenades, fencing and parlour games, as well as staging operas, plays and hosting extravagant parties.

Louis summoned André Le Nôtre to create and renovate the gardens at Versailles and the architect Louis Le Vau and painter Charles Le Brun to work on the palace, with baroque architect Jules Hardouin-Mansart working on the expansion of the palace in the late 1670s. The gardens and palace were designed and constructed simultaneously and Le Vau was commissioned to extend the original brick and stone château to form the King's and Queen's Apartments. On the garden side he covered the original brick with white cut ashlar stone, which became known as Le Vau's *envelope*, forming a modern and distinctive feature that unites the facade with the gardens below.

Le Nôtre was working on the gardens of Chantilly in Picardy when he was summoned by the king. He is considered to be the father of the 'French-style' garden, which is based on long tree-lined avenues set out on strong axes, with formal straight lines and symmetry, stretching far into the distance, interspersed with parterres, groves, water features, fountains, flower borders and low hedges. It is a masterpiece of garden design that has been copied around the world for centuries. Originally inspired by Italian Renaissance garden design and the use of geometry with large areas subdivided into smaller squares, Le Nôtre formalized his style of garden design over a 25-year period, while working on Versailles. A pupil at Les Tuileries gardens in Paris, he created the vast perspective for which the Champs-Elysées is famous. Later, his work at the baroque chateau Vaux-le-Vicomte in Seine-et-Marne for finance minister Nicolas Fouquet between 1656 and 1661 became a celebrated aesthetic.

UNFOLDING SCENES

Versailles is a garden of huge proportions and a prodigious amount of earth had to be dug, reshaped and moved by hand and carthorse. Thousands of men, sometimes entire regiments, took part in this ambitious project. Jean-Baptiste Colbert managed the project, with the king overseeing and checking every detail. It took almost 40 years to create but, like every garden, it required and still requires maintenance, restoration, replanting and a great deal of time and investment. Trees were brought from different regions of France. Le Brun provided many of the drawings for the statues and fountains. Le Nôtre's plan comprised three avenues forming a trident or *trivium*, leading to the palace, to which he added fountains, canals, and several square flower beds. Near the palace, on the site of King Louis XIII's garden, Le Nôtre created two large parterres to the north and south, and redesigned the east-west axis by extending the perspective far into the distance – his acclaimed 'art of perspective' – creating an 'infinite' vista. *Bosquets* (groves) provided shady places to meet and sit, while open spaces were turned into parterres. It is nearly impossible to see Versailles all at once. The landscape reveals itself slowly, like the succession of scenes within a play.

Le Nôtre introduced trellises and arbours forming living green walls that strengthened perspectives, while diagonal or winding alleys led to *bosquets* designed to surprise visitors. Water features contrasted with the areas planted with trees. While adhering to geometric principles they provided an open aspect, flooded with natural light. Within the overall scheme, Le Nôtre set up a grid of smaller areas, each with its own individual design, using plants such as bergamot (*Monarda didyma*) and lily of the valley (*Convallaria majalis*). Surrounding the palace were several parterres. These, like the principal avenues, were dotted with statues and topiarized yews. (It is worthy of note, however, that the current parterres are reconstructions of ones dating from the 1920s. Old etchings show that, unlike the lawns bordered by small hedges that we see today, the parterres were intricately shaped lawns traced directly onto gravel.) The Water Parterre, Latona's

ABOVE OPPOSITE *BELOW OPPOSITE*
The Palace   The Grand Trianon

Parterre, the North Parterre, the Middle Parterre (also referred to as the Flower Garden), which is on the roof of the Orangery, and the South Parterre – best viewed from the higher Middle Parterre – are some of the most stunning examples, decorated with box and flowers in the typical scrolling patterns known as arabesque.

Farther away from the palace there were *bosquets*, wooded outdoor 'rooms' or *cabinets de verdure*, in geometric patterns. Some were formal while others were less constrained in imitation of nature. There were eight *bosquets* on the north side of the central *tapis vert* of the Royal Way and six on the south, all of which were created between 1680 and 1690.

THE IMPORTANCE OF WATER

The 1.5 kilometre (almost 1-mile) long Grand Canal at Versailles is truly a marvel of design and engineering. Louis XIV sailed small craft, including gondolas, on it. Le Nôtre's task was to create a perfect visual harmony; in fact, the Grand Canal has two lateral canals that are unequal in width; one is 62 metres (200 feet) and the other 80 metres (260 feet). On paper, the design looks asymmetrical but when the king arrived in person at the Latona Basin everything appeared perfectly harmonious and symmetrical. Le Nôtre had relied on an optical illusion to give the impression that the canal is much larger than it is. The technique, known as anamorphosis, is a distorted projection or perspective in which the observer is required to occupy a specific vantage point to resolve the view. Trees now obscure the view from the Latona Basin.

Water features played a key role in French gardens, and were often considered more important than the plants or groves. Versailles' garden is designed around avenues running parallel or perpendicular to the Royal Way. Eleven main fountains animate the gardens with their sound and display of water cascading over statues, or spraying from the mouths of dolphins, horses and other themes from Greek and Roman mythology. Closest to the palace is the *parterre d'eau*, in fact two water parterres or large pools that reflect the palace facade itself. Le Nôtre masterfully designed the pools so that they also reflect light into the windows of Versailles' famed Hall of Mirrors. Down a stairway leading away from the palace is the Latona Fountain, set in the middle of the Latona Basin. The fountain was inspired by Ovid's *Metamorphoses*. The Apollo Basin, originally known as the Pond of the Swans, was constructed during the reign of Louis XIII and later adorned by Louis XIV with sculptures of Apollo, the sun god. It is located at the end of the two *allées*, one on either side of the central *tapis vert* that forms the Royal Way, before they meet the Grand Canal. In total there are 55 fountains at Versailles, including four dedicated to the seasons, and others adorned with mythological and allegorical figures such as the Neptune Fountain and – tallest of all – the Dragon Fountain with a main water jet that spouts 27 metres (88 feet). Among Versailles' other allegorical water features are the reflective Mirror Basin, the Bath of the Nymphs, the Basin of the Pyramid, and, on the edge of the grove, the Golden Children's Basin.

THE PORCELAIN TRIANON AND THE GRAND TRIANON

In 1668 Louis XIV built a smaller palace some distance from the main residence, where he could spend time away from the crowds and formality of court. He purchased the village of Trianon which adjoined the park, and constructed a pavilion covered with blue and white porcelain in the fashionable Chinese style. It became known as the Porcelain Trianon. This he replaced, in 1687, with the Grand Trianon, a larger and more classical pavilion designed by Mansart.

THE ORANGERY AND LABYRINTH

Like other royal gardens, the Orangery at Versailles was built for cultivating citrus trees and protecting them during the winter; however, it covers a staggering 3 hectares (7½ acres). Today, it houses more than 1,000 trees including citrus trees, such as *Citrus x aurantium*, that are more than 200 years old, originally imported from Italy, Spain and Portugal. During the summer, gardeners move many of the plants from the orangery to the gardens outside.

ABOVE OPPOSITE   *BELOW OPPOSITE*

The Petit Trianon   Yew topiaries

There was a labyrinth at Versailles, located just west of the Orangery in the southern part of the gardens. It was created by Le Nôtre in 1665 as a plain, undecorated maze. In the 1670s, the statesman and writer Charles Perrault transformed it with 330 lead animals, depicting Aesop's fables, and 39 fountains. It proved difficult to maintain the labyrinth; it was neglected in the eighteenth century and finally destroyed in 1774 to be replaced by a grove in the English garden style, more to the liking of Marie Antoinette (1755–93). Only fragments of Perrault's fountains have survived.

FRUIT AND VEGETABLES FIT FOR A KING

Of great importance to the palace was the Potager du Roi (the king's kitchen garden), located south-east of the palace, where fresh vegetables and fruit were grown for the royal table. It covers an astounding 9 hectares (22 acres) and was developed by Jean Baptiste de la Quintinie. On the site of a swamp known as 'stinking pond', Mansart designed the original layout with 29 regular plots with walls for training fruit trees. To overcome the swampy conditions, an underground aqueduct, rubble drains and raised beds were constructed between 1678 and 1683. The green-fingered La Quintinie cultivated rare fruits and vegetables and the individual microclimates of the different sections of the garden allowed him to raise produce out of season, such as asparagus in mid-winter and strawberries in early spring. His system for providing figs in early summer involved keeping 700 potted fig trees in a sunken garden to be heaved into the adjacent *figuerie* building in winter. La Quintinie produced 50 varieties of pears and 20 varieties of apples. Herbs played a large part in the potager, among them chervil, rocket, tarragon,

RIGHT AND OPPOSITE
The Petit Trianon

mint and lemon balm. After La Quintinie died in 1688, three generations of the Le Normand family tended the potager for 90 years from 1691. Louis Normand, who took responsibility in 1723, introduced the Dutch greenhouse, which resulted in the first pineapples in France being grown in the potager in the 1730s. Today, the École Nationale Supérieure du Paysage continues to cultivate some 130 apple varieties and as many pears, a wide range of small red fruits, and traditional and heritage vegetables.

PERIOD OF NEGLECT AND SUBSEQUENT YEARS

After Louis XIV died in September 1715, the court moved back to Paris and Versailles entered a long period of neglect. Peter the Great (1672–1725; see page 197) visited twice in 1717, and upon his request Louis XV (1710–74) returned to Versailles where he eventually died. To maintain the design, the garden needed to be replanted approximately once every hundred years. Louis XVI (1754–93) undertook this task at the beginning of his reign, as did Napoleon III (1808–73).

Louis XVI, who became king before the age of twenty, was also born at Versailles. He married the Archduchess of Austria Marie Antoinette in 1770, and offered her, in 1774, the Petit Trianon, a rustic hamlet built by Louis XV for his mistress Madame de Pompadour. Marie Antoinette made the Petit Trianon her private domain.

The gardens were prohibitively expensive to maintain, and as the formality of the seventeenth-century garden fell out of fashion, Louis XVI ordered the creation of a new informal garden. This was never achieved and eventually the royal family was forced to leave Versailles for Paris. The fall of the monarchy in August 1792 ushered in a period of uncertainty.

In 1830, Louis Philippe I (1773–1850) transformed the by-

now empty Palace into a museum devoted to 'All the Glories of France'. Napoleon IIII resided in the Trianon and used the palace for celebrations, including a visit from Queen Victoria in 1855.

From the mid-nineteenth century to the early twentieth century, Versailles was plagued by devastation. In 1870, a violent storm uprooted hundreds of trees, which required the implementation of a massive replantation programme. After the First World War, lack of funds meant that maintenance of the palace and gardens was rarely undertaken, until huge donations by the philanthropist John D. Rockefeller allowed restoration work to resume. On 14 June 1940 the Nazi swastika flag was raised over Versailles (and the Eiffel Tower) to show that France was in German hands.

RECENT RESTORATION OF THE GARDENS

Another violent storm, in February 1990, resulted in 1,500 trees being blown over or uprooted across the gardens and the garden of Trianon. That same year a vast restoration was initiated; Pierre-André Lablaude was appointed architect in consultation with Jean-Pierre Babelon, director of the Versailles museum. Lablaude was believed to be the first architect with sole responsibility for the gardens since the French Revolution in 1789. Initially, some 250 storm-ravaged or rotten trees in the woods of the North Parterre had to be removed. Four hundred remaining trees were preserved and eight hundred new ones planted. All of the avenue trees had suffered. Among the damaged trees were two specimens of tulip tree planted by Marie Antoinette in 1783 in Trianon and a Corsican pine planted by Napoleon. The storm of 1990 and another in 1999 highlighted the advanced state of deterioration of the vegetation. In the words of Lablaude: 'the aim of the renovation was to return to the spirit and original landscape of the Sun King's brilliant gardener Le Nôtre where possible.' The Jardin Anglais designed by Louis XVI was respected and renewed.

In 2003, a new restoration initiative – the Grand Versailles project – began by replanting the gardens. While carrying out research for the restoration, an estimate for the amount spent to build Versailles was found. During the *Ancien Régime*, leading up to the Revolution, the equivalent of a staggering US$2 billion was spent, but this was felt to be an under-evaluation.

Jean Chaufourier, a leading French illustrator and landscape painter, had sketched, drafted and painted Versailles many times. His plan of 1720 was used to restore the pleasure garden. The Romantic style of the nineteenth and twentieth centuries had completely obscured Le Nôtre's intricate designs. By removing these, the palace's gardeners could start on the major earthwork operations, necessary for setting out the large shell and scroll motifs in Latona's Parterre. Using modern-day GPS, the area was plotted out with plaster as they did in the seventeenth century, which marked where the metal strips needed to be laid that are then used to position the rolls of turf. Avenues were covered with crushed flint and finally the box hedges and topiarized shrubs were restored. An article in the *Guardian* of February 2013 stated:

'Forty kilometres of hornbeam hedges – trimmed to a height of eight metres and reinforced by fencing held together by the traditional copper wire – mark the outlines of the garden, some dead straight, others forming complex arabesque designs. About 900 ornamental yew trees, sporting 70 different outlines – balls, cubes and cones – set off the white marble statues. Quite a few of the latter were taken from Vaux-le-Vicomte, once the property of finance minister Nicolas Fouquet, who was imprisoned by the youthful Louis XIV on suspicion of trying to outdo his master, such was the splendour of his country estate.'

In 2018, at a cost of £326 million, the Petit Trianon was restored, based on Marie Antoinette's vision of a countryside farm with box hedging bordering vegetable beds, scented climbers hanging from the rustic pergola and potted plants lining the pathways.

Regardless of the cost, Versailles offers a stunning visual history of French architecture from the seventeenth century to the end of the eighteenth century.

OPPOSITE

The Potager du Roi

ROYAL PALACE OF CASERTA

ITALY

The ROYAL PALACE OF CASERTA in southern Italy is the former residence of the House of Bourbon when its dynasty ruled Southern Italy and Sicily (1734–1861). After two centuries of Spanish rule, the Bourbons introduced a stable political and municipal environment.

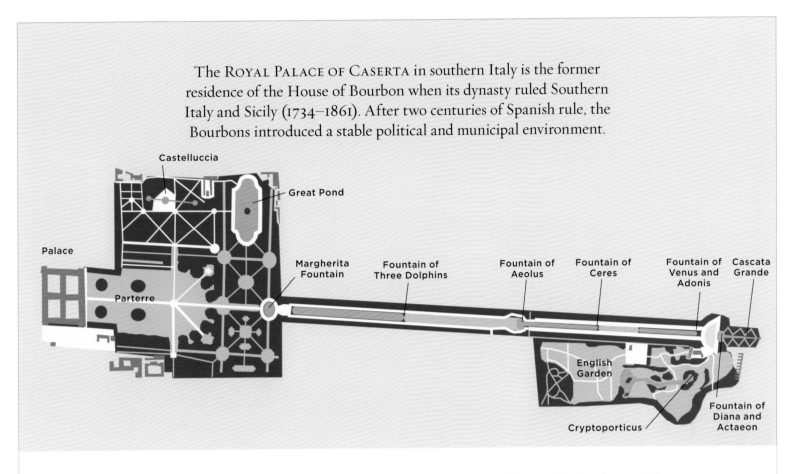

The Royal Palace (*reggia*) was at the heart of this new set of ideals and the city of Caserta went from dilapidated to opulent. The palace is among the world's largest royal estates, its surface area exceeding 23.5 hectares (58 acres), while the garden stretches for 120 hectares (296 acres). During the eighteenth century, the king's love of mathematical order based on strict geometry, and the sheer scale of the palace and gardens meant that the architects, following the intellectual and philosophical ideas of the Enlightenment, had to support their technical assessments with greater mathematical and mechanical evidence. The palace and imposing gardens at Caserta are perfect examples of this.

LUIGI VANVITELLI

Dutch painter Caspar Van Wittel, known as Vanvitelli, spent most of his life painting urban landscapes in Italy, gaining recognition and patrons among the aristocracy. Wittel's son Luigi Vanvitelli became one of the most admired architects in Naples. He designed many secular buildings in Naples, Rome, Milan and other Italian cities, worked on the construction of the Trevi Fountain in Rome and stabilized the dome of St Peter's Basilica in the Vatican. Vanvitelli worked in the late baroque style, but he was open to many influences and his approach transitioned to become neoclassical. Vanvitelli possessed a large library, mainly left to him by his maternal grandfather Giovanni Andrea Lorenzani, and was an avid reader. His continual search for harmony, comparison and evaluation possibly resulted in his various stylistic approaches.

He was commissioned by the King of Naples, Charles VII (1716–88), or Charles of Bourbon, to work on the summer residence of the Bourbons at Caserta, 25 kilometres (15 miles) north of Naples. Vanvitelli was to spend most of his life designing and constructing the Royal Palace of Caserta, which was to be modelled on the Palace of Versailles (see page 90). Other royal palaces took their inspiration from Versailles (Charles' father, Philip V of Spain, 1683–1746, was Louis XIV's, 1638–1715 grandson). Work began in 1751 when Charles VII was just 35 years old and the project was also much

PREVIOUS PAGES   *OPPOSITE*
The cascades   The Cascata Grande

influenced by Charles' wife, the well-educated Maria Amalia of Saxony (1724–60). Charles himself laid the foundation stone amid much festivity on 20 January 1752. His reign of benevolent despotism was popular among his Neapolitan subjects and he was hailed as an Enlightenment king.

Caserta is located on the inland plains of Terra di Lavoro in the Campania region and originally it was a small hunting lodge. The region reminded Charles of central Spain where his father's summer residence, La Granja de San Ildefonso, was located.

BAROQUE MEETS NEOCLASSICAL

Vanvitelli's design for the Royal Palace of Caserta proved to be a triumphant mix of baroque and neoclassical styles, its gardens combining the traditions of the Italian Renaissance with the French garden design principles that André Le Nôtre had so successfully used at Versailles, with influences from Rome and Tuscany. This is a royal garden, not one full of flowers but of large theatrical spaces filled with large expanses of manicured lawn and dramatic waterways. Opulent and imposing, it has fountains and cascades, parkland and woodland with hunting lodges – even a silk factory. The entire palace complex extends for some 4 kilometres (2½ miles), but including the Caroline Aqueduct (constructed by Vanvitelli between 1752 and 1764) its overall length exceeds 42 kilometres (25 miles).

South of the palace is Piazza Carlo III which, at 130,000 square metres (1,400,000 square feet) is the largest square in Italy; however, the gardens in the square had lost its historical connection as a result of the introduction of modern intersecting roads and high ongoing maintenance. Yet, in 2018 a memorandum of understanding was signed authorizing its restoration back to the original designs by Vanvitelli.

The gardens and park are partly on hilly terrain and include several water features, including a waterfall, cascades, ponds and fountains and an English-style landscape garden, the *giardino inglese*, the first garden in Italy to be created using plants from every corner of the world. Amid ponds and temples stands

the Cryptoporticus – a fake ruin, built soon after the discovery of Pompeii – decorated with original statues discovered during the excavations at Pompei and from the Farnese collection of items of antiquity. The structure is a circular nymphaeum (a shrine to water nymphs) made of tufa. Its floor is made from broken coloured marble tiles and from the roots of a large yew, planted by the German gardener John Andrew Graefer. Gushing water feeds a picturesque lake where a marble sculpture (the work of Tommaso Solari) of Venus portrays the goddess emerging from bathing in the water. In this area the vegetation is rich in ferns, surrounded by laurels, oaks and yews.

Commissioned in *c.*1753 by Charles, after whom its name derives, the 38-kilometre (23-mile) long Caroline Aqueduct took nearly twenty years to complete. The result is a magnificent three-tiered arched aqueduct, designed by Vanvitelli, that supplies water to the village of St Leucio as well as the Royal Palace of Caserta and its fountains. The aqueduct, reminiscent of Roman structures, was admired around the world and seen as an incredible achievement both in terms of architecture and engineering.

VANVITELLI AND THE TELESCOPIC EFFECT

From the palace the gardens extend as far as the eye can see. Optical observation and the 'telescopic effect' of a distant view were of particular scientific interest to Vanvitelli. He produced a court publication in 1756 entitled *Dichiarazione disegni del Reale palazzo di Caserta* (Declaration of the Drawings of the Royal Palace of Caserta), which described and highlighted this telescopic or perspectival effect.

To create this effect, Vanvitelli designed a 3-kilometre (almost 2-mile) straight avenue starting in Naples and ending at the waterfall (which is 75 metres/246 feet high) at the far end of the garden on Briano Mountain. This incredibly long avenue lined with evergreen holm oaks (*Quercus ilex*) with strips of lawn surrounding rectilinear basins of water, is broken up by cascades, large expanses of lawns, further pools of water, mythological statues and fountains. Seen from the palace, an optical illusion is formed, as the distance

ABOVE OPPOSITE   *BELOW OPPOSITE*

The Piazza Carlo III   The English Garden

between the first fountain, the Margherita Fountain, in the parkland – or even the Fountain of Three Dolphins in the avenue – and the bottom of the waterfall appears to be short.

Work commenced in the garden, with the first planting in 1753. The late baroque style was to adorn the immediate surroundings of the palace, but lack of funds meant that this was not realized. In fact, the 120-hectares (296-acre) garden seen today is a reduced adaptation of Vanvitelli's original design. In 1773, Vanvitelli died and work on the garden was stalled. Then, in 1777, Vanvitelli's son Carlo was appointed director of the works.

THE PARTERRE

Luigi Vanvitelli's original design showed intricate parterres and groves immediately to the rear of the palace, and while much of the general shape has remained, today there is a simplification of the layout, with a reduction of ornamental features, in particular fountains, both in the first and second parts of the garden. The parterre outside the palace's main gallery formed the first part of the garden (the second being the long avenue ending with the waterfall) and followed French formal designs, with shapes filled with flowers to resemble embroidery (the classic *parterre de broderie*). The French head gardener Martin Biancourt was responsible for setting out the garden. However, the intricate parterres were replaced, again due to lack of funds, with four wide areas of square lawn that were 'adorned' in the nineteenth century with circular beds in their centres, comprising yew and laurel. The form does not really follow a *parterre à l'anglaise* since there are no flower borders around the perimeter of the lawns. Pathways intersect the four lawns. At the far end of the lawns five radial pathways with further lawns between them, lead out to the perimeter of *bosquets* of hornbeams, limes and holm oaks. These *bosquets* are in the characteristic 'chair-like' form, meaning double-height trees. At the end of the central pathway is a circular area where the Margherita Fountain is situated. It is at the junction where the first part of the garden ends and the second

(the long avenue) begins. Surrounding it are 16 white marble busts known as 'terminal figures' or terminus.

To the west of the parterre is old woodland, *bosco vecchio*, which Vanvitelli decided to leave, but added holm oak, ivy and butcher's broom. The dense woods created a secret garden, a place for respite from court life. A tower, designed as a small castle or bastion, Castelluccia, is set in an octagonal pool with bridges to the pathway at the front and a formal garden to the rear. Two curved staircases lead from the tower's bridge to the formal gardens, set out with hedge-bordered lawns, citrus trees, palms and ivy. On one of the corners of the boundary walls of the formal garden is a chinoiserie metal parasol in red and green with bells and topped with a weather vane. Originally the tower was built as a place to entertain and became a lodge in 1818. Surrounding the tower, and reflecting in the pool, are magnolia, tall *Araucaria* (monkey puzzles) and palms. To the north of Castelluccia is the elliptical Great Fishpond. It was constructed in 1769 by Francesco Collecini (who collaborated with Vanvitelli) and has a raised stone surround and a circular island at its centre. This large expanse of water, measuring 270 metres by 105 metres (885 by 344 feet), and being 3.5 metres (almost 11½ feet) deep, offered further scope for entertainment in the form of recreated naval battles.

FOUNTAINS

There are many fountains at the Royal Palace of Caserta, set out along the long avenue. Leading from the Margherita Fountain, the first is the Fountain of Three Dolphins. Here, two smaller dolphins flank a larger dolphin with clawed feet, set on top of a rocky outcrop. Water cascades from the dolphins' mouths into a vast straight-edged waterway. Using his father's drawings, Carlo Vanvitelli designed the fountain, which was sculpted from travertine by Gaetano Salomone between 1776 and 1779. The fountain also marks a change in land height. The level waterway ends with the fountain, backed by a series of travertine arches and a semi-circular metal balustrade on top. Steep inclines either side of the waterway make their way

ABOVE OPPOSITE

The Cryptoporticus

BELOW OPPOSITE

The Margherita Fountain

to the top of the arches, so that the fountain can be viewed from above.

Heading towards the waterfall, and passing a huge expanse of lawn, the next is the magnificent Fountain of Aeolus, signifying another change in level. This fountain is quite an overwhelming sight, with sculptures depicting 28 winged zephyrs and gods set among rocks (there were 54 in the original concept). Aeolus, the divine keeper of the winds and king of the mythical floating island of Aeolia (represented by the basin at the front), is urged by Juno to unleash the winds against Aeneas and the Trojans. Several sculptors were involved with the creation of this fountain: Salomone, Angelo Brunelli, Andrea Violani, Paolo Persico and Tommaso Solari the Elder. At the centre of the scheme is a waterfall, fed by the next waterway on the level above. On either side of the fountain and basin is a curved stone balustrade with additional sculptures.

The Fountain of Ceres (the goddess of the fertility of the fields), is a much calmer and a less dramatic fountain than the Fountain of Aeolus. It was created in 1783–85; Salomone carved the statues from Carrera marble and travertine and depicts Ceres, sea nymphs, tritons or mermen and a dolphin. From it a small waterfall cascades into the long waterway below.

At the top of a series of cascades is the Fountain of Venus and Adonis, while at the end of the gardens, at the base of the waterfall, is the Fountain of Diana and Actaeon, reached by either a series of steps or ramps. Distinctive against the backdrop of trees and water is a group of white sculptures by Persico, Pietro Solari and Brunelli.

THE ENGLISH GARDEN

While much of the garden at Caserta adheres to French design principles, in the area to the north-east is the 24-hectare (60-acre) *giardino inglese*, the English Garden, dating from 1785, which is recognized as the first Italian landscape garden. It is similar to the naturalistic landscapes created by English landscape architect Lancelot 'Capability' Brown and was to eclipse the Petit Trianon at Versailles. It was designed by Queen Maria Carolina of Austria (1752–1814), the sister of Marie Antoinette, Queen of France (1755–93), and wife of Ferdinand IV (1751–1825). Her garden was realized by Carlo Vanvitelli and Graefer. The latter trained at the Chelsea Physic Garden, England, and was recommended to the queen by the botanist Sir Joseph Banks. Graefer was responsible, among many things, for introducing the variegated form of Japanese laurel (*Aucuba japonica*) in 1783, initially as a heated greenhouse plant. He also introduced the Bollwyller pear (*Pyrus bollwylleriana*) and the Siberian wild crab apple (*P. baccata*, later *Malus baccata*).

Founded in 1807, the English Garden became the Royal Botanic Gardens of Caserta, with the Herbarium Neapolitanum housed within it. Nicola Terracciano was director of the Royal Botanic Gardens from 1861 to 1903, while his son Achille and a colleague Giovanni Gussone made a huge contribution to plant knowledge. Within the Herbarium are two collections belonging to Gussone, which contain up to 20,000 samples and one collection to Terracciano, which includes 3,500 samples. The gardens are dotted with temples, statues, bridges and ruins. Pathways and small rivers

Fountain of Diana and Actaeon

Bath of Venus, the English Garden

wind through groves of holm oak and between large specimens of Lebanese cedar, palm, holly, eucalyptus, maple, ferns, rose beds and what is believed to be the first camellia, *Camellia japonica*, to arrive in Europe from Japan.

There are several glasshouses. By the Rose Garden is an eighteenth-century greenhouse built to house begonias and succulents; another, known as the Serra Moderna (modern greenhouse) is a barrel-vaulted greenhouse that dates from 1785. To the north of the latter, in an area surrounded by woodland and tall specimen palm trees is an old iron-and-glass greenhouse, the Serra Borbonica, commissioned by Nicola Terracciano, neoclassical in design with Doric columns and large floor-to-ceiling windows, the now somewhat shabby shell, once used for the most delicate of plants, contains a large specimen of *Ceiba speciosa*, the silk floss tree from Brazil.

Graefer resided in the English Mansion (built between 1790 and 1794), which is not far from the old greenhouses. He continuously travelled to Campania, Capri and Palermo to stock up on plants, and through his contacts with English botanists, obtained many specimens and seeds from Australia, China and Japan, from which he created hybrids and numerous rarities, which were kept in the greenhouses. Graefer published in England a descriptive catalogue of more than 1,100 species and varieties of plants and herbaceous perennials. He also catalogued the plants at Caserta in *Synopsis plantarum regii viridarii Caserti* (Naples, 1803). He left the Royal Palace of Caserta on 23 December 1798 when he became bailiff of Admiral Horatio Nelson's estate at Bronte, Sicily, where he died in 1802.

Caserta is huge, and through clever design and placement of ornamentation, primarily statues and fountains, it became a large theatrical space in which to display the wealth and influence of the Bourbon dynasty. With its fake ruins and temples, it is truly a 'Parc à fabriques'. Intricate parterres may have been replaced with large expanses of lawn, but *bosquets* remain, along with the remarkable central waterway, leading the eye from the palace to the countryside beyond. While the plant selection in the late baroque garden and down the central avenue is limited, within the English Garden where the function of studying, experimenting and conserving plants is paramount, plants from local and distant shores abound.

OPPOSITE
The Bagnero di Venere

LEFT
The Castelluccia

LA VENARIA REALE

ITALY

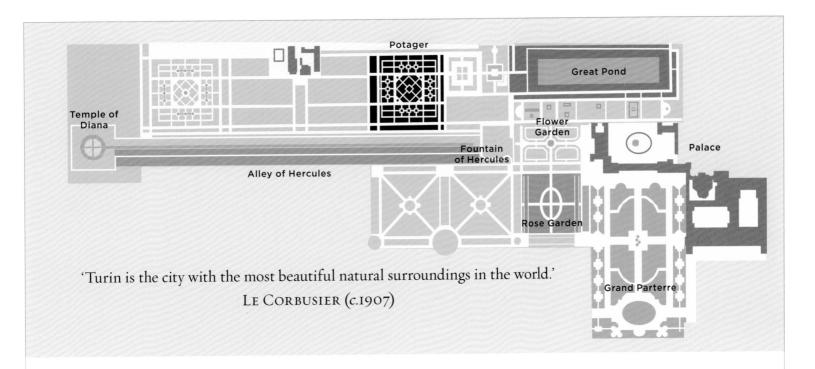

Temple of Diana

Potager

Great Pond

Flower Garden

Fountain of Hercules

Palace

Alley of Hercules

Rose Garden

Grand Parterre

'Turin is the city with the most beautiful natural surroundings in the world.'
Le Corbusier (c.1907)

After the Royal Palace of Caserta (see page 102) La Venaria Reale is Italy's second-largest royal palace (*reggia*). It is located in the town of Venaria Reale, a municipality of Turin, situated where the River Stura di Lanzo meets the Ceronda creek in Piedmont. The palace is a beautiful example of Italian baroque architecture, art and landscape design dating primarily from the seventeenth and eighteenth centuries, and yet it was forgotten for about 200 years and even risked demolition in the 1970s. Although the origins of the palace and gardens are from the Renaissance period, the baroque architecture and landscape seen today are the result of eight years of restoration, costing some €255 million euros, completed in 2007.

The House of Savoy, a dynasty dating back to the eleventh century, was the longest-surviving royal house of Europe. In 1562, Emmanuel Philibert, Duke of Savoy (1528–80) moved his capital from Chambéry (in present-day France) to Turin and began a programme of construction initiatives, which his successors would continue. One of these initiatives was the creation of a luxurious complex of gardens and woods. The ensemble of palaces, residences and ecclesiastical buildings (known as the Corona di Delizie, 'crown of delights') made it one of the biggest in the world, visually unified, with the help of leading architects and artists, by a single style and choice of materials.

In order to link the various areas of the vast palace complex an interconnected system of courtyards and historical gardens was designed by Amedeo di Castellamonte, Michelangelo Garove and, later, Filippo Juvarra. The architect and engineer Castellamonte was commissioned by Charles Emmanuel II, Duke of Savoy (1634–75) to design and build the white Chianocco marble *reggia*. (The imposing red-brick wing that runs east to west was later added by Garove.) The duke was inspired by the Castle of Mirafiori, another of the House of Savoy residences. Between 1658 and 1679 Castellamonte created a series of *maisons de plaisance* (pleasure houses), parks and hunting lodges and grounds surrounding the city of Turin, principally for Charles Emmanuel's leisure, but with the strategic advantage of being able to control politics and trade in the areas close to the ducal capital.

The palace was built on the site of a village called Altessano Superiore. To achieve the duke's desire for uniformity of design he purchased the village of Altessano Inferiore from a wealthy Milanese family. The enlargement of the royal palace, gardens and hunting park led to the palace being renamed Venaria Reale, taken from the Latin words for 'royal hunt'.

It was in the early eighteenth century, when Victor Amadeus II, Duke of Savoy (1666–1732) appointed Juvarra as chief court architect in 1716, that the palace

PREVIOUS PAGES
The Potager

OPPOSITE
The Rose Garden

and gardens reached their greatest baroque grandeur. As director of works Juvarra's ambitious task was to rival Versailles. He added the southern wing – the vaulted Great Gallery (Galleria Grande) conceived by Garove, connecting the royal apartments – a huge south-facing Orangery (Citroniera) and a stable block.

During the eighteenth century, under the reign of Charles Emmanuel III, Duke of Savoy (1701–73), when the family was given royal status, La Venaria Reale was further enlarged by Benedetto Alfieri. French principles continued to influence the design of the *reggia* when Michel Bénard, a garden designer who had worked at Versailles, was charged with the management of the gardens. But, at the end of the eighteenth century, following the abolition of the French monarchy, the great palace fell into disuse.

The gardens

The gardens of La Venaria Reale follow mathematical rules with an emphasis on geometric layouts. They are neither French nor 'picturesque', the hallmark of English landscape design. The *reggia* of the House of Savoy and the formal gardens, dating from the sixteenth and seventeenth centuries, follow baroque principles of perfect symmetry, axial geometry, avenues, geometric shapes, large vistas, manicured lawns and artificially trimmed shrubs and trees, reflecting harmonic rules and humans' power over nature.

A bird's-eye view of the palace and gardens reveals an area of 95 hectares (234 acres); the gardens alone cover 60 hectares (148 acres). The complex lies at the heart of a vast estate, including a walled reserve in the nearby La Mandria Park.

The gardens comprise the Parco Basso (Lower Park) and the Parco Alto (Upper Park). In the Lower Park the remains of the Fountain of Hercules (built 1669–72) and the Temple of Diana mark the ends of the Alley of Hercules, the central canal. To the north of the *reggia* is the truly vast sunken rectangular Great Pond (Peschiera) surrounded by large strips of lawn, a wide pathway on the longer southern side and bordered on all sides with high trimmed hedging. Gentle slopes lead up from the Great Pond to another wide pathway,

so that it can be viewed from above. Alongside the Central Alley the 10-hectare (24-acre) Potager Royal – the largest potager in Italy – carefully restored to its original layout, contains the east and west vegetable, fruit, flower and herb gardens, interspersed with pergolas and fountains. Interestingly, the vegetables are now grown in raised beds. An orchard, also in the Lower Park, has 1,700 espaliered fruit trees – apple, pear, fig, apricot, peach and cherry – planted in 2010.

The Rose Garden and Flower Garden are found in the Upper Park. In the Rose Garden, on three sides of the garden 'room', are arch-topped pergolas smothered with climbing roses, and at its centre an oval-shaped lawn (which appears round to the viewer standing within this space) surrounded by large sweeping curved borders planted with bush roses. The Flower Garden is composed of four sections with a central cruciform water feature, which is in line with the central canal. Low trimmed yew and box hedges define the spaces, while perennials and annuals represent varieties found in the Piedmont area, as well as the symbolic and iconographic flowers seen in the paintings and stuccoes inside the *reggia*, such as blue gentian, white saxifrage and pink rock jasmine. More contemporary planting schemes are being introduced into the Flower Garden with the use of ornamental grasses and herbaceous perennials. There used to be a large semi-circular loggia to the west of the Flower Garden but it was demolished during the eighteenth century to open up the space and the vista beyond.

The Grand Parterre is an interpretation of the eighteenth-century plans for this area of the garden according to Juvarra. To connect the architecture with the garden he designed two axes, the first focused on the Great Gallery, and the second on the Orangery, which forms the Royal Avenue (Allea Royale). The area covers a staggering 6 hectares (15 acres). Over a two-year period, 248 conical yews and 18,000 box plants were laid out to form the perimeters of the grass parterres. An astonishing 5,500 hornbeams were planted to create small *bosquets* with circular interiors. The shapes that form the Grand Parterre echo ones found elsewhere in the garden, connecting it to the wider landscape.

ABOVE OPPOSITE
The Alley of Hercules

BELOW OPPOSITE
The Flower Garden

THE GARDEN'S PROGRESSION

Castellamonte's design drew the eye down the garden along the Alley of Hercules. Fountains, reliefs and sculpture reflected the ornamentation of the palace interior. To the north of the remains of the Fountain of Hercules nine tulip trees have been planted in an arc formation, suggesting the arches and columns of a former finely adorned portico. The canal is indeed long at 800 metres (more than 2,600 feet) and was once lined with a single row of oaks (*Quercus robur*). These have since been replaced with field maples, which contrast with the limes used in the Upper Park. Hedgerows of berberis, deutzia, elaeagnus, spiraea and viburnum add colour throughout the year.

When Juvarra added the Orangery and stables to the south of the palace, the central axis design formed by the Alley of Hercules with symmetrical shapes and patterns on either side was lost. Suddenly, the southern side of the gardens was deeper than the northern side, where the Potager and the Great Pond are located. Garove, along with French garden engineers, restored this central design by removing monumental works and structures along the east–west axis, opening up the distant views. Such an approach adhered to French garden design principles. The Alley of Hercules was lined with *bosquets* in the Upper Park and lawns in the Lower Park, laid out symmetrically, while the supporting wall of the Upper Park, parallel to the Alley of Hercules, was replaced by a grass embankment. As a result, Castellamonte's Temple of Diana and the Fountain of Hercules were demolished. Waterfalls connect ponds at different levels and serve to animate the surface, oxygenate the water and provide sound.

LA MANDRIA PARK

Charles Emmanuel II was a keen huntsman and established a reserve in the sixteenth century called La Mandria Park. Victor Emmanuel II (1820–78) built a 30-kilometre (18-mile) long brick wall in the nineteenth century to enclose the 3,125-hectare (7,700-acre) park. It represents the second-largest enclosed nature reserve in Europe. La Mandria is a remnant of a mosaic of wooded and open areas, and it has a rich ecosystem. The trees in the reserve today are typical of those that covered the Po Valley a thousand years ago, namely various oaks (sessile, northern red, holm and pedunculate), hornbeam, ash, lime, sweet cherry, black alder and elm.

RESTORATION AND RECONSTRUCTION

In 1999 the *reggia* of the House of Savoy embarked on its journey of restoration, following original eighteenth-century plans and layout. The gardens had become so neglected and severely damaged that restoration seemed almost impossible. Aerial photography, however, revealed the remnants of the garden, including the pathways, tree-lined avenues, embankments and woodlands. Through archaeological excavation, marble artefacts and motifs were found and restored, and the Great Pond in the Lower Garden was reconstructed, together with the seventeenth-century remains of the Fountain of Hercules and the Temple of Diana. The Grand Parterre south of the palace was also restored.

At the front of the palace is the Court of Honour where the foundations of the Fountain of the Stag were also found during the archaeological work, but as part of the restoration and refurbishment, a modern 'water theatre' has been installed. Designed by a company specializing in water features, architect Carlo Fucini installed water nozzles, projectors and steam pipes to create a modern 'fountain', mesmerizingly choreographed using lights and music.

The restoration project involved myriad experts, architects, archaeologists and landscape designers, charged with the difficult task of reinventing the baroque garden with a contemporary layout. La Venaria Reale Project has become the largest restoration project in European history.

ABOVE OPPOSITE   *BELOW OPPOSITE*

The Potager garden   The Flower Garden

THE ALHAMBRA

SPAIN

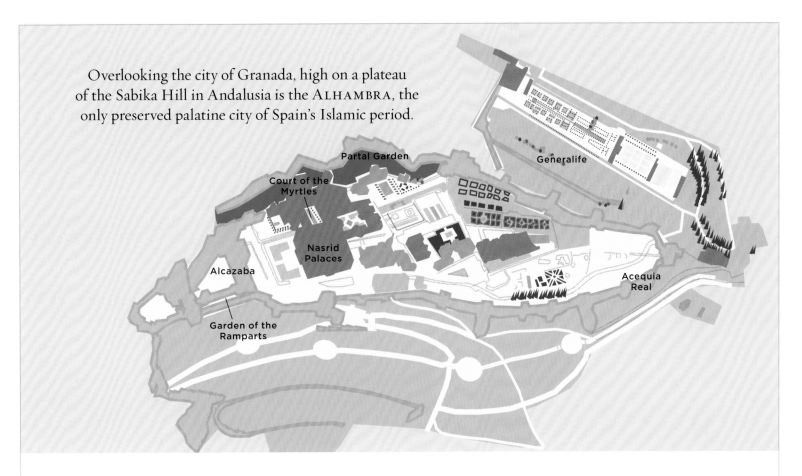

Overlooking the city of Granada, high on a plateau of the Sabika Hill in Andalusia is the ALHAMBRA, the only preserved palatine city of Spain's Islamic period.

Against a backdrop of the Sierra Nevada mountains, the Alhambra provides a rich history of Moorish planning and architecture of the Nasrid dynasty, as well as insight into construction in Christian Spanish Renaissance and baroque styles. To the east of the Alhambra itself is Generalife, the former residence and gardens of the emirs who ruled Granada in the thirteenth and fourteenth centuries.

The name Alhambra means 'red fort' from the Arabic *Qa 'lat al-Hamra*, derived from the colour of the sun-dried *tapia*, or adobe, bricks made from fine gravel and clay.

Alhambra stands on the site of a small fortress dating from 889 CE. What is seen today was built between 1232 and 1354 by the founder of the Nasrid dynasty, Abu Abdullah Muhammad Ibn Yusuf ibn Nasr, also known as Ibn al-Ahmar (1195–1273), and the complex has been continuously occupied throughout its history. The oldest part is the walled Alcazaba (fortress), built to protect the Nasrid stronghold against the Crusaders. It was not until the reign of Yusuf I, Sultan of Granada (1318–54) that the Alhambra

became a royal palace. Its 1,730 metres (more than a mile) of fortified walls and 30 towers enclose a 10.5-hectare (26-acre) city within a city.

King Ferdinand II of Aragon (1452–1516) and Queen Isabella I of Castile (1451–1504) made the Alhambra the Royal Court following almost 780 years of the Christian Reconquista (reconquest) between 711 and 1492, which marked the end of the Nasrid dynasty.

In 1526, the building of a Renaissance Palace in the Alhambra by King Charles V (1500–1558, Holy Roman Emperor from 1519) changed the aspect of the complex, altering its internal structure and its connection to the city.

During the seventeenth and eighteenth centuries Granada went into a long decline, as did much of Spain. Europe was at war and William and Mary were fighting Louis XIV. The region suffered the Spanish War of Succession in the early eighteenth century when the Bourbons were fighting with Archduke Charles of Austria over the Spanish throne. As a result the Alhambra fell into neglect, and Napoleon Bonaparte (1769–1821) used it as barracks between 1808 and 1812.

PREVIOUS PAGES
The Court of the Myrtles

OPPOSITE
The Generalife

In 1870, however, the Alhambra was declared a national monument, with subsequent restorations.

THE ISLAMIC GARDENS AND THE USE OF WATER

The different parts of the Alhambra complex are connected by paths, gardens and gates and, just beyond its walls, is the medieval garden Generalife, taking its name from the Arabic *Jannat al-arifa*. The word Jannat means 'paradise' and, by association, 'garden'. It incorporates the Moorish gardening tradition, the aesthetic use of water and gardens as a place of cultivation, relaxation and entertainment. Its water channels, fountains and greenery can be understood in relation to passage 2:25 in the Koran, '... garden, underneath which running waters flow ...'

Nasrid Islamic art, architecture and garden design used water as a central, integral and repeating feature in the form of fountains, canals and pools. Water feeds, cleans, cools and is aesthetically stunning and audibly calming. People valued it greatly and therefore wanted it as a constant feature, in close proximity to where they lived and worked.

THE GENERALIFE

Generalife was a true royal palace, designed according to the layout and style of enclosed gardens of Persia (albeit with more ornamentation) as well as country palace gardens of the Menara and Agdal in Morocco. In its gardens there is a constant play between openness and enclosure. As the art historian D. Fairchild Ruggles describes:

'Although [many] sources rarely describe actual gardens and never the royal palace gardens ... as a group they tell of a landscape undergoing dramatic transformations and, equally as important, allow a glimpse of how those changes were perceived by a variety of persons at the time.'

The Generalife gardens were created in the thirteenth century and redecorated by King Abu I-Walid Isma'il (1313–24), but those seen today were recreated over a 20-year period starting in 1931 by Spanish architect Francisco Prieto Moreno. No documentation has survived of the original layout and they have been altered and rebuilt over the years, but by following designs found in other Islamic gardens and with the help from historians and restorers the gardens were given a new life.

The walkways are paved with a mosaic of pebbles from nearby rivers, which is a traditional Granadian style. Sometimes the patterns are cross-hatched, other times they are six-sided star formations and others more plain with expanses of pebbles and bricks laid sideways to form edging. The outer gardens include fruit and nut trees, such as pomegranate and walnut, a vegetable garden and a vineyard. The lower gardens are filled with roses, salvias, geraniums, fountains and topiarized cypresses.

The Generalife is comprised of several distinct gardens. The Water Garden Courtyard (Patio de la Acequia) is an enclosed courtyard with walls lined with archways. It measures 49 metres by 13 metres (almost 160 feet by 42 feet) and, although designed as a garden to be enjoyed from within, its eighteen arches reveal the gardens beyond and stairways lead to the lower and upper gardens.

The central feature, dividing the courtyard longitudinally, is a long water canal with symmetrical fountains, with water drawn from the Royal Canal. The jets of water appear to quiver. At either end are two stone cups. Cloaked in bougainvillea and climbing roses, the high walls of the Generalife resonate, adding to the acoustics of the space within. Archaeological excavation of 1958 revealed that at some point the canal had twelve spouts, though it is also believed that the water was still, reflecting the light and sky above, like the pool found in the Court of Myrtles (Patio de los Arrayanes) or the Partal Gardens (Jardines del Partal).

The original layout was in the shape of a transept, with a rectangular area, the Acequia Real (royal irrigation channel) crossing the main axis of the Patio de la Acequia. The royal irrigation channel took water from the Darro river by means of a dam, 6 kilometres (more than 3 miles) from the Alhambra. It travelled along the right bank of the river, crossed it via an aqueduct and continued along the left bank where it

ABOVE OPPOSITE   *BELOW OPPOSITE*

The Partal Garden   The Garden of the Ramparts

divided into two – one channel towards the Generalife, the other to Tercio – to supply the fountains, pools and other water features.

The Sultana's Garden (Jardin de la Sultana) or Courtyard of the Sultana's Cypress (Patio del Ciprés de la Sultana), another enclosed courtyard, is cooled by a central pond surrounded by a neatly trimmed myrtle hedge. In the centre is an island divided into three equal sections by two large oleander trees (*Nerium oleander*). The two outer sections are square flower beds surrounded by a myrtle hedge. Between these beds is a small pond with a central stone water bath. The ponds are edged with mirrored fountains, trickling into the still water. There are also the remains of a Mediterranean cypress (*Cupressus sempervirens*), which, according to botanists Jose Tito and Manuel Casares, was planted during the Moorish period and lived for 600 years. Leading away from this is an *escalera del agua* (water stairway), a set of brick steps with three flights and landings, each with the familiar pebble mosaics and low fountains. Surrounding the steps the walls have been hollowed out as runnels, acting as a handrail, and giving a handmade feel. Laurel hedges overhead create a vaulted green roof.

Near the entrance of the Alcazaba to the west of the complex is the Garden of the Ramparts (Jardin de los Adarves), located on the parapet walk. From this garden, with its cypresses, flowers and fountains, there are magnificent views over the modern city below.

Gardens of Daraxa

In contrast to the white-walled patios, the Gardens of Daraxa, also called Garden of the Orange Trees, are mellowed by apricot-pink plastered walls. This irregular trapezoid garden was constructed between 1526 and 1538 in a garden that already existed between the fortress and the ramparts. In addition to its citrus trees (*Citrus medica* and *C.* x *aurantium*) there are lofty cypresses and acacias. Box hedging surrounds the large central Renaissance marble fountain, which is decorated around its sides with a poem in Arabic. The fountain was placed here in 1626, using the great basin formerly found in the courtyard of the Comares Palace.

The Partal Gardens

Muhammad III (1257–1314) built the Partal Gardens (Jardines del Partal) on the eastern side of the main palace as a belvedere looking over Granada. It comprises a large pool, a portico and a cupola with relief carvings known as *mocarabes*, which are believed to be the oldest example in the Alhambra. The slender round columns below the arches of the portico do not look substantial enough to hold up the arches. Yet, cleverly, the effect of such slim supports is to draw the eye upwards to appreciate the incredible craftsmanship of the portico, as well as the sky above. Originally, one area of the gardens was laid out as terraces, with an upper pavilion and a U-shaped pool. Only the pool remains. Unlike many of the walled gardens, this garden is open and sun lit.

Archaeological work and pollen analysis

Archaeological work during 1959 showed that from its creation, the Patio de la Acequia was an ornamental garden. This was shown by an organic-mineral layer of old cultivated soil, 60 centimetres (2 feet) below the present soil level, containing pollen remains from myrtle, cypress, laurel, citrus trees (*Citrus medica* and *C.* x *aurantium*), as well as rose, jasmine, honeysuckle and meadow grass (Poaceae). The lower (medieval) strata lacked pollen remains.

Excavation also revealed that the Patio de la Acequia was a sunken garden, some 40 centimetres (15 inches) below the level of the walkways, with grassy areas (comparable to lawn) and flower beds interspersed with trees. *Myrtus communis* subsp. *baetica* (a rare species of myrtle) was arranged as bordering hedges concealing the ceramic pipes of the irrigation system. The patio was filled with earth towards the end of the sixteenth century, losing its sunken form, and was planted with new flowering species from America, the Far East and South Africa.

A small garden like this one was to be enjoyed from within, being close to nature and focusing on the smallest features. The colour and scent of the plants and flowers and sound of trickling water were the main focus. Plants from around the world, not adapted to the climate of southern Spain, were carefully pruned and watered to produce the most flowers and fruit.

The myrtle has been considered the emblematic plant of the Alhambra and the surrounding area of Generalife. Interestingly, in 1564 Flemish botanist Carolus Clusius proposed the name *Myrtus baetica*, stating: 'I have never seen this kind of myrtle in any place except in ... the splendid Moorish gardens of Granada, next to pools and lakes where all hedges are always made from this type of myrtle.'

Research published in 2016 in the *Journal of Agricultural Science and Technology* identified and genetically authenticated subsp. *baetica*. The genetic identification offers the opportunity to restore a key element of this fourteenth-century garden.

AN EARTHLY PARADISE

The Alhambra and the Generalife are both works of art and symbols of victory and of paradise. The way water was used differed dramatically from the way Renaissance designers used it or the way we use it today. Water was seen as something to be sculpted, like marble, creating shapes and patterns, or as an integral element to the overall design, offering stillness and contemplation. There is a strong sense of geometry and discipline found at the Alhambra. Elegant lines, the play of light and shade, vistas and the constant presence of water reflect an earthly paradise.

RIGHT
The Avenue of the Cypress Trees

OPPOSITE
The Gardens of Daraxa

SCHÖNBRUNN

AUSTRIA

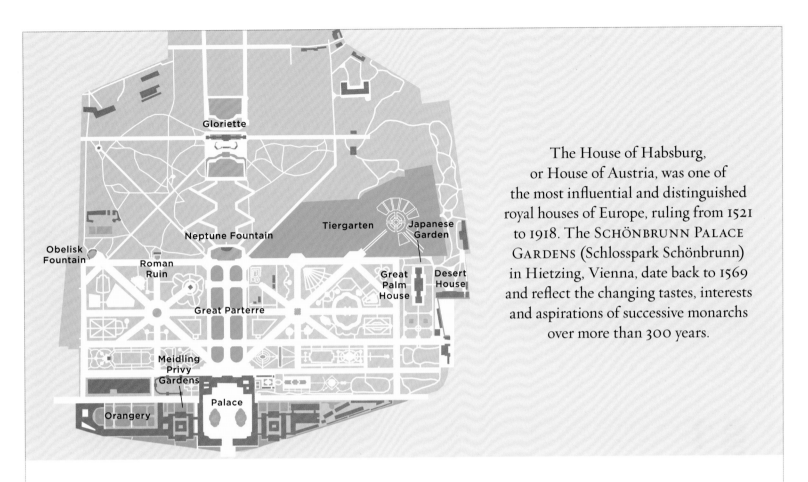

Gloriette

Tiergarten

Japanese
Garden

Neptune Fountain

Obelisk
Fountain

Roman
Ruin

Great
Palm
House

Desert
House

Great Parterre

Meidling
Privy
Gardens

Palace

Orangery

The House of Habsburg, or House of Austria, was one of the most influential and distinguished royal houses of Europe, ruling from 1521 to 1918. The SCHÖNBRUNN PALACE GARDENS (Schlosspark Schönbrunn) in Hietzing, Vienna, date back to 1569 and reflect the changing tastes, interests and aspirations of successive monarchs over more than 300 years.

The Holy Roman Emperor Maximilian II (1527–76), a keen huntsman, wanted to create a game reserve as well as pleasure gardens. In 1569 he purchased a large section of floodplain of the River Wien where a mansion called Katterburg had been erected in 1548. In 1605, Hungarian forces destroyed the gardens, but they were restored by Holy Roman Emperor Matthias (1557–1619) who, in 1612, discovered a 'beautiful spring' (*Schöner Brunnen*) issuing from an artesian well, which later gave the estate its name. Matthias' successor Ferdinand II (1578–1637) and his wife Eleonora of Gonzaga (1598–1655) loved hunting and held extravagant hunting parties, but after Ferdinand's death the residence became a *château de plaisance* (country house or summer residence), and its name Schönbrunn was first documented in 1642.

GARDEN PLANS

Between 1638 and 1643 Eleonora of Gonzaga added a palace to the mansion. She had a rare understanding of art, design and plants and had large formal gardens created around the palace, which became the ideal setting for the frequent court celebrations and festivities. Her niece and successor, also Eleonora of Gonzaga (1630–86), continued to extend the gardens. During the seventeenth century the Holy Roman Emperor Leopold I (1640–1705), a keen composer and actor, created open-air performances, which took place in the '*famose parco di Scheenbrunn*'. However, in 1683, Ottoman forces brought an abrupt end to this indulgent lifestyle, when Vienna was besieged and the palace and park at Schönbrunn devastated. In 1686, both were returned to Leopold; he bequeathed them to his son and successor Joseph I (1678–1711), who commissioned a magnificent new palace for the future, forward-thinking emperor, Charles VI (1685–1740).

The architect Johann Bernhard Fischer von Erlach, who trained in Rome, was invited to submit designs to the imperial court. His original designs were complex, rather utopian and followed outdated ideas on landscape design from the Mannerist (late Renaissance) villas of Italy. The palace, set on top of the hill, was to outshine Versailles (see page 90),

PREVIOUS PAGES

The Great Palm House

OPPOSITE

The Crown Prince Garden

but the scheme could never have been achieved. He eventually came up with a practicable design for a large hunting lodge, which started construction in 1696. Although it took only four years to build, unfortunately the lodge was not fully completed by the time of Joseph I's death in 1711.

Designs for the gardens by Jean Trehet, a pupil of André Le Nôtre (see page 11), date from as early as 1695, but the work did not begin until 1705 and only partly observed Fischer von Erlach's scheme. Along the main axis of the building Trehet placed a central parterre, accentuated by a pool where the paths intersected and flanked by lateral *boskets (bosquets)*, formal plantings of trees and shrubs interspersed with small enclosures. Wide avenues are reminiscent of early baroque gardens, as well as a maze – an almost obligatory feature for gardens of this type and age – and an Orangery. The maze (Irrgarten) was a network of pathways lined by yews with a central raised pavilion. The pathways, comprised of six sections, extended over 3.5 kilometres (2 miles). Over time, the paths fell into disrepair and were altered and simplified until 1892, when the last section was cleared.

When Joseph I died in 1711, the unfinished lodge became the dower house of Empress Wilhelmine Amalia of Brunswick-Lüneburg (1673–1742). The Holy Roman Emperor Charles VI adopted the lodge in 1728, but his imperial intentions to wage war against France and the Ottoman Empire meant he visited Schönbrunn only for its game reserve to shoot pheasant. After the early death of his son, he gave the palace and gardens as a wedding gift to his daughter, Maria Theresa (1717–80), who had a great affection for the place. While she was in residence the park was extended with a new, stelliform (star-shaped) system of avenues with many walks and pleasing vistas, as well as two main diagonal avenues which meet at the dominant central axis of the palace. The baroque gardens were an impressive symbol of imperial power and were seen as an organic extension of the interiors, a concept known as *Gesamtkunstwerk*, a masterly fusion of many artforms.

THE GREAT PARTERRE

In front of the south facade is the Great Parterre, laid out using box hedging on coloured gravel arranged in intricate patterns using embroidery motifs (*parterre de broderie*). On each side of the parterre ornamental *bosquets* were interspersed with small enclosures. The avenues of trees clipped to form tall hedges bordering the parterre acknowledged the State Chancellor, Prince Wenzel Anton of Kaunitz-Rietberg (1711–94), who was especially interested in French garden design; the diagonal avenues and diverse shapes of the areas of ornamental shrubbery are after the French architect and writer Jacques-François Blondel, who was known especially for his monumental four-volume encyclopedia of French buildings, *L'Architecture Française* (1752–6).

In the western part of the park the Schönbrunn menagerie was founded in 1752 by Emperor Franz Stephan of Lorraine (1708–65), who was deeply interested in natural history. The following year the Dutch Botanic Garden was established near the village of Hietzing. Then, two years later, Maria Theresa bought Schloss Hof, some 60 kilometres (40 miles) from Schönbrunn, from Prince Eugene of Savoy (1663–1736). Schloss Hof consisted of a two-storey palace, gardens and estate farm in Lower Austria, which, during the 1770s, was substantially altered by the court architect Franz Anton Hillebrandt.

SCHLOSS HOF AND SCHÖNBRUNN HILL

The Paradise Garden at Schloss Hof was designed by garden landscaper Johann Anton Zinner in the French style. The vertical central axis with its fountains divides the garden on each terrace into two laterally reversed areas with seven terraces. The main drive to the palace, embellished with trophies, takes up the first terrace, with the palace on the second. In common with other baroque gardens, *parterres de broderie* flank the palace on both sides, with box hedging, flowers and multi-coloured gravel. (Today, this second terrace has been extended to include meadows and

fruit trees.) The third terrace has *parterres de broderie* that spread, carpet-like, with intricate flowing lines; espaliered trees supported by a high bastion wall form the fourth terrace; and the outer areas of the fifth terrace are defined by clipped sweet chestnut and lime trees forming avenues. Originally, the rows of chestnuts enclosed a wide arbour path into which four garden pavilions were integrated. The arbours and gazebos were built mainly of wood and festooned with climbers. These gazebos were removed during the nineteenth century, although the foundations are still visible. *Parterres à l'anglaise* – ones made in grass, also known as cut-grass parterres – flank the sides of the central axis. A *bosquet*, with coppiced field maple, and niches for benches, invites strollers to linger on the sixth terrace. At the end of the terrace are more lime trees with their crowns clipped to the shape of a hive, a typical feature of baroque gardens. On the final terrace is the most extensive section of garden, with a central crossing path dividing it into four rectangular zones, with *bosquets* surrounding *boulingrins* (bowling greens), or sunken lawns.

By 1760 the palace and gardens were nearing completion, but Schönbrunn Hill, the 60-metre (almost 200-foot) slope rising behind the Great Parterre was no more than an ornamented passage cut through the surrounding woods. Johann Ferdinand Hetzendorf von Hohenberg had grand schemes for the hill and designed elaborate plans with terraces, but Maria Theresa, now widowed, decided on a simplified solution: the Neptune Fountain at the foot of the hill, and a Gloriette (small building, usually commanding a view) at its summit. This Gloriette, constructed from recycled otherwise 'useless stone' left from the remains of Schloss Neugebäude, was designed to exalt the Habsburgs' power (the same stone was used for the folly that is the Roman Ruin).

FURTHER WORKS

The Great Parterre was redesigned towards the end of the 1770s and included statues of mythological figures, the work of Johann Wilhelm Beyer. Numerous architectural features were erected, including the Roman Ruin (previously known as the Ruin of Carthage), the Obelisk Fountain, which symbolizes stability and perpetuity, the Fair Spring (a pavilion housing a well fed by spring water) and the Small Gloriette (another pavilion). All were completed in 1780, the year in which Maria Theresa died.

DUTCH BOTANIC GARDEN AND OTHER ATTRACTIONS

In order to accommodate the imperial family's extensive botanical collections, glasshouses were built. To the east of the palace is an Orangery, erected around 1755, recalling the one at Versailles. Adjacent to the eastern end of the Orangery is a semi-circular Citron House (Cedrathaus), while to the front of it is a kitchen garden, which, until 1744, included a historic vineyard, Liesenpfennig.

More land to the south was acquired in 1753. Established by Franz Stephan I, this area became the Dutch Botanic Garden, which was expanded to accommodate the growing collection of plants. Part of the garden was cleared for the monumental glass construction of the Great Palm House. Modern technologies, such as a steam heating system, meant plants from all over the world could be grown. When the Great Palm House opened, on 19 July 1882, it was the largest in the world and the last of its kind across continental Europe. Other attractions were soon added to the garden. The menagerie of 1752 became a zoo (Tiergarten), which is believed to be the oldest in the world, while the western parts of the park and gardens were redesigned in the English landscape garden style between 1828 and 1852.

RESTORATIONS OF THE TWENTIETH AND TWENTY-FIRST CENTURIES

Schönbrunn, like many royal gardens, had smaller, more private spaces, away from the court, for the family to enjoy. On the palace's eastern facade, adjacent to Crown Prince Rudolph's (1858–89) apartment, is the Crown Prince Garden (Kronprinzengarten), and the Garden on the Cellar

ABOVE OPPOSITE   *BELOW OPPOSITE*

The Bosquet   The Garden on the Cellar

(Garten am Keller), which is raised above the cellar. These gardens, known as the Meidling Privy Gardens (Meidlinger Kammergarten), date from the mid-eighteenth century and are among the oldest parts of the park and gardens. They served as privy (meaning private) gardens for the imperial family until the end of the monarchy in 1918. The Garden on the Cellar, bordered by a horseshoe-shaped pergola, underwent a baroque restoration between 1750 and 1755, consisting of a *parterre de broderie* arranged around an octagonal pool. Its intricate design of bedding plants and coloured sands was restored again, between 2000 and 2003, and the ensemble is framed by topiary trees, including box and yew.

Five trelliswork pavilions have been incorporated into the pergola covered in *Parthenocissus quinquefolia* (Virginia creeper). The original pavilion at the centre, removed in the mid-twentieth century, has been replaced by one with a viewing platform. The historical pavilions are elaborately carved wooden structures crowned by a painted dome. As early as 1770, the pergola's trelliswork was replaced by an iron structure.

Gardeners are the lifeblood of any garden, and from time to time they enjoy the opportunity to create new spaces. During the early twentieth century, gardeners at Schönbrunn built a Japanese garden (Japanischer Garten). However, it subsequently became disused and overgrown until, in 1998, it was restored to its three separate areas: the Tea Garden (Teegarten) with a paved area (Teeplatz); next to the Teegarten, the Stone Garden (Steingarten) and, beyond that, a dry landscape garden (Karesanui).

VALUABLE PLANTS

Along with tulips, daffodils were among the most precious decorative plants at Schönbrunn.

These plants were imported from the Ottoman Empire during the sixteenth century, and today around 10,000 varieties bloom every spring in Schloss Hof and Schönbrunn. During the eighteenth century many tropical plants were growing at Schönbrunn, thanks to the efforts of Franz Boos. The former under-gardener became a plant collector, sending succulents (*Fockea capensis*) and bulbs (*Veltheimia capensis and Haemanthus amarylloides*) from South Africa and other plants from his expeditions to the Americas.

In 1904, the Sundial House (*Sonnenuhrhaus*) housed the plant collection of Emperor Franz Joseph I (1830–1916). He was born at Schönbrunn, spent much of his life, and eventually died there, aged 86. Until 1989, the Sundial House served as a conservatory and for overwintering plants native to Australia and South Africa. Today, renamed the Desert House (Wüstenhaus), it contains specimens from the valuable collection of succulents, including the prickly pear (*Opuntia* spp.) and the hedgehog cactus (*Echinocereus engelmannii*).

Following the downfall of the Habsburg monarchy in November 1918, Schönbrunn was passed to the newly founded Austrian Republic and became a museum. It has provided the location for film and television productions, including *A Breath of Scandal* (1960) and, briefly, *The Living Daylights* (1987). The maze of 1720 underwent considerable restoration work and, in 1999, the first section was opened as a classical maze with false turns and a viewing platform. One thousand yews were planted forming a 630-metre (over 2,000-foot) long, 1.9-metre (6-foot) tall hedge. The Liesenpfennig vineyard was resurrected, and enjoyed its first harvest in 2012.

RIGHT
The Japanese Garden

OPPOSITE
The Columbary

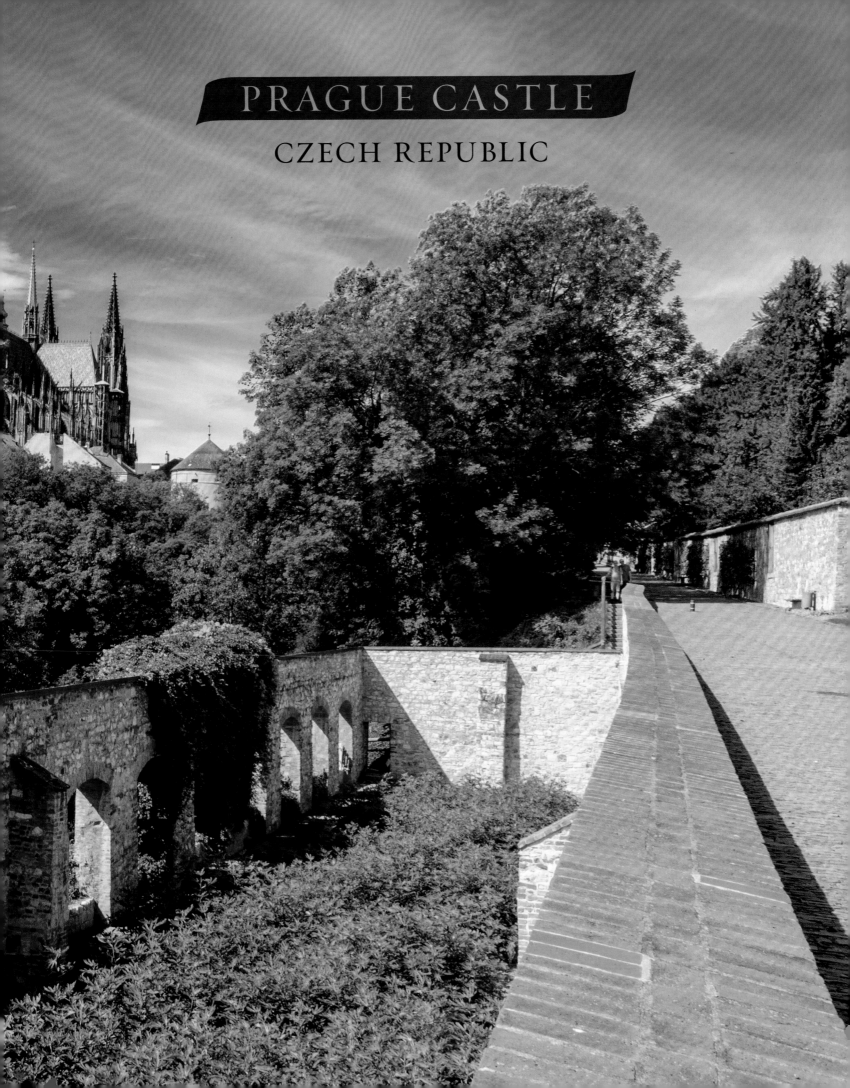

PRAGUE CASTLE

CZECH REPUBLIC

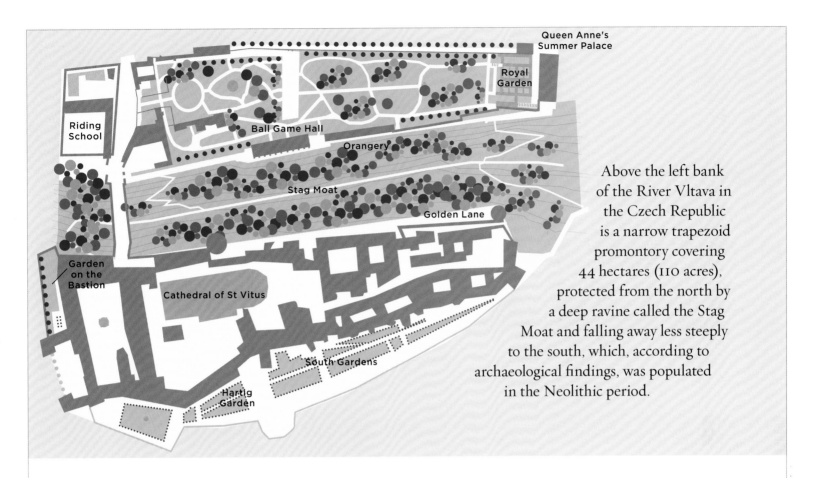

Queen Anne's
Summer Palace

Royal
Garden

Riding
School

Ball Game Hall

Orangery

Stag Moat

Golden Lane

Garden
on the
Bastion

Cathedral of St Vitus

South Gardens

Hartig
Garden

Above the left bank
of the River Vltava in
the Czech Republic
is a narrow trapezoid
promontory covering
44 hectares (110 acres),
protected from the north by
a deep ravine called the Stag
Moat and falling away less steeply
to the south, which, according to
archaeological findings, was populated
in the Neolithic period.

This hilltop is the site of the largest castle complex in the world, Prague Castle, also known as Hradčany, a collective name for an assembly of churches, offices, fortifications, gardens, offices and palaces. For more than a millennium it has been the traditional and only seat of Czech rulers and state representatives, as well as being a religious and spiritual centre of the country.

ARCHITECTURE THROUGH THE CENTURIES

Changing needs, demands and taste over the centuries are reflected in the architecture of the secular as well as the religious buildings of Prague Castle. Its history begins in 875, when the first Christian prince of Bohemia, Bořivoj I (852–89) of the Přemyslid dynasty, moved his seat from Levý Hradec, a fortified wooden settlement on the Vlatava, to what is now Prague. At the end of the tenth century the significance of Prague Castle was reinforced when it became not only the domicile of the head of state, but also the seat of the Prague Bishop. At the same time the first

Bohemian monastery was founded by St George's Basilica (in 920). In this period the castle and its grounds took up about 6 hectares (almost 15 acres). The original wooden settlement was then rebuilt as a fortified medieval castle in the Gothic era and continued to expand. The biggest development came in the fourteenth century when the Holy Roman Emperor Charles IV (1316–78) made Prague Castle his imperial residence and began construction of a Gothic cathedral. In 1344 the foundation stone was laid on the Hradčany Hill, with master builder Matthias of Arras and later Petr Parléř building the chancel with its ring of chapels, St Wenceslas Chapel, the Golden Gate and the lower part of the Great South Tower of the Cathedral of St Vitus. During Charles' rule, the castle fortifications were strengthened and some of the roofs were covered with gold-plated metal sheets.

After the Hapsburg ascension to the Czech throne (in 1526) the castle underwent further reconstruction, this time in the Renaissance style. The New Royal Palace was built during the late sixteenth and early seventeenth centuries in the reign of the Emperor

PREVIOUS PAGES   OPPOSITE

The Fig Tree House   The Royal Garden

Rudolf II (1552–1612), who chose Prague as his seat of residence and returned it to the centre of the Empire, as a hub of European culture and science. The Castle was then transformed into a representative 'château-style' seat under Maria Theresa (1717–80), who reigned for 40 years, and it gained the late baroque style visible today. Substantial reconstruction and repairs ensued as part of the so-called Teresian attempts to give the castle a unified facade. The only female ruler of the Habsburg dominions, Maria Theresa was also one of the most significant rulers to exercise authority. On her death, the Habsburgs moved their royal residence to Vienna. At the end of their monarchy, in 1918, Prague Castle became a seat of Czechoslovakian (and later Czech) presidents.

Interestingly, after more than 1,100 years of modification and reconstruction, the castle has retained, in essence, the layout of the Přemyslid settlement from the ninth and tenth centuries. The grounds can be entered from three sides: the main (western) entrance from the Hradčany Square, the side (northern) entrance from U Prašného mostu street and the eastern entrance from the Old Castle Steps.

THE RENAISSANCE AND THE ROYAL GARDEN

Leisure time, beautiful environments and well-arranged gardens were the choice of sovereigns and aristocrats during the Renaissance period. Symmetry and harmony were key, and spaces had to contain various fountains and waterworks. It was fashionable to grow exotic plants or breed animals among nobility at the time. This way of life was introduced to Prague by Holy Roman Emperor Ferdinand I (1503–64), who chose an area of vineyards for his Royal Garden (Královská zahrada), and work commenced in 1534. Ferdinand I was interested in exotic plants, and, inspired by Italian gardens, Mediterranean plants such as orange trees, including sweet (*Citrus* x *sinensis*) and bitter (*C.* x *aurantium*) varieties, mandarins (*C. reticulata* 'Blanco') and fig trees (*Ficus carica*) were soon growing in the Prague Royal Gardens. By 1554, the royal garden collection included tulips brought from Turkey. These

flowers became so admired that they were introduced to the rest of Europe.

Work began on an important building, the Royal Summer Residence, in 1538 as a gift from Ferdinand I for his wife Anna Jagellonica (1503–47). Architect Paolo della Stella and, later, stonemason Bonifac Wohlmut brought progressive ideals and attitudes and did not fully follow Renaissance rules of architecture; which can be seen in the building's unique Gothic roof. In front of the residence is the Singing Fountain, the water from its spouts falling rhythmically to the bronze plate below, which dates from 1568. The Royal Ball Game Hall (Ballhaus), built by Wohlmut between 1567 and 1569, was used by the emperor's courtiers, along with a shooting range and skittle alley.

The Royal Garden was seriously damaged during the Thirty Years' War (1618–48). In the late seventeenth century it was restored, following the Renaissance style, by Leopold I (1640–1705; Holy Roman Emperor, King of Hungary, Croatia and Bohemia). By the early 1700s the baroque style was fashionable and the Royal Garden was graced with a new glasshouse built by Bohemian architect Kilian Ignaz Dienzenhofer and statues by Austrian-born sculptor Matthias Bernard Braun, one of which, *The Night*, is seen in front of the Ballhaus. A similar piece, *The Day*, was destroyed by the Prussians in 1757.

After Ferdinand V (1793–1875), the last Czech king and a member of the Habsburg-Lorraine dynasty, was forced to abdicate in 1848 he lived in Prague Castle for the rest of his life. Ferdinand loved music, spoke five languages and was particularly interested in botany. He and his wife, Maria Anna of Sardinia (1803–84) became interested in the strip of land above Stag Moat, the ravine that provided the castle with its natural defence. Ferdinand had three greenhouses built, one of which was devoted to growing their highly prized and expensive camellia, rhododendron and azalea species.

A style that was finding favour across Europe was the picturesque or English landscape garden of the nineteenth century, which was introduced to the royal gardens at Prague. Ornamental flower borders were replaced with sweeping areas of grass; it became an English park, which remains the dominant feature of

ABOVE OPPOSITE
The Paradise Garden

BELOW OPPOSITE
The Rose Garden

the garden with glorious traces of the Renaissance and baroque periods.

THE ROYAL GARDEN TODAY

The Royal Garden is dotted with lemon trees, a legacy of Ferdinand I's interest in exotic plants, and surrounded by sixteenth-, seventeenth- and eighteenth-century buildings. It is a geometric and formal Renaissance garden, designed with abundant shrubbery and fountains. The new Orangery, on the site of the old Empire Greenhouse, the most recent building in the Royal Garden, is a glass-and-steel structure, almost 90 metres (295 feet) long, and was designed in 1999 by the Czech architect Eva Jiřičná and commissioned by Olga Havlová, the first wife of President Václav Havel. Citrus trees, palms, yuccas, phormiums and figs all thrive in its humid interior.

To the west of the Royal Garden lies the Garden on the Bastion (Zahrada Na Baště), first created in 1861 and redesigned in 1930 by Slovenian architect Jože Plečnik, who introduced features inspired by Japanese and Italian gardens. The South Gardens comprise three smaller gardens – the Paradise Garden (Rajská zahrada), the Garden on the Ramparts (Zahrada Na valech) and Hartig Garden (Hartigovská zahrada) – spread along the facade of Prague Castle for 500 metres (almost 550 yards), culminating in the St Wenceslas vineyard and the neoclassical summerhouse Villa Richter (now a restaurant). Collectively, the three gardens represent a unified landscape, preserving the majestic trees. Laid out as a private garden for Ferdinand I, the Paradise Garden covers 0.38 hectares (almost an acre). A lawned area in the shape of a trapezoid edged with granite is dominated by a Greek-style basin, designed by Plečnik, using Mrákotín granite. The Hartig Garden only became part of the castle's complex in the 1960s. It is the smallest baroque garden with trellised walls and a balustrade adorned with decorative vases. The Terrace of the Riding School has a large stone terrace affording some of the best views over Prague. The garden is formally laid out as a symmetrical parterre with three oval pools.

A Renaissance pavilion built during the reign of Emperor Matthias (1557–1619) in 1614 marks the entrance to the Garden on the Ramparts. This is a long and narrow garden with several other pavilions, featuring wall paintings dating from 1848 by the leading Czech painter Josef Navrátil. The oldest woody plant in the castle, a yew specimen estimated to be about 400 years old, is to the right of the staircase and interestingly the stone border purposefully bypasses it. Two baroque obelisks are a reminder of the defenestration of imperial governors on 23 May 1618. The Bull Steps, also the work of Plečnik, divide the Garden on the Ramparts from the third castle courtyard, the Hartig Garden, the final and most recent of the trilogy, having been redesigned during the 1960s, and contains a music pavilion.

THE PALACE GARDENS

In addition to the royal gardens at Prague Castle, there are surrounding gardens of importance, leading down to the River Vltava. Running the length of the castle, extending along the steep terrain is a series of interconnected gardens, created in 1697, often referred to as the Palace Gardens (Palácové zahrady) under Prague Castle: Ledeburská Garden, Malá and Velká Pálffyovská Gardens, Kolowratská Garden and Fürstenberská Garden. These gardens are rich in architectural elements, including terraces, garden houses, balustrading, ornamentation and decoration. In 2000, HRH Prince Charles was present when the Palace Gardens were reopened after years of cleaning and reconstruction.

In Malá Strana, or the Lesser Quarter, of Prague itself is the Wallenstein Garden, designed in early baroque style as part of the Wallenstein Palace complex built between 1623 and 1630. Dominating the garden is a large wall with artificial stalactites imitating a limestone cave (*grotta*). Greek mythological sculptures, including the marble fountain in the middle of the pond, were by Dutch sculptor Adriaen de Vries. The ones seen today are replicas; the originals, plundered by the Swedish army in 1648, are now in the garden of Drottningholm Palace (see page 164).

ABOVE OPPOSITE
The Fürstenberská Garden

BELOW OPPOSITE
The Vrtba Garden

The gardens that surround Prague Castle also extend to the slopes of Petřín Park where the baroque Vrtba Palace is situated. It was designed by František Maxmilián Kaňka in 1720. Between 1990 and 1998 the Vrtba Garden underwent complete reconstruction. It is not large, but it contains the very essence of a baroque garden – elegant staircases, decorated handrails and balustrading, terraces, flower beds, hedges and statuary by sculptor Braun.

Petřín Park itself was established as a royal hunting park in 1268 by the King of Bohemia Otakar II (1233–78). During the sixteenth century the park was newly planted; however, during Maria Theresa's reign (1740–80) almost all the trees in the park were cut down and burned. The park reopened in 1804. As part of the World's Fair hosted by Prague in 1891 a tower resembling the Eiffel Tower was erected in the park and some of its vineyards and fruit trees were removed to create a 6-hectare (15-acre) Rose Garden (Růžový sad Petřín), 320 metres (more than 1,000 feet) above sea level. Designed and built between 1932 and 1934 in the shape of a rosette and fan, it contains around 12,000 roses of various species that bloom from June until the first frosts. In 2002 Prague was flooded, causing the park to close. Renovation work started and the Rose Garden reopened in April 2003.

PLANTS: A HISTORY OF SELECTED SPECIES

An article published in *Natural Sciences in Archaeology* in 2012 looked at the archaeobotanical evidence of particular species from sites in the area of Prague Castle and Hradčany, over the preceding two decades. Many of the plants were imported to Prague from south Europe and Asia, as well as the Americas. They included: *Cucumis melo* (melon), *Oryza sativa* (rice), *Buxus sempervirens* (box), *Ficus carica* (brown Turkey fig), *Nicotiana rustica* (Aztec tobacco), *Cucurbita pepo* (pumpkin), *Ribes rubrum* (redcurrant), *Datura stramonium* (Jimson weed) and medicinal herbs, such as *Coriandrum sativum* (coriander) and *Foeniculum vulgare* (fennel), which are rarely represented in archaeobotanical assemblages. Other medicinal plants, among them *Cannabis sativa* (hemp), *Papaver somniferum* (Opium poppy), *Anethum graveolens* (dill), *Lepidium sativum* (pepperwort), *Majorana hortensis* (marjoram), *Ocimum basilicum* (basil) and *Satureja hortensis* (Summer savory), were also identified. Larger samples revealed plums, hazelnuts, walnuts and grapes. Among the less common species recorded in the archaeobotanical complex were *Olea europaea* (olive), *Prunus dulcis* (sweet almond), *Castanea sativa* (sweet chestnut), *Arachis hypogaea* (peanut), *Pistacia vera* (pistachio nut) and *Coffea arabica* (coffee). All of these species are unique in the archaeobotanical context in central Europe.

Based on this analysis, the researchers were able to reconstruct the social life in the Early Modern period of Prague Castle itself and the agricultural activities around the castle and further afield. The introduction of plants from the Mediterranean, Asia, Africa and the Americas can be interpreted as the first wave of globalization, which in turn affected the environment of royal courts in central Europe.

ABOVE OPPOSITE *BELOW OPPOSITE*
The Royal Ball Game Hall   The Wallenstein Garden

HET LOO PALACE

THE NETHERLANDS

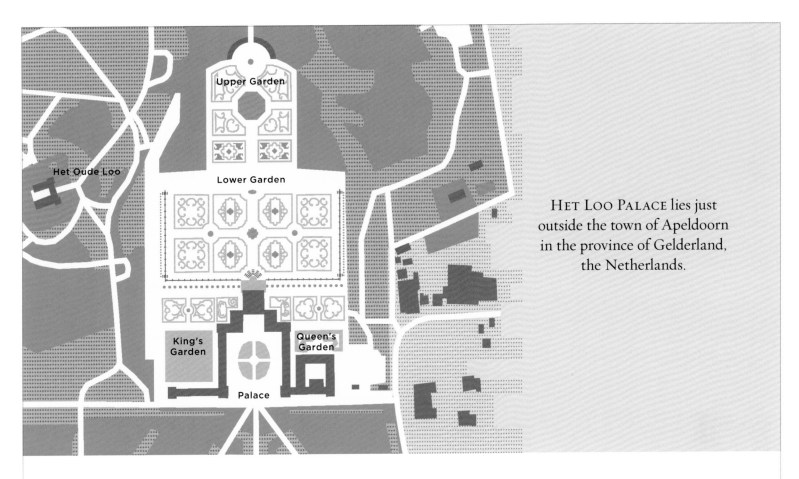

HET LOO PALACE lies just outside the town of Apeldoorn in the province of Gelderland, the Netherlands.

The word 'loo' means deciduous forest in old Dutch and Het Loo translates as *'open space in the forest'*. Het Loo was the summer palace of the Dutch House of Orange-Nassau from its construction in the 1680s by Stadtholder (servant of the state, the equivalent of Chief Magistrate or Lord Lieutenant) King William III (1650–1702) and his wife, Mary Stuart, Mary II of England (1662–94), until the death of Queen Wilhelmina of the Netherlands (1880–1962).

This symmetrical Dutch baroque masterpiece was built not as a palace but as a simple country retreat or pleasure house (*Lust-hof*). From the 1600s it became fashionable for the nobility and the wealthy to build estates in the countryside with surrounding large tracts of forest, which provided an income and acted as hunting grounds. William III chose the open area of the Veluwe, a ridge of hills where he already owned hunting rights, for his retreat. The medieval castle of Het Oude Loo (which still exists) suited his purpose: cool, surrounded by lush countryside, with abundant water flowing from natural springs and a high water table. All in all, the area lent itself perfectly to his desire

to create a showcase for his dynasty. Het Loo gardens and park cover a staggering 10,000 hectares (more than 24,700 acres) and the baroque-style garden covers 7 hectares (17 acres).

Naturally flowing, gravity-driven streams powered numerous watermills during the sixteenth century. Watercourses were dug that increased the flow towards the mills, and ponds helped to regulate water levels. The difference in height in the terrain along with this system of watercourses and ponds meant that the water pressure was ample, and could support and maintain the large garden with fountains, cascades, rills and running water. Prudently, the Stadtholder bought up water rights to the entire area, demolishing the watermills purely for the creation of water features, which were the height of fashion in late seventeenth-century Europe. An extensive network of ceramic pipes over a distance of 5 kilometres (3 miles) from Orden and 10 kilometres (6 miles) from Assel was used to divert water from the springs issuing from the ground higher than Het Loo in order to feed the myriad water features needed to create a style of garden

PREVIOUS PAGES

The Upper Garden

OPPOSITE

The Lower Garden with the *berceau* beyond

not seen before in the Netherlands – one of sufficient splendour to match the country residences of other European rulers.

GARDENS ON A HUMAN SCALE

Het Loo is laid out on a north–south axis and its formal gravel walks, parterres with vases, fountains, basins and statuary create a unified whole. From the southern facade (the front of the palace) a *patte d'oie* (goose foot) radiates out as a simple, elegant beech avenue. Initially this was a central straight avenue towards the palace; two diagonal avenues were added at a later stage. The gardens to the north are very much on a human scale, created as a form of art. The effects were achieved by the use of parterres, enclosure and rigid symmetry adhering to baroque principles. Over the centuries, the gardens at Het Loo changed to reflect fashion and the taste of the royal owners, but a programme of painstaking reconstruction since the 1980s has reinstated the walks, vistas and fragrant planting that William and Mary would have enjoyed two centuries earlier.

THE DUTCH GOLDEN AGE

The original work was carried out by skilled architects and garden designers – Daniel Desmarets, Jacob Roman and Romeyn de Hooghe and, later, the French-born architect Daniel Marot – under the supervision of Hans William Bentinck, the Stadtholder's right-hand man. Construction began in 1685 with the garden and palace being conceived as a single harmonious design, both the internal and external spaces melding seamlessly together. Het Loo reflected the prosperity of the period: this was the Dutch Golden Age. Dutch naval power had risen rapidly from the late sixteenth century, and by the second half of the seventeenth century the Netherlands dominated global commerce. Merchant ships returned with magnificent paintings and porcelain, rare plants and even a menagerie of exotic animals. Through the monopolies of the Dutch East India Company, the West India Company and an increasingly international network of plant

and garden enthusiasts, William III built up a unique and spectacular collection of rare and exotic plants. Desmarets, Super-intendent of His Highness's Country Houses, Plantations and Gardens, carried out an inventory of plants in 1713, and more than 200 exotic plants were recorded, including myrtle, fig, oleander and pomegranate. Many plants depicted in wall paintings, tapestries, on furniture, vases and other ornaments that decorate Het Loo give other clues to the species that were introduced.

THE GARDENS

In 1686, construction started on the rectangular sunken garden, the Lower Garden, surrounded on three sides by walls and terraces with two smaller enclosed gardens flanking the side wings of the palace, the King's Garden (with parterre, bowling green and fruit trees) and Queen's Garden (a private space filled with columbines and lilies, with a *berceau*, or arbour walkway, framing the entire garden). The *berceau* was planted with Dutch Elm (*Ulmus* spp.) on either side. As the trees grew their canopies fused across the roof, forming an intimate green tunnel around an elaborate arrangement of parterres, ponds and arbour seats.

It is not known who designed the *berceau*. De Hooghe, Marot's rival at Het Loo, named Bentinck as the designer, but the curves of the feature are entirely different from Bentinck's typical use of squares and geometric forms. His travels throughout Europe to gather inspiration may explain the change in style, or perhaps it was the fruit of a Dutch–French collaboration, with Bentinck responsible for the traditional Dutch elements of the outer square tunnel, central pond and arbour seats and Marot for the sweeping curves of the inner *berceau*. The *berceau* and gardens pay homage to the dominant French style, but the outcome was the result of different forms of expertise, remodelling and creating, not a single concept by one designer; the 1686 design of Het Loo echoes the earlier gardens of the House of Orange-Nassau, created by William's grandfather Prince Frederik Hendrik (1584–1647). Only after the ascension of William and Mary to the English throne were the

OPPOSITE

The *berceau* interior

gardens altered in the French style, with a strong vista and grass parterres, the so-called *parterres à l'anglaise*.

THE LOWER GARDEN
AND BOTANIC SPECIMENS

The Lower Garden was built around eight partly symmetrical parterres: clipped hedges, usually of box, and topiarized juniper pyramids. Four inner *parterres de broderie* were planted in a style unique to Het Loo, with elaborate patterns. The four outer *parterres à l'anglaise* were plainer, being filled primarily with grass. The box edging the parterres is impressive, 27 kilometres (almost 17 miles) in its entirety and it provides a glossy contrast to the loam walkways and coloured materials – grey gravel, black slate and red granite – used to decorate the inner parterres. In the centre is a magnificent fountain of Venus accompanied by four Tritons and four swans.

All eight parterres were edged by *plate-bandes*: borders that showcased single free-standing plant species. These *plate-bandes* were spaces for the palace gardeners to exhibit their particular expertise and resources, such as the famous tulip collections which epitomize Dutch taste, and which could be taken out and replaced to ensure colour and pattern in every season.

A NEW REGAL STATUS

In 1689, William and Mary ascended the throne of England in the Glorious Revolution (1688–9) which cemented Protestantism in the country, and greatly enlarged the status of the Netherlands and its royal house. (The Netherlands remained a republic, so there was a princely family of Orange Nassau who served as the first 'servants' of the State.) While in England, William sent Bentinck back to Holland to inspect the garden at Het Loo, instructing him: 'Do not forget Het Loo, nor to go there and sort out what remains to be done; you know how that place is close to my heart.'

The gardens were expanded in 1689, including the Upper Garden, and redesigned to reflect their new regal status. A new fountain was installed – Europe's highest at the time – the 'King's Leap', a few years later. However, the height of its jet (13 metres/43 feet) was surpassed by a fountain built at Herrenhausen (see page 54). An avenue of oak trees and a water rill separated the Lower Garden from the Upper Garden, with their canopies lifted so that the entire length of the garden could be seen from the palace, providing a vista of the King's Leap and a semi-circular colonnade on a red brick platform beyond, which encloses the far end of the Upper Garden. Large terracotta pots filled with topiarized shrubs and palms were set out as theatre, a feature that continues today. *Reposoirs*, resting spots where those who had walked the distance from the palace might catch their breath, were positioned at the bottom of the formal garden. Together the Upper Garden and Lower Garden formed the central part of a much larger garden that included landscaped parkland, kitchen gardens and garden 'rooms'. To the west of the baroque garden near Het Oude Loo a labyrinth promised entertainment and opportunities for flirtation. As an ensemble, the gardens formed an impressive public space in which the majesty of the rulers and the power of the Dutch nation could be celebrated and affirmed in ceremonies, parties, concerts and receptions. These decorative elements for pleasure and exhibition were complemented by spaces dedicated to more domestic purposes, such as the kitchen gardens and orchards.

REFINEMENTS TO THE GARDEN

With the patronage of their royal master and supported by the wealth of the Dutch Empire, the gardens' first designers continued to refine and perfect their work. The borders around the parterres became ever more decorative and the borders filled with flowering plants in the hands of Marot, a promoter of the late baroque style. He was a Huguenot who fled France after the Edict of Nantes in 1685 and was both an interior and exterior designer as well as an architect, and although Hampton Court was to be his masterpiece, Het Loo provided an opportunity for him to hone his skills for the far grander English project.

ABOVE OPPOSITE

The *parterres de broderies*

BELOW OPPOSITE

The *parterres de gazon*

By the time William V (1748–1806) became the last Stadtholder of the Dutch Republic in 1766, the baroque symmetry of the gardens was no longer fashionable. In 1780, he commissioned architect Philip William Schonck to reflect the new vogue for landscaped parkland. Schonck's plans were only partially completed, however, when the Netherlands were invaded by French revolutionary troops in 1795. The Stadtholder fled to England and the gardens at Het Loo were plundered and then abandoned. In 1808, Louis Bonaparte (1778–1846), Napoleon's brother and briefly king of Holland, levelled the old gardens, destroying the elaborate baroque design and in its place he commissioned Alexandre Dufour to build a landscaped park of winding alleyways. The Dufour's scheme was never executed; however, it did inspire the Dutch garden architect J. P. Posth to create a landscape park near the palace.

The palace remained a summer residence but the gardens did not regain their prominent place in court life until the second half of the nineteenth century when it passed into the hands of King William III of the Netherlands (1817–1890), who had a love of plants and trees, and his daughter Queen Wilhelmina. Although the garden and parkland were not drastically altered, numbers of rhododendrons were planted under William III, some of which survive today. Wilhelmina was passionate about Het Loo: her memoir *Eenzaam maar niet alleen* ('Lonely but not alone'), published in 1959, describes in affectionate detail the time she spent in the boathouse and the tea pavilion, and the landscaped park which she loved to paint.

During the nineteenth and twentieth centuries the garden team had three subdivisions: the florestry division (*De Bloemisterij*) took care of the greenhouses and the gardens closest to the palace; the park division (*Het Park*) maintained the 650 hectares (more than 1,600 acres) of land; and the kitchen garden division (*De Moes-en Fruittuin*) provided for the palace household. This team was disbanded in 1952 and the current garden team consists of the former floristry division and has sixteen specialist gardeners.

BAROQUE SPLENDOUR RESTORED

The palace has not been used as a royal residence since Wilhelmina's death in 1962, when the decision was made to turn it into a national museum. During the 1980s work began to restore Het Loo and its grounds to its baroque splendour, with the more recent additions pulled down and interiors redecorated to reflect the taste of its seventeenth-century occupants.

When J. B. Baron van Asbeck began the reconstruction of a baroque garden behind the palace, he consulted designs dated *c*.1725 by Christiaan Pieter van Staden. When the foundations of the fountains, the edgings of the parterres and other seventeenth-century remains were uncovered, the accuracy of Van Staden's map was confirmed. There was one deviation from the overall design detailed by Van Staden. In the Upper Garden, large trees were still growing, and the design of this section was adapted so that these could be incorporated into the reconstruction.

A four-year programme of work began in 1980 to uncover and rebuild the original walls and colonnades. An innovative method of reconstructing the elaborate parterre designs was created by the Het Loo garden team: photographic slides were used to project the outlines onto a wall, which were then traced onto large sheets of paper to be pinned to the ground for use as patterns. Once all the designs had been traced out and connected, they were fixed with a type of plastic edging. The strong patterns and symmetry became visible with the planting of the box. In 1989 it was decided that, given the cold Dutch winters, the *Buxus sempervirens* 'Suffruticosa' would be replaced by a hardier variety of box. In addition, the original planting of the *berceau* had been affected by Dutch elm disease and as part of the 1980s restoration programme the elms were replaced with hornbeams.

Renovations continued from 2007 to 2015 in four phases, with work on the Upper Garden starting in 2007. Remedial works were necessary to make good the 1980s constructions. The irrigation pipes had sprung leaks, the plastic edging had perished, the soil

OPPOSITE

Van Staden's map of 1706

DOOR mÿ Christiaan Peter van Stadin. WEST OOST Rÿn Lanse JO ROEDE

Het Jot Con Afiere

of the flower borders was exhausted and some trees in the landscape garden had died. The opportunity was taken to rebuild the Upper Garden with increased accuracy, following Van Staden's map (and the more accurate map of Henry Reetz, dated 1706), but this time using Corten steel rather than plastic.

All of the plants in the Upper Garden that were to be retained were dug up and stored so the parterre layout could be repaired and adjusted. During the planting, *Calonectria pseudonaviculata* (box blight) was discovered. After a rainstorm in April 2019, the garden was flooded, and the blight spread through the whole garden. The entire 27 kilometres (17 miles) of box hedging had to be removed and replaced with the box-leaved holly (*Ilex crenata* 'Dark Green'). Trials started at the end of 2019 with the *Buxus* cultivars 'Heritage' and 'Babylon Beauty' to replace the box-leaved holly. The second phase, in 2003, encompassed work on the *reposoirs* uncovered by archaeological excavation and these were reinstated.

In 2012 attention turned to the renovation of the King's and Queen's Gardens, particularly to the *parterres de broderie*. These designs were more intricate than those elsewhere, and so another method for demarcating them had to be developed. Templates were cut from perforated steel, their elaborate patterns taken from the Van Staden map and welded *in situ*. These were then fitted with Corten steel edges.

The final phase saw the renovation of the Lower Garden between 2013 and 2015. First, perforated steel templates were deployed to replicate all the outer *parterres à l'anglaise* and inner *parterres de broderie*. For the first two years work concentrated on the left-hand side of the garden, followed by the right-hand side over the following two years. This meant that between the two stages of renovation the symmetry of the Lower Garden was broken for the first time in the history of the palace. Close study of the Van Staden map led the twenty-first century designers to re-evaluate the meaning of the colours used in the parterres. Grass was reinstated as the material of the outer *parterres à l'anglaise* and an internal flower border filled with perennials.

ORIGINAL SPECIES AND REPLANTING

Replanting proved to be a major element in the renovation works. A special garden committee was convened between 1975 and 1984 to study original species and planting patterns. Botanical texts, prints and manuscripts dated between approximately 1680 and 1702 were collected, including a colourful memoir left by Walter Harris, who, in a visit in 1699, recorded:

'pyramids of juniper and box, and with shrubs of Marshmallows of all colours, but contain a variety of the finest tulips, Hyacinths, Ranunculi, Anemone, Auricula ursi, Narcissus, Junci, etc. In the summer there are double poppies of all colours, Gilliflowers, lark-heels etc. In the autumn, sun-flowers, indian cresses, the stockrose, Marygolds, etc. On the walls of these gardens do grow great variety of most excellent fruit, as the best peaches, apricots, cherries, pears, figs, plums, muscat grapes of all sorts.'

On the committee's list of plants were the espaliered fruit trees characteristic of Dutch gardens – apple, pear, peach, apricot, nectarine, cherry and plum – known to have been grown on the south walls of the Lower Garden. The list also featured the famous tulips, parrot and striped varieties especially, that were the height of fashion during the seventeenth-century 'Tulipomania' when gamblers bet vast sums on the colour varieties of new bulbs, and gardeners made fortunes by producing variations of shade and pattern.

The reconstructed grounds now include many specimens and varieties of *Citrus x aurantium* (the bitter orange tree) which had adorned the Queen's Garden during the seventeenth century and were emblems of the king's family, the House of Orange, some of which – now part of the Dutch National Plant Collection – are more than 300 years old. Since 1984 further studies on plant introductions during the sixteenth and seventeenth centuries have been undertaken and published. As a result, the list of suitable (exotic) plants that can be used in the baroque garden of Het Loo Palace trebled.

OPPOSITE

Aerial view

DROTTNINGHOLM PALACE

SWEDEN

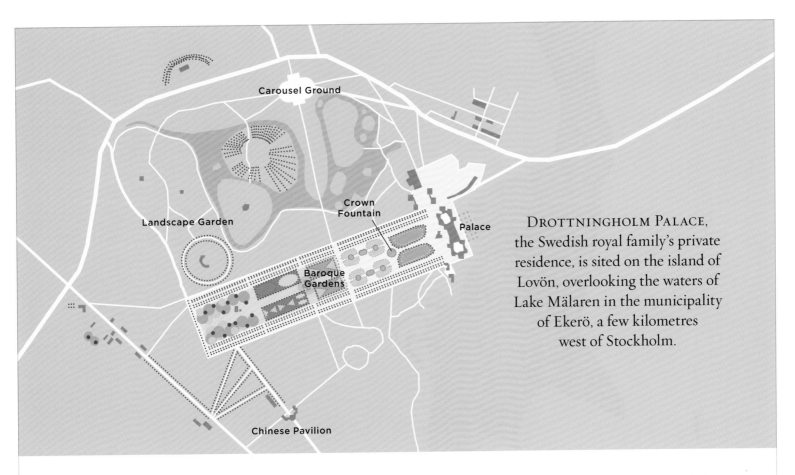

Carousel Ground

Landscape Garden

Crown
Fountain

Palace

Baroque
Gardens

Chinese Pavilion

DROTTNINGHOLM PALACE, the Swedish royal family's private residence, is sited on the island of Lovön, overlooking the waters of Lake Mälaren in the municipality of Ekerö, a few kilometres west of Stockholm.

It was constructed to emphasize the greatness and power of the Swedish monarchy. Its 127 hectares (314 acres) of gardens take inspiration from Italian and French baroque styles, as well as the more naturalistic planting and design of the English landscape style. Drottningholm, which translates as 'Queen's islet', was originally a royal mansion called Torvesund, built in the sixteenth century by King John III (1537–92) for his wife Queen Catherine Jagiellon (1526–83). The mansion burnt down however in 1661. Dowager Queen Hedwig Eleonora (1636–1715), widow of Charles X Gustav of Sweden (1622–60) from the age of 23, ordered the design of her new palace. As the layout and design of the former architecture did not exist, a new palace could be constructed.

THE DOWAGER QUEEN AND HER NEW PALACE

Following the Thirty Years' War (1618–48) Sweden had become a leading European state with a population of about one million. The regent Queen Hedwig

Eleonora, over the infant Charles XI (1655–97), ruled as head of state, a position that even after Charles was crowned king in 1672 was a powerful one. To match such a position a new residence needed to be built. She commissioned leading architect Nicodemus Tessin the Elder to design a baroque-style park with influences from André Le Nôtre's work at Vaux-le-Vicomte in France. This grand vision was to include formal avenues, a clear main vista, sculpture, fountains, cascades, canals and *parterres de broderie* and the overall concept for the gardens and park was based on symmetrical axiality. Eleonora, however, was not pleased with the design and work on the exterior space was delayed until the royal palace was complete.

NICODEMUS TESSIN THE YOUNGER AND EUROPEAN INSPIRATION

Following in his father's footsteps, Nicodemus Tessin the Younger took over the position in 1681, after familiarizing himself with European landscape architecture, in particular French and Italian, having

PREVIOUS PAGES AND OPPOSITE

The Baroque Gardens

visited Chantilly, Versailles (see page 90), Marly, Villa d'Este and Villa Aldobrandini. Given the queen's response to his father's design, Tessin changed it to the extent that it is considered his own work.

THE BAROQUE GARDENS

The baroque gardens, started in 1681, extend south-west in four sections, with paired rectangular parterres and *bosquets*. The gardens stretch for 800 metres (more than 2,600 feet); viewed from above they look long and narrow because Tessin's original plans included a large rectangular water basin to the north and a cascade to the south, following the natural topography. The overall length is double that of his father's design.

Between the eastern facade and Lake Mälaren is a smaller parterre with *tapis verts* and shrubs trimmed in the shape of cubes with curved beds of salvia. A prominent statue of Poseidon points to the lake, a gesture conveying Sweden's powerful navy in the seventeenth century.

An estate map from 1698 shows an Orangery to the north of the palace with a large kitchen garden with fruit trees. No traces remain of the building in this area, but an Orangery was moved closer to the English Park during the reign of Gustav III (1746–92) and is therefore not part of the symmetrical composition.

Through a series of outdoor 'rooms', the palace's interior is visually extended from the western facade into the landscape. On either side of two avenues are four rows of trimmed lime trees, each row offset to the centre from the preceding row, forming a three-dimensional framework to reinforce the longitudinal axis of the baroque gardens. A total of 792 limes were planted, beginning in 1684, and it took 40 years to complete the scheme.

PARTERRES, SCULPTURE AND WATER

The wide pathways of the *parterres de broderie* closest to the palace, edged with box, consist of gravel, crushed brick and black hyperite (a form of dolomite).

Drottningholm Palace is built so it appears to be on a terrace of red brick when viewed from the gardens and park. Although these two parterres are now *tapis verts*, during the seventeenth century they were *parterres de broderie*, surrounded by *plate-bandes* (flower beds) in delicate patterns. In the corner of each parterre, at the end closest to the palace, is a circular fountain adorned with sculptures.

A change in level coincides with the next section of garden, which contains two water parterres with five fountains on each side. The parterres are surrounded with low trimmed hedges of box and squared-off obelisks of yew that give height to an otherwise flat landscape. the focal point is the Crown Fountain, with a sculpture of Hercules slaying the hydra. Water for the fountains and cascades at Drottningholm needed to be transported from springs located 1.5 kilometres (almost a mile) away, using a system of interconnected hollowed wooden logs. However, because the difference in height between the location of the springs and the palace was little more than 12 metres (40 feet) there was insufficient pressure to ensure that all the fountains in the gardens worked properly.

The bronze sculptures and fountains in the baroque garden are created by the Dutch sculptor Adriaen de Vries, who also worked at Prague Castle (see page 142) and Frederiksborg Palace (see page 184); many of his figures that formed the cascading spouts for the fountains were brought to Sweden as spoils of war from Prague in 1648 and from Denmark in 1659.

BOSQUETS: THE TAMING OF NATURE

Farther from the palace and with another change in topography, at the terrace bordered by Tessin's octagonal water cascade, the vegetation becomes denser and taller, with pine hedges creating secluded garden 'rooms'. The main axis continues with four *bosquets* placed along it. The northern *bosquets* are the more recent, dating from the 1780s, and have flowing lines and pathways, whereas the older southern *bosquets* have a symmetrical layout. Before the long axis of the baroque garden ends there is a

ABOVE OPPOSITE   *BELOW OPPOSITE*

Chestnut trees   The Chinese Pavilion

dense grove, at the centre of which is an open space the shape of a 'star' with radiating paths and sightlines. The garden terminates with an avenue of lime trees.

THE CHINESE PAVILION AND GARDEN

From 1720 to 1792, the palace was often taken up by the Royal Court. Between 1715 and 1744, Queen Ulrika Eleonora of Sweden (1688–1741) and King Frederick I (1676–1751) resided in the palace. It was then given to Crown Princess Louisa Ulrika of Prussia (1720–82), who later became queen when she married Adolf Frederick of Sweden (1710–71; King of Sweden from 1751).

Queen Louisa Ulrika, who loved art and natural history, was given a wooden Chinese Pavilion (Kina Slot) as a gift from the king. Architecturally, its style was French baroque with Chinese elements, which were the height of fashion and reflected trade associations with the Far East through the East India Company. The pavilion, built in 1753, stands on a rise in the hunting park south-west of the palace. The queen recalled in a letter to her mother: 'He led me to one side of the garden and suddenly to my surprise, I found myself gazing upon a real-fairy tale creation, for the king had had a Chinese palace built, the loveliest imaginable.'

The garden surrounding the Chinese Pavilion was built at the same time in the English landscape style and provided a natural transition from the rigid geometry and straight lines used elsewhere. It represents a freer, late baroque style. An avenue of chestnut trees was planted to open up vistas around the buildings and trellis was covered in honeysuckle, lilac and mulberry. The wooden building itself was replaced in 1769 with a brick pleasure palace adorned with a green roof and 'exotic' ornamentation.

FREDERIK MAGNUS PIPER AND THE ENGLISH PARK

During the 1770s, a period characterized by weak royal power, bad harvests and food shortages in Sweden, many of the country's formal parks were in disrepair. The involvement of Russia and France in domestic politics led to political and social unrest as a Russian–Danish alliance grew stronger. In 1777, Gustav III assumed possession of Drottningholm Palace. The king had an interest in garden design and drew up a general plan for an English landscape garden. Inspired by Tsarskoye Selo in Russia, the former home of the Romanov imperial family, he commissioned Swedish architect Carl Frederik Adelcrantz, who was the 'First Surveyor', responsible for overseeing royal construction and 'to provide the Kingdom with lasting and neat buildings.' Most of the work focused on Drottningholm and other palaces and castles. The king's plan was revised in 1780 by Frederik Magnus Piper, the Swedish landscape architect responsible for Haga Park, part of Stockholm's Royal National City Park.

Pieces of sculpture acquired by Gustav III during his travels were carefully positioned within the natural landscape. Buildings and monuments were added towards the end of the eighteenth century, including a Turkish-inspired copper tent (originally designed by Adelcrantz for the palace guard) in 1782 and a Gothic tower in 1792.

Piper was introduced to William Chambers, a Scottish-Swedish architect based in London, and, while he was staying in England, Piper visited Stourhead, Painshill and the Leasowes and became familiar with the English landscape style. At Drottningholm, he was commissioned to create a landscape garden and in 1797 he produced his master plan of the gardens and grounds with ponds, canals, islets, bridges, lawns, tree-lined avenues and *bosquets*. Sinuous pathways lead through meadows and fields are punctuated with specimen trees and classical sculptures. Despite strong support from Gustav III, it is reported that Piper's plan was disregarded in favour of the king's own.

To the north of the 'star' in the baroque garden, in the bottom south-west corner of the English landscaped park there is a 'labyrinth'. Although some of the *bosquets* are sometimes described as mazes, the 'labyrinth' is circular, surrounded by tall trees and can clearly be seen in Piper's watercolour (dating from the 1790s) of the gardens and park. During the eighteenth century it had 3-metre (almost 10-foot) tall hedges, but after Gustav's death it deteriorated. Now it has been restored as a grass labyrinth. It is not a maze,

ABOVE OPPOSITE
Aerial view of the *bosquets*

BELOW OPPOSITE
The statue of Poseidon

as it has only a simple single path to follow. At the centre is a semi-circle of trees and a white statue.

RESTORATION AND ONGOING WORK

The nineteenth century was not kind to the gardens. However, between 1907 and 1911, Gustaf V (1858–1950) started a renovation project of the palace. In 1911, the palace returned to royal use and has since remained a royal residence. Further restoration was undertaken during the 1950s and 1960s on the initiative of Gustaf VI Adolf (1882–1973). In 1981, King Carl XVI Gustaf (b. 1946) and Queen Silvia (b. 1943) moved from their apartments in the Royal Palace of Stockholm and Drottningholm became their main residence.

The daily maintenance of the gardens and park at Drottningholm requires the input of many individuals. Historically, military regiments, farmers and crofters who lived in the area gave their labour. The gardens were cut with scythes or hooks and the clipped hedges and shaped trees were trimmed with scissors, knives or hedge sabres. Gravelled areas were shovelled or raked by hand. Large potted plants were taken in and out from the glasshouse several times a year. Today, of course, lawn mowers, motorized hedge clippers and tractors have replaced the scythes, knives and scissors.

THE PLANTS

Plants that struggle in the Swedish climate have needed replacing many times over the centuries. Some of the plants in the parterre have today been replaced by more suitable alternatives; the northern white cedar (*Thuja occidentalis*), a native of eastern Canada and the north of the United States, is one ornamental that does well in colder conditions and aesthetically it works well planted with extensive lawns.

The common limes, *Tilia* x europaea 'Pallida' (historically and collectively known as 'Dutch lime'), have also undergone replanting. Between 1997 and 2011, the trees were rejuvenated, section by section. Cuttings were taken from trees close to the palace and propagated following historical methods, such as mound layering, then force-grown until they were large enough to be transplanted. As castle gardener Dan Haubo explained at the start of the fourteen-year restoration:

'Throughout the years, rot, fungal infestations and harsh pruning, in combination with poor plant-site conditions, had weakened the winds in the park and it was decided that every one should be replaced in different stages.'

The 350 winds [limes] planted closest to the castle are [propagated] by cuttings from the old [ones in] the park. The other winds in the park are of the kind Tilia x europaea *'Pallida' whose clone is known from the early 17th century.*

As Drottningholm was not subjected to the disruption and devastation of two world wars, many of its tree-lined avenues and *bosquets* survived. During the seventeenth and eighteenth centuries, lime trees would have been pruned as part of the overall scheme, opening up vistas and emphasizing the layout of the garden. Later trees would have been left to grow to their natural shapes or pollarded. It is therefore a difficult task for restorers to decide the correct pruning practices in the twenty-first century.

The Drottningholm Palace gardens have been restored and conserved impeccably. Their three distinct styles – baroque, the Chinese pavilion with its less formal late-baroque gardens and the English romantic landscaped park – chart their royal owners' tastes and ideas down the years as well as garden design itself.

OPPOSITE

The *bosquets*

FREDENSBORG PALACE

DENMARK

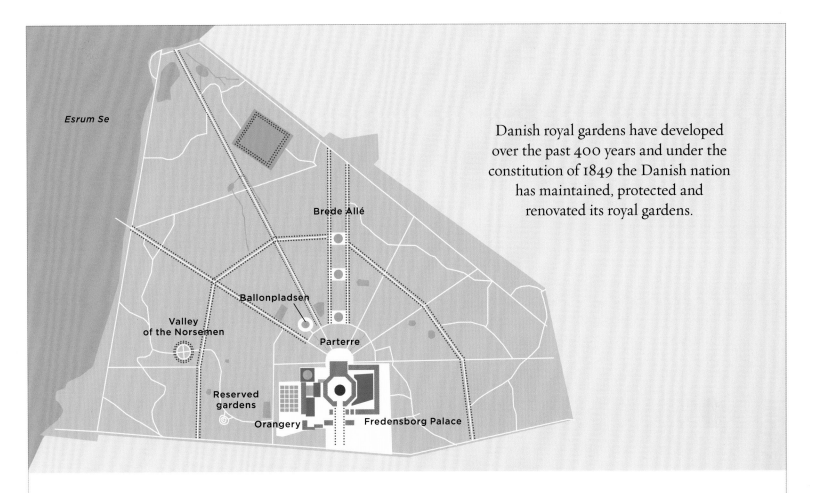

Esrum Se

Brede Allé

Ballonpladsen

Valley
of the Norsemen

Parterre

Reserved
gardens

Orangery

Fredensborg Palace

Danish royal gardens have developed over the past 400 years and under the constitution of 1849 the Danish nation has maintained, protected and renovated its royal gardens.

Collectively Danish royal gardens provide insight into the evolution of garden design from the early seventeenth century to the present day.

Garden design reflects the trends, loves and hates of the times just as much as architecture or fashion. During the seventeenth and eighteenth centuries, monarchs and courtiers would have travelled and seen gardens which left an impression. Court architects or head gardeners were also sent on Enlightenment tours to gather inspiration, knowledge, plants and art. Ideas were often copied, modified, adapted and shared to fit into the local environment and landscape.

Gardens are not frozen in time, however. Trees and plants mature and die, sculptures degrade and buildings need repair. As the years pass, new styles bring changes to the gardens and the necessity to adapt to fresh uses, different elements and alternative materials. Gardens are therefore like crystal balls, offering glimpses of the past as well as future needs and requirements.

PLANTS AS GARDEN ARCHITECTURE

At the end of the seventeenth century and the beginning of the eighteenth century, two kings of Denmark and Norway, Christian V (1646–99) and his son Frederik IV (1671–1730), began to use plants to create garden architecture, following the popular trend in Germany, Italy, France and Holland. The king, after all, was pivotal in society and gardens were designed with a well-planned structure and order; the baroque style was particularly in vogue across Europe. Frederik IV became so enthusiastic that, with the desire to demonstrate his power, he commissioned elaborate gardens at Frederiksborg Palace (see page 184) and the palaces of Frederiksborg and Fredensborg.

Fredensborg Palace was built by Frederik IV in the 1720s on the east banks of Lake Esrum Sø, on the island of Zealand, 8 kilometres (5 miles) from Frederiksborg in the north of Zealand. Before the palace and gardens were built, the site was a farm named Østrup. The king wanted to create a summer

PREVIOUS PAGES

Reserved (private) gardens

OPPOSITE

Aerial view

palace for pleasure and hunting amid a lovely garden surrounded by rolling hills and forests. In 1720 he commissioned leading architect Johan Cornelius Krieger (royal gardener to the court at another of Christian IV's (1577–1648) residences, Rosenborg in Copenhagen) and General Building Master Johan Conrad Ernst. The palace was built in the Palladian style with Italian and French influences, and became occupied in 1722. It took six years to design and build the French-inspired baroque style garden. To commemorate the end of Denmark's eleven-year participation in the Great Northern War, the palace was named Fredens Borg, which means 'palace of peace'.

During the reigns of Christian VI (1699–1746) and of Frederik V (1723–66) and his queen, Juliana Maria of Brunswick-Wolfenbüttel-Bevern (1729–96) the palace was rebuilt and expanded by the architects Nicolai Eigtved, Lauritz de Thurah and Caspar Frederik Harsdorff. Following Juliana Maria's death, the palace was rarely used; not until the reign of Christian IX (1818–1906) and Queen Louise of Hesse-Kassel (1817–98) did Fredensborg became the setting for the royal family's life, and for any lengthy durations.

A SETTING FIT FOR A STAR

Set within 120 hectares (297 acres), the square palace block was built on the highest ground as a centrepiece of seven avenues laid out in the form of a fan, known as the 'hunting star' (*jagtstjerne*), radiating into the distant surrounding forest. Today, the palace affords a view of the countryside and the lake, along each of the avenues, extending for over 9 kilometres (6 miles), to the beautiful Gribskov, Denmark's fourth largest forest. These avenues, planted between 1720 and 1765, stretched for 15 kilometres (9 miles) in Frederik V's day.

PLEASURE PALACE

At his pleasure palace Christian enjoyed sailing on the lake in his miniature frigate, which was berthed in the Chaluphus (boathouse or covered harbour). Horses and deer grazed on the meadows, a three-storey menagerie housed bears, wolves, tigers and rare birds,

and there were enclosures for ducks, pheasants, hares, rabbits and squirrels. The royal family would lunch in one of the garden's pavilions, with produce from the large fruit and vegetable garden. Hunting was another, well-planned pleasure activity.

The hunt *par force* required each participant to have a specific role. Many nobles hunted *par force* for many reasons, but above all because it was considered the purest and noblest form of hunting.

In front of the palace, to the north, was a semi-circular *parterre de broderie* of box, with trimmed hornbeam hedges. Members of the royal family and courtiers would walk through this space, but due to the length of the avenues they would invariably use horses or horse-drawn carriages to enjoy the rest of the grounds.

INSPIRATION FROM ENGLAND AND FRANCE

During the 1750s four pavilions were added at the corners of the square block to extend the palace and accommodate the entire royal family. In the 1760s, the new King Frederik V moved in, and as the palace had been enlarged considerably over the years it was necessary to expand the large octagonal section in front of and to the south of it, to make the proportions match the facade. Inspiration came from Hampton Court Palace (see page 12), and the gardens at Versailles (see page 90). Frederik V wished to change the main purpose of the garden from a productive garden, supplying food to the palace, to an aesthetic and artistic experience. During his reign, the palace gardens were in their prime.

Reorganization of the gardens was undertaken in the 1750s in the prevailing French fashion by the French architect Nicolas-Henri Jardin who preserved the main structure but took inspiration from Versailles. He wanted to remove fences and introduce a main axis with a double avenue filled with sculptures overlooking the lawn or *tapis vert* (green carpet). The central *allée* (an avenue or walk, bordered by clipped trees or hedges planted in straight lines to emphasize the perspective) was widened to mirror the enlarged

ABOVE OPPOSITE

The Brede Allé

BELOW OPPOSITE

The Queen Mother's Rose Garden

building. Originally, the *tapis vert* was framed by a double *allée* of limes and spruces. Working with the Danish neoclassical sculptor Johannes Wiedewelt, Jardin created a masterpiece of garden architecture where palace, garden and sculpture would 'create an unprecedented entity – a gem of artistic unity'.

TO MAINTAIN, RATHER THAN RESTORE

The gardens were well maintained for a further twenty years, but by the beginning of the nineteenth century they were in a poor state. The spruces had been felled and the limes, hedges and flower beds were in disarray. During the 1840s it was clear something had to be done: the garden needed to become a more modern landscape garden to reduce costs. Many *allées* were felled, and new paths laid. Trees were left to grow to their natural height, only being pruned to secure the views of the landscape. The sculptures in the Brede Allé (Broad Avenue) started to disappear under the dense foliage of the trees.

In the past hundred years, many of the garden's features had either been removed or badly neglected. Since the early twentieth century, however, there has been a dedicated effort to restore the gardens, often as a simplification of Frederik V's original baroque garden. By 1930 the trees surrounding the palace had grown so tall and dense they almost concealed it. Then, during the 1940s, a tree collapsed, killing a man in the forecourt. This terrible accident resulted in the rest of the trees being felled to avoid further risk and marked the start of the huge renewal plan.

NEW GRASS CARPETS

The *parterre de broderie* along the palace front (north) facade facing the garden was reconstructed as a semi-circle, divided into six sections of large grass carpets framed by low yew hedges and adorned with marble figures and vases. Jardin was enthusiastic about enormous lawns (his *tapis verts*) which he designed in various forms with gravel areas between. This type of decoration was new in the mid-eighteenth century.

The garden was a direct response to the palace architecture. The front courtyard was like an entrance hall, the parterre an elegant outdoor room, while the Broad Avenue could be seen as an impressive knights' hall. There were, however, a number of smaller garden rooms located around the outer arc of the semi-circular parterre. These were called 'cabinets' and each one was decorated differently. One example is the existing Ballonpladsen (Balloon Court), which is framed by tall lime trees and decorated with a round basin. A bridge links to a square island with an obelisk in remembrance of Frederik V. The name 'Balloon Court' references an area used to play balloon – or ball – with an inflated pig's bladder.

The name Brede Allé (Broad Avenue) hints at its sheer scale: 74 metres (more than 240 feet) wide with four rows of trees flanking a *tapis vert*. At the entrance are two huge monuments in tribute to Frederik IV's great empire, which consisted of Denmark, Norway, Iceland, the Faeroe Islands, Greenland and a number of dukedoms in northern Germany. Along the rows of trees are eight large groups of sculpture. Four are inspired by Greek and Roman mythology with themes of love, war, fire and abduction and the other four are war trophies portraying collections of weapons and military paraphernalia guarded by a lion with a cannonball representing the king's strength and power.

THE VALLEY OF THE NORSEMEN

In a valley between Fredensborg Palace and Esrum Lake lies the Nordmandsdalen – the Valley of the Norsemen – a truly unique attraction. Whereas most royal gardens display statuary of deities, this valley features 70 life-size sandstone sculptures depicting Norwegians and Faeroe Islanders – farmers and fishermen and women in period clothing with various tools such as scythes, fishing gear and rifles, sculpted by Johan Gottfried Grund. The gathering of ordinary people was a bold attempt to bring the king's subjects closer – the king could easily walk among his people – and in this regard the sculptures are quite unique among European royal gardens. Other features are two pavilions, one on either side, and a central column.

ABOVE OPPOSITE *BELOW OPPOSITE*

The Valley of the Norsemen Tree-lined avenue

THE RESERVED GARDEN

The Reserverede Have (Reserved Garden), otherwise known as the Marble Garden, is the royal family's current private sanctuary. It was created by Frederik V in front of the royal apartments at Fredensborg. Vegetable and herb gardens yield produce and flowers for the royal tables, continuing the 300-year tradition. Twenty-four equally sized square plots are divided in half lengthways, twelve aside, by a pathway with arched frames for climbers. To the south, the Orangery, built in 1995, houses many species, among them lemon, orange, laurel, myrtle and pineapple. The Reserved Garden differs from the rest of the baroque garden. Large expanses of lawn and beds of rhododendrons and azaleas prevail, with free-standing exotic trees. The loose, organic style using perennials was designed in the 1930s by Queen Ingrid (1910–2000), drawing inspiration from the Romantic landscape garden favoured during the late 1700s, a style that quickly took hold at both Fredensborg and Frederiksborg and which has provided inspiration to gardeners and garden designers down the years.

From the Reserved Garden a small bridge leads over an octagonal pond to an octagonal garden, the Rose Garden. Each segment of the octagon displays roses in a single colour with topiarized shrubs in wooden pots positioned on each corner of both octagons. In the centre, keeping watch over the roses, is the Flora statue, which has been a feature here since the 1770s. (A new rose garden, located between the Valley of the Horsemen and the Balloon Court, was created in 2011, marking the seventieth birthday of Queen Margrethe II, b. 1940, the previous year.)

RESTORATION WORK

Restoration of the gardens began in the mid-1940s and continues today. From aerial photographs, it was possible to see where the main *allée* had been. The seven *allées* are planted with limes and horse chestnuts and a tree survey was required to consider the health of each tree. Replanting the *allées* represented a huge investment, leaving insufficient funds for maintenance. As a result, rather than pruning the trees in baroque forms, the crowns were lifted on the inside flank of the *allées*. Fifty years after planting the trees, money was raised to prune the trees to reveal the original layout.

In 2009, the decision was taken to honour Jardin by restoring the baroque garden to his design. It was, however, unrealistic to attempt a full reconstruction. Several of the sculptures were in such poor condition they had to be replaced. Restoration efforts focused on the garden's main structure and geometric form, and the trees. Tree restoration was coupled with research to establish their original genotype. Of the original 220 lime trees planted along the main *allée* only 115 remained but researchers were keen to identify the specific clone that had originally been planted. Studies and DNA testing of lime trees in other Danish royal gardens laid out at approximately the same time revealed 106 of them to be *Tilia* x *intermedia* 'Zwarte Linde' and five to be T. x *europaea* Pallida.

To restore and recreate a historic garden requires more than funding: it also requires an understanding of garden design as art. Christine Waage Rasmussen, landscape architect at the Royal Gardens, Agency for Culture and Palaces, found that she was helped by studying the German philosopher Hans-Georg Gadamer, author of *Truth and Method* (1960). He observed that, 'to understand and to interpret is a productive approach which is always qualified in our own time and has a starting point in our own horizon. The goal is to bring us in contact with the old truths seen from our viewpoint,' what he calls a 'fusion of horizons'.

It is a complex task to preserve, restore and develop a living artwork, especially one that is almost 300 years old. Fredensborg Palace gardens accommodate many historical layers and landscape design features. It is an evolving piece of art. What we see is a garden that continues to grow with a modern outlook, while clearly revealing and showcasing its history.

OPPOSITE

The Rose Garden

FREDERIKSBORG PALACE

DENMARK

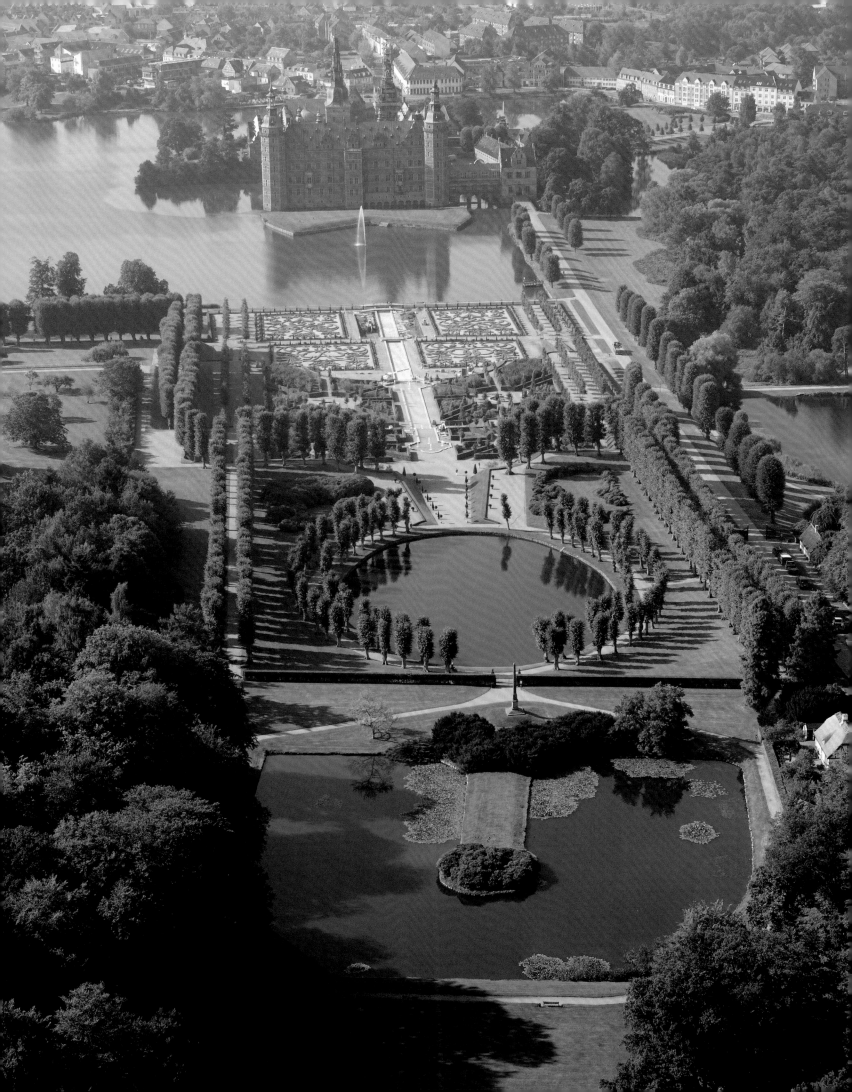

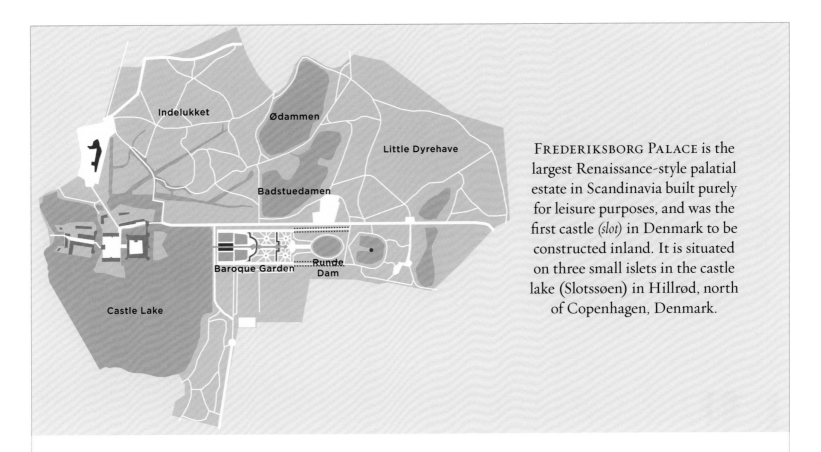

Indelukket

Ødammen

Little Dyrehave

Badstuedamen

Baroque Garden

Runde Dam

Castle Lake

FREDERIKSBORG PALACE is the largest Renaissance-style palatial estate in Scandinavia built purely for leisure purposes, and was the first castle (*slot*) in Denmark to be constructed inland. It is situated on three small islets in the castle lake (Slotssøen) in Hillrød, north of Copenhagen, Denmark.

Like many palaces of the time, it was built to display and reinforce the king's status as a powerful monarch (the lineage of the Danish royal family is the oldest in Europe, dating from at least the tenth century). The castle is richly adorned with symbolic and decorative elements, with gardens to match.

NORTHERN MANNERISM

During the sixteenth century, Frederik II (1534–88), Duke of Schleswig and King of Denmark and Norway, acquired Hillerødsholm Manor from the Gøyes, one of Denmark's noble families, and constructed the first part of Frederiksborg Castle because the original dwelling, a two-towered manor house, was deemed too small for the king. Road systems were developed linking Frederiksborg with Copenhagen. However, Frederik's son Christian IV (1577–1648), who had a residence on the opposite side of the lake, razed the castle between 1600 and 1620, and replaced it with a new palace inspired by the Flemish-Dutch late Renaissance- (or Northern Mannerism-) style, based on drawings by the Flemish architect Hans van Steenwinckel the Elder.

A LOVE OF BOTANY

Christian IV had an intense passion for botany and gardens. As a child he would visit the garden of his grandparents Christian III (1503–59) and Queen Dorothea (1511–71) at Koldinghus Castle, Jutland, which is regarded as one of the first true royal castles and gardens in Denmark, dating from the mid-thirteenth century. It had a monastery garden where plants for medicinal and culinary use were cultivated.

At Frederiksborg, Christian IV subdivided the garden into 'rooms', one containing a vegetable garden, another for growing medicinal herbs, as well as a fruit garden. He collected beautiful plants, exotic spices, pots and sculpture from all over the world and cultivated more than 1,300 different species.

SWEDEN AND DENMARK

During the mid-seventeenth century, Sweden and Denmark were engaged in informal trade wars, aside from the Second Northern War, and Frederiksborg was captured by the Swedes in 1659. During the Swedish

PREVIOUS PAGES
Frederiksborg Palace

OPPOSITE
Aerial view

occupation, the Queen of Sweden, Hedwig Eleonora of Holstein-Gottorp (1636–1715), used the palace and hunted in the woods with Malcolm Sinclair, the English envoy to Sweden.

The chequered history of Christian IV's palace and gardens continued. In 1720, his gardens were replaced by a stunning baroque garden by Frederik IV (1671–1730). (The palace itself was renovated in the 1730s but ceased to be used as a royal residence by the end of the eighteenth century.) Then, in the 1850s, it was again used as a residence by Frederik VII (1808–63). He married Louise Rasmussen (1815–74), who became known as Countess Danner. As part of the castle renovations, new fireplaces and stoves had been installed to heat the large rooms. On a cold night in December 1859, the king asked for a fire to be lit in an upstairs room. Unfortunately, the chimney was under repair and it resulted in a major fire breaking out that quickly spread to other parts of the building.

CARLSBERG AND FREDERIKSBORG

Following the fire, the reconstruction of Frederiksborg was funded by public subscription, a lottery fund, with substantial contributions from the king and state, as well as the prominent philanthropist J. C. Jacobsen of the Carlsberg Brewery. The royal family decided it would no longer use the palace as a residence, Jacobsen proposed the establishment of a museum of national history and offered to pay both for the reconstruction and for the museum's further expenses. On the basis of old plans from the archives, as well as detailed paintings and drawings by Heinrich Hansen, restoration and reconstruction began a year later and opened to the public as the Museum of National History in 1882.

By the time work was completed under the guidance of historicist architect Ferdinand Meldahl in 1864, Frederiksborg resumed its original appearance. The stepped gables, orange-red brick and sandstone facades are among the most striking features. In the outer cobbled courtyard is a copy, by Hansen, of the Neptune Fountain, paid for and donated by Jacobsen (the original, cast bronze figures from Prague, by

Dutch sculptor Adriaen de Vries, were taken to Sweden following the Treaty of Roskilde of 1658 and now stand in the gardens of Drottningholm Palace, outside Stockholm (see page 164).

ITALIAN INFLUENCES AND J. C. KRIEGER

The formal baroque style evolved in Italy and France in the early seventeenth century and dominated European garden design until the mid-eighteenth century. Although Christian IV's gardens still existed, court gardener Johan Cornelius Krieger was commissioned by Frederik IV to create a baroque park with waterfalls, harmonious symmetry, wide pathways, parterres, clipped and topiarized hedges and lawn-terraced embankments. It was inspired by the Italian terraced gardens that the king admired on his travels. The gardens were conceived as 'architecture in the open' – without a roof. Most royal gardens were created so that the nobility could leave their residence and step immediately into the gardens, whereas at Frederiksborg the gardens to the east and north are separated from the castle by the lake. This physical separation made it difficult to create the desired connection between them, but Krieger used this to his advantage and sited the garden on the main axis of the castle, accentuated by a long canal.

TERRACES, PARTERRES, *BOSQUETS* AND TOPIARY

The garden comprised four terraces which descended downwards towards the lake. Meticulous hedges of hornbeam, manicured grass slopes and topiarized box balls and yew pyramids and hedges emphasize the straight lines. Because stone was scarce, the terraces in the garden were held back by turf banks rather than retaining walls.

Along the central axis runs a water feature that cascades into the lake. Using an extensive system of lakes, streams, pipes and channels – and at vast expense – the feature runs from the second-highest terrace down to the lake.

The lowest terraces also contain the monograms

ABOVE OPPOSITE   *BELOW OPPOSITE*

The Cascade   The Baroque Gardens

of the four monarchs mostly closely involved in the garden – Frederik IV, its creator, Frederik V, Christian VI and Margrethe II (b. 1940), who recreated it. Their monograms, set within a bed of white and red gravel, are designed in expertly trimmed hedges, *bosquets* and parterres, surrounded by dome-shaped box trees, and framed by flower beds filled with exotic and native plants, including peonies, carnations, amaranths, fragrant lavenders, yellow *Hemerocallis* (day lilies), scented sweet peas and irises. In spring yellow and white daffodils fill this space, as well as tulips and hyacinths, which were the height of fashion in the seventeenth century. (Tulip bulbs, especially two-coloured varieties, traded at exorbitant prices in the seventeenth century and were therefore seen as a symbol of great wealth.) Set on a slight slope, the parterre is visible from the castle and resembles a Persian carpet.

On the next two, the highest, terraces are *bosquets* of hornbeam hedges laid out in a star shape. Gravel paths connect the 'rooms', adorned with plants and fountains to form a grove or *bosquet*. Sculptures, de rigueur in a baroque garden, were made not of marble or granite, but of painted oak, a far cheaper option. (Today they are cast in zinc.) Plants such as scented lilacs and laburnum were popular. Privet was imported, and at Frederiksborg it was allowed to grow freely, displaying its white flowers and black fruits in different seasons. More exotic plants, too, were brought to Denmark from gardens and nurseries throughout Europe, including agapanthus, pomegranate, fig, myrtle, bay laurel and citrus trees.

FRENCH BAROQUE INFLUENCE

Gardens from this period are on a scale unimaginable by modern standards and at Frederiksborg tens of thousands of plants have been cultivated, shaped and pampered for centuries. In common with other baroque gardens, including Versailles (see page 90), the palace or residence is normally the focus of the garden. This is particularly so when viewed from the upper terrace, looking back towards the castle. André Le Nôtre aggrandized the Renaissance Italian-style gardens at Versailles, a style that was observed, copied and 'improved' upon by many visiting nobility. Garden design and gardens represented a new art form and continued the acknowledgement as a mark of monarchical status. The gardens at Frederiksborg, clearly inspired by those at Versailles, were created as spaces in which to socialize and entertain. Closer to the palace planting was kept purposely low as parterres, ornamental flower gardens, or, further away, as patterns cut into turf as a cut-grass parterre. A geometric plan with symmetry was paramount to the baroque garden. Today Frederiksborg's avenues and clipped hedges are breathtakingly beautiful, especially when a low sun shines through the autumn foliage. The plants become living statues, creating a delightful cadence that punctuates the landscape. These natural sculptures of trained trees and shrubs were a typical feature of Dutch gardens (see Het Loo, for example, page 152) and at Frederiksborg rhythm and balance result from the three-dimensional arrangement of elements and materials. Seen today, the shape and reflection of the canal and lake add to the symmetry and tranquillity of the scene.

THE ART OF PERSPECTIVE

Krieger, again borrowing from Le Nôtre, also used false perspective, creating a garden that looks larger than it is in reality. Ramps that led visitors from one terrace to the next were wider at the bottom than at the top, which made them look longer. The same device was used for the cascade's steps. Also, repeating garden elements, such as terracotta pots, became smaller and smaller the further away they were positioned from the castle, which similarly extended the view. At the top of the terraces the Runde Dam, the Circular Pool, is in fact an oval basin but it appears perfectly circular from the garden's main axis. Pollarded limes surround and are reflected in the basin.

ABOVE OPPOSITE *BELOW OPPOSITE*

The Baroque Gardens Runde Dam

THE ENGLISH-STYLE ROMANTIC LANDSCAPE GARDEN

All woody plants, deciduous and evergreen, need constant pruning to keep their shape and gardens that rely on many kilometres of tree-lined avenues and clipped hedges, and hundreds of square metres of flower beds and lawns require excessive maintenance. Frederik IV's successors realized that it was almost impossible to maintain his gardens to the exacting standard required by the baroque style. Several of the avenues were left to grow, which meant the precise geometrical forms were lost. To one side of the Baroque Garden, north of the castle, is the Romantic Garden where plants are left to grow more organically as nature intended, in the style of an English landscape garden. This is also the location of the small Bath House, a miniature version of the castle, built in 1580 by Frederik II as a hunting lodge.

The Romantic Garden has several lakes, the largest of which are Ødammen and Badstuedamen, and pathways that meander beneath the canopies of trees and alongside the meadows. It is in direct contrast to the rigid lines and acute angles of the Baroque Garden. This was a place for leisurely strolling, as well as hunting. Whereas baroque gardens showcase human capacity to impose order on the natural world, the English-style garden celebrates the forms of nature.

A PERIOD OF NEGLECT

The gardens at Frederiksborg were maintained until the early nineteenth century, when the shrubs became overgrown, although the paths and terraces were still visible. It was not until 1993, when financial aid was provided, that work could begin to recreate the gardens and Krieger's restored Baroque Garden was inaugurated in 1996. An astonishing 65,000 box plants and 166 pyramid-shaped yews were planted in the parterre, while 375 lime trees with cone or sphere crowns and 7,000 hornbeams were used to recreate the avenues and *bosquets*. The cascade floor alone is half a kilometre (a third of a mile) of dressed granite stones. There is a saying in Denmark that the 'colour green is easy on the eye', and this is at the heart of the royal gardens at Frederiksborg.

ABOVE
Frederiksborg Castle and Garden 1718, engraved by I.A. Corvinus after a drawing by C. Marselius

OPPOSITE
A view of Frederiksborg Palace over the Baroque Garden

PETERHOF PALACE

RUSSIA

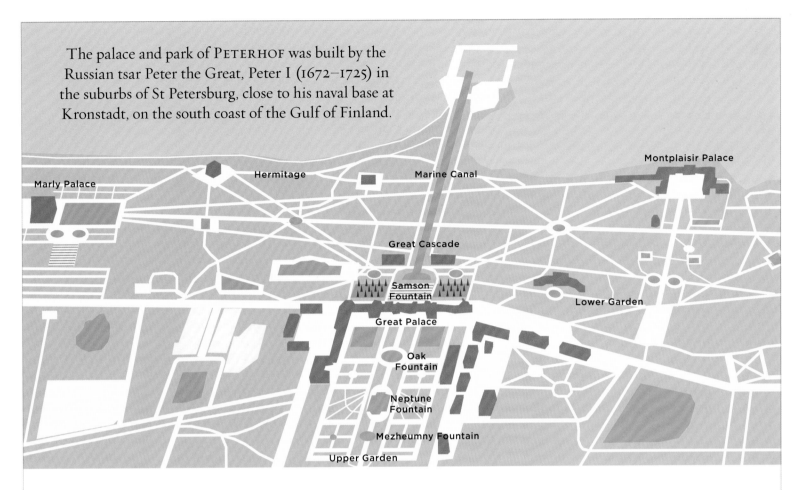

The palace and park of PETERHOF was built by the Russian tsar Peter the Great, Peter I (1672–1725) in the suburbs of St Petersburg, close to his naval base at Kronstadt, on the south coast of the Gulf of Finland.

Peter sought to demonstrate the power of his great nation and as such he required a residence that would rival the French masterpiece at Versailles (see page 90). His large urban project started in 1703 and the magnificent gardens, fountains, water basins, cascades and sculptures Peter created are an outstanding example of eighteenth-century garden design.

EXTENSIVE REFORMS AND PETER THE GREAT

Peter the Great ruled the Tsardom of Russia and later the Russian Empire from 1682 until his death in 1725. Before his reign, the Renaissance and the Reformation swept through Europe, but such westernization had been rejected; Russia remained isolated. When Peter's joint ruler, his brother Ivan (1666–1696), Peter was officially declared Sovereign of all Russia. He travelled across northern Europe focusing his efforts on art, science and education, and proved to be a great reformer. He modernized the Russian alphabet,

introduced the Julian calendar and produced the first Russian newspaper. His new gentrified bourgeoisie population mirrored western culture.

In 1717 Peter the Great visited the French Court at Versailles, which was to be the inspiration for his own palace. Preferring Dutch and Italian styles of architecture, he commissioned the Swiss-Italian Domenico Trezzini as the master builder to create an imperial residence. Although Trezzini was influenced by German baroque, he grew up in northern Italy so he was also influenced by the Lombard baroque style and its focus on classicism. Trezzini's style represented a drastic break from traditional Byzantine architecture and it became known as Petrine baroque, the style favoured by Peter. In 1710, Trezzini was given the title of Lieutenant-Colonel of Fortification and Architect.

Majestically perched on a hill, the 300-metre (almost 1,000-foot) long, 16-metre (52-foot) high yellow facade and golden domes of Peterhof Palace overlook the expansive grounds that stretch as far as the eye can see.

PREVIOUS PAGES

The Great Cascade

OPPOSITE

The Lower Garden

THE GARDENS

The size and opulence of the estate at Versailles, its water features and the clever use of perspective, made more of an impression on Peter the Great than the palace architecture. The French architect and master garden planner Jean-Baptiste Alexandre Le Blond was engaged to design the palace's gardens. He was a pupil of André Le Nôtre, and given the title 'General Architect'. Peter the Great became interested in Le Blond's work when he visited France, but he also read Le Blond's book on the theory and practice of gardening, which was published in 1709 in twelve different countries.

The gardens and parks, which were later enlarged in 1752 by the Italian architect Francesco Bartolomeo Rastrelli are split into Upper and Lower, and following the topography, the architects, master builders and gardeners created a series of terraces. The Upper Garden, which is 100 metres (328 feet) above sea level, forms the grand entrance – a green *cour d'honneur* (court of honour)– to the palace, while the Lower Garden, also known as the Lower Park, initially forms a comparatively small formal garden with the Great Cascade, then extends into Nizhniy Park down to the shoreline, set out as a baroque formal garden. Nearby is the Garden of Venus, Peter the Great's orchard of apple and cherry trees. East of the Lower Garden on the shores of the Gulf of Finland is Alexandria Park, a romantic picturesque English-style park constructed in the second half of the nineteenth century.

The Upper Garden covers around 16 hectares (40 acres) and is designed as a formal, geometric approach to the Palace. Johann Friedrich Braunstein, who drew up the site plan for the palace and whose documents still exist today, containing instructions on tree species, how to create the avenues and even build drainage systems, and Le Blond originally designed the Upper Garden as a kitchen garden producing vegetables, fruit and herbs for the palace, with fish in the fountain basins. It was replaced in the second quarter of the eighteenth century with a far grander design with avenues of clipped trees and sculpture. Around three sides is a wooden railing painted green with gold

tips, separated by plastered brick white and yellow pillars with lion masks and rounded tops. Three paired columns with Corinthian capitals mark the entrance to the garden and, just beyond the entrance itself, are two white-topped pavilions, rows of clipped trees on either side and a formal large grass parterre made up of six square enclosures, each with a distinctive pattern – square, radial and circular – and two square pools. Box balls, strategically placed down the central alley, draw the eye towards the palace. In addition to the rows of clipped trees, a belt of trimmed trees and shrubs further enhances the formal nature of the space. Geometry, a strong axis, wide avenues, lawned areas, clipped shrubs and trees, fountains and large expanses of water emphasize French garden design principles. Between 1754 and 1760, the last major adjustment of the Upper Garden was the work of Rastrelli, who widened the entire area to fit the altered facade of the Great Palace.

FOUNTAINS AND POOLS OF THE UPPER GARDEN

Walking from the Upper Garden towards the palace the first fountain is the Midway (Mezheumny) Fountain. This name belies the fact that the fountain is not placed centrally within the garden. The name 'Mezheumny' is said to refer to 'a bit of this, a bit of that' and signifies the many permutations of the fountain. It was built between 1737 and 1739 and is 30 metres (almost 100 feet) in diameter. The sculptor Bartolomeo Carlo Rastrelli (Francesco Bartolomeo's father) created a central group of figures for it. Destroyed in the 1940s during the Nazi occupation, the fountain seen today is a reconstruction. (Most of the statues and fountains at Peterhof are replicas or restored; the area was bombed during the Second World War.) In 1957 the sculptor Alexey Gurzhy created a replica of five of Rastrelli's figures, a dragon and four dolphins, based on drawings from the 1770s.

The fountain that is central to the garden is the Neptune Fountain. The largest of all the fountains, with approximately 40 jets, its basin is a staggering 92 metres (300 feet) in length by 33 metres (more than

ABOVE OPPOSITE
Winter's Avenue

BELOW OPPOSITE
The Upper Garden

100 feet) wide and edged with dolomite. A bronze statue of Neptune in a chariot, again using a cast by Rastrelli, was installed in 1737. It was dismantled during the Second World War and the statue of Neptune was recovered from Germany in 1947. In 1956 eight dolphins were cast, and in 1973 Vladimir Tatarovich recreated the horsemen in the western section of the pool.

The last fountain is the Oak Fountain, built between 1733 and 1735, which is the same size as the Midway Fountain, and edged with the same limestone. The bottom of the pool has a chequerboard pattern using light and dark granite. Rastrelli designed a group of tritons and dolphins in lead under the gilded branches of an oak tree but after the Second World War the fountain was completely reconstructed to a simpler design of dolphins surrounding the figure of Cupid seated on a starfish-shaped base of tufa.

On either side of the central avenue are the two Square Pools, in the centre of which is a marble statue of Apollo and Venus with six dolphins spouting tall jets of water. Despite their names, the pools are in fact symmetrical rectangles, measuring 54 by 45 metres (177 by 147 feet). Their position, however, in front of the south facade of the Great Palace means their longer sides are less noticeable in the overall scheme.

THE LOWER GARDEN AND PARK

The area to the north of the Great Palace was designed as a formal baroque garden and took ten years to create, beginning in 1714. Peter the Great sketched what he desired with fountains and palaces positioned at the end of each avenue. Further concepts by Braunstein, Le Blond, Nicola Michetti and master gardeners Leonardt van Harnigfelt and A. Borisov (and later by architects Mikhail Zemtsov and Rastrelli) were created to form a 102-hectare (252-acre) park consisting of bosquets and woodlands dissected by four radial avenues and the central Marine Canal, that leads the eye from the palace to the sea in the distance. A 'trident' set of avenues – the Marly Avenue, the Maliebaan Alley and the Birch Walk – cross the garden from west to east. In total, there are 150 fountains in the Lower Garden.

The highlight of the Lower Garden is the Great Cascade, the link between the palace and the Marine Canal. It is the main component of the entire fountain system: with this centrepiece Peter the Great wanted to rival Versailles and designed an elaborate scheme that included two grottos faced with tufa and a cascade stairway on either side, each step decorated with gilded scenes from mythology, and rich in sculpture, urns and statuary, with 176 jets of water. At the base of the water feature stands a sculpture of Samson crushing the lion's jaw (an allegory of Russia's victory over Sweden in the Great North War), to form the Samson Fountain. The gilded ornamentation is entirely extravagant, but set against the yellow-and-white facade of the palace a sense of unity and harmony is created. In the centre of the Great Cascade, and in front of the grottoes, is the Basket Fountain. A series of jets rises from a circle of tufa to form the basket shape, while eight vertical jets, set within an inner circle of tufa, form the shape of the flowers. There are also a series of fountains and stepped cascades along the length of the terrace, either side of the Great Cascade. Another in the Lower Garden is the Sun Fountain, with sixteen jets. A hidden mechanism, powered by the water, allows the fountain to rotate, causing the water jets to catch the sun. Perhaps one of the most remarkable secrets of the Peterhof Palace is that all of the fountains throughout the garden are supplied with water without the use of a pump. Gravity drives the water through an elaborate 20-kilometre (12-mile) network of pipes and valves, hidden underground, from the large reservoirs of water in the Upper Garden. A third of the pipes are originals from the eighteenth century.

THE MARINE CANAL

The Marine Canal, the work of Braunstein, Le Blond and Michetti, is a remarkable feat of engineering and much manual labour. It is approximately 600 metres (almost 2,000 feet) long, running from the Great Cascade to the Gulf of Finland and spanning the entire breadth of the Lower Garden. Like the rest of the gardens, the canal is based on a drawing by Peter the Great. Records from August 1721 indicate that this canal could take 115 small vessels at a time. The slope from the Lower Garden to the sea is considerable. In order to overcome this, engineer Vassily Tuvolkov built a sluice, 40 metres (over 130 feet) long by 3 metres (almost 10 feet) high, as a single chamber closed by oak gates. In 1770 the sluice walls were rebuilt from ashlar blocks of granite; not until 1962 was the canal finally faced with granite. Twenty-two white shallow circular basins set in the lawns have been positioned along the length of the canal. As the basins fill with water a gilded mask in each one sends out an arc of water. After restoration work, fourteen of the basins are made from Carrara marble; the remainder have retained their original Pudost limestone.

THE GREAT PARTERRES

The Great Parterres in front of the Great Cascade were created between 1716 and 1723 by Harnigfelt and Borisov, following designs by Le Blond and Michetti. They are laid out as *parterres de broderie* with clipped boxwood. (During restoration work, many of the box plants were replaced with lingonberry (*Vaccinium vitis-idaea*).) Between 1755 and 1760, when the palace was greatly expanded, Rastrelli and Bernhard Fock created new parterres with patterns of crushed marble, brick and shells. Colourful china vases and gold-trimmed painted tubs displayed rare plants alongside topiary. In 1769 these baroque parterres were extended and replaced by lawns in the English style. The parterres were devastated during Second World War. It was not until 1953, following designs by Rastrelli, that garden designer Regina Kontskaya recreated and harmonized the parterres using red brick and crushed white marble and shells to create decorative patterns within the lawn. With the Samson Fountain

Marly Palace

in the centre of the Lower Garden, a mirrored parterre formed of four quadrants is on either side of the fountain. Located in the centre of each quadrant is a circular pool with a decorative urn and a tall jet of water.

THE PERSPECTIVE AND MARLY PALACE

The Perspective, or the Marly Avenue, is the main avenue of lime trees in the Lower Garden which runs for 2 kilometres (a little over a mile). During the Second World War the 200-year old trees were cut down. However, after the liberation of Peterhof in 1944, lime saplings were planted, and when their crowns grew they were clipped in the formal style. The Perspective is an astonishing design element. It is straight and cuts across the Lower Garden from west to east, intersected by the Marine Canal, and, although of considerable length, it makes the garden feel even wider. The dense planting of the *bosquets* and woodlands stops where it meets the wide pathways and regimented planting of pleached lime trees. Taking a straight line along the top of the limes and along the base of the trunks the 'art of perspective' is clearly seen.

At the very edge of the Lower Garden on the Baltic coast is Marly Palace, an elegant, white, two-storey property. It takes its name from Marly-le-Roi, a hunting lodge and Louis XIV's (1638–1715) private retreat from Versailles, which Peter the Great had seen when he visited the French king. He wanted to create something similarly secluded and quite distinct from the rest of the estate, along with gardens, orchards and a cascade. The Marly Cascade was created between 1722 and 1732 using a natural slope and has a 14-metre (46-foot) wide stairway of 21 steps, with a small formal-shaped basin at the bottom. The Marly Cascade is sometimes called

Montplaisir Palace

Golden Hill, owing to the gilded lead masks of Medusa, by the sculptor Rastrelli, which spurt water down the steps.

MONPLAISIR

Deep in the grounds, through a labyrinth of trees, lies Peter the Great's pet project at Peterhof, a small, charming summer palace built between 1714 and 1723, which the tsar designed by and for himself, although he sought the help of several architects. Sited in the eastern corner of the Lower Garden, right on the shore of the Gulf of Finland, Monplaisir Palace is a single-storey brick building with a high, multi-tiered roof resembling a Dutch colonial mansion, flanked by two galleries that end in pavilions. It became Peter's preferred retreat, where he entertained only his closest friends and advisers.

A courtyard, surrounded by the building, contains a quadpartite parterre with intricate patterns set within crushed red brick, which ties in with the red-coloured roof of Monplaisir, with a central fountain, Kolokola, set in a circular pool surrounded by hostas. Neatly trimmed hedges, conical topiarized yew, conical obelisks covered in Virginia creeper (*Parthenocissus quinquefolia*) and topped with gilded balls and statues create a very formal space. Blue-and-white ceramic urns are placed in each quadrant and are filled each autumn with pumpkins and squashes as a decorative composition. To the west and east of the parterre are three rows of lime trees pruned like lollipops.

EIGHTEENTH- AND NINETEENTH-CENTURY WORK

After Peter the Great's death in 1725, and following a decade of neglect at Peterhof, Empress Elizabeth (1709–62) continued to expand her father's palace (Bartolomeo added the wings from 1745–55) and extend the water features. She loved hunting and gardening and, for her, aesthetics reigned supreme. Elizabeth, who was childless, named her nephew Peter of Holstein-Gottorp (1728–62) as her successor. He became Peter III of Russia until a coup that saw his

wife Sophia Augusta Frederica (1729–96), who was later known as Catherine the Great, become Empress of Russia. She was an avid collector of illustrated books and engravings of English parks and oversaw the creation of Alexandria Park, the first English-style landscape garden at Peterhof, designed jointly by Scottish landscaper James Meader, the former gardener at Alnwick Castle in Northumberland, and the Italian architect Giacomo Quarenghi. During Catherine's reign imperial gardeners were sent to Hampton Court to learn from Lancelot 'Capability' Brown.

To the south of the Upper Garden lies Kolonistskiy Park, which, in the nineteenth century, underwent significant earth-moving operations with the creation of Olga Pond. The excavated earth formed three islands, Olgin, Tsaritsyn and Krolichy. Andrey Stakenschneider built two pavilions, the Tsaritsyn Pavilion between 1842 and 1844 and the Olgin Pavilion between 1846 and 1848. The former is a Pompeian-style villa (its floor tiles were taken from Pompei) with formal gardens, parterres and a central fountain in white marble with a chequerboard base. A statue of Narcissus looks into the water and a semi-circular seating area is adorned with white marble statues and busts. On the north side of the pavilion lies another formal parterre garden divided into four quadrants with pathways in red brick dust and borders filled with seasonal planting. The Olgin Pavilion was built for the emperor's daughter Olga Nikolaevna (1895–1918) and resembles an Italian villa with a belvedere and peacocks. Balconies and niches with marble busts overlook lawns and winding paths with borders brimming with lilac, jasmine, strawberry and berberis.

DESTRUCTION AND RECONSTRUCTION

Peterhof suffered greatly in the Second World War. The palace was captured and occupied by the Germans and by the time it was liberated in 1944 it was in ruins. The palace was looted, fountains and sculpture stolen, the gardens and orchards torn down. However, the bulk of the damage came from Stalin, when he ordered Peterhof to be bombed to stop Hitler and the

OPPOSITE

The Marine Canal

German troops. The name itself was de-Germanicized in 1944, becoming Petrodvorets. Yet through the efforts of military engineers and more than 1,000 volunteers the Lower Garden was resurrected and opened in 1945. The facades of the palace were restored in 1952. The meticulous task continues to this day.

PLANTS

When seen as a historic garden Peterhof cannot be considered as a single garden, but as several gardens spanning the last three centuries. Garden history in Russia prior to the eighteenth century is almost impossible to uncover. Russia was, however, among the first countries to compile a pharmacopoeia. In 1778, the *Pharmacopoeia Rossica* was published in St Petersburg by the Russian Academy of Sciences founded by Peter the Great. This work contains 770 monographs, including 316 texts relating to herbal medicinal preparations. Russia's first *National Pharmacopoeia*, written in Russian, was published nearly a century later, in 1866.

Many members of the Russian nobility travelled across Europe, observing, collecting and bringing home plants. Peter the Great travelled far and wide and, by examining inventories from the eighteenth century and Braunstein's site plan, it is an educated guess that many of them were grown at Peterhof. Species include alder, buckthorn, grey alder, silver birch, guelder rose, white and mauve lilacs, as well as European blueberry, peppermint, fennel and flowers such as common foxglove, yellow foxglove, jimson weed, wild pansy and imperforate St John's wort. At Peter the Great's other residence of Strelna Palace, east along the shores of the Gulf of Finland from Peterhof, an inventory from 1736 listed cherries, pears, figs and apricots, and these were undoubtedly used, if not grown, at Peterhof too. Tunnelled arches, pergolas (*berso*) at Peterhof were covered with plants such as alder and hornbeam to create green corridors. In 2004, when Maria Ignatieva and Galina Konechnaya carried out floristic investigations into historical parks in St Petersburg and in Alexandria Park they found: lesser celandine, the yellow-star of Bethlehem, *Gagea minima*, wood anemones and fumewort.

Given its latitude, Peterhof's green expanses can be snow-covered from November to March, and its fountains and cascades covered. Therefore, there is an emphasis on spring and summer displays of flowers and flowering shrubs and trees bringing colour and scent to an otherwise overtly formal garden. Daffodils and tulips, as well as wood anemones and celandines bring heartfelt colour after the blanket of snow. However, the myriad lines of trimmed trees in the Upper Garden, the *bosquets* in the Lower Garden and the woods of Alexandria Park bring structure and wildlife to this estate. It is extravagant and vast, and yet by dividing the garden spaces into smaller areas, linked by tree-lined avenues and water features, Peterhof's gardeners and garden designers in the eighteenth century triumphed in making their 'Russian Versailles'.

OPPOSITE

The Samson Fountain

TAJ MAHAL

INDIA

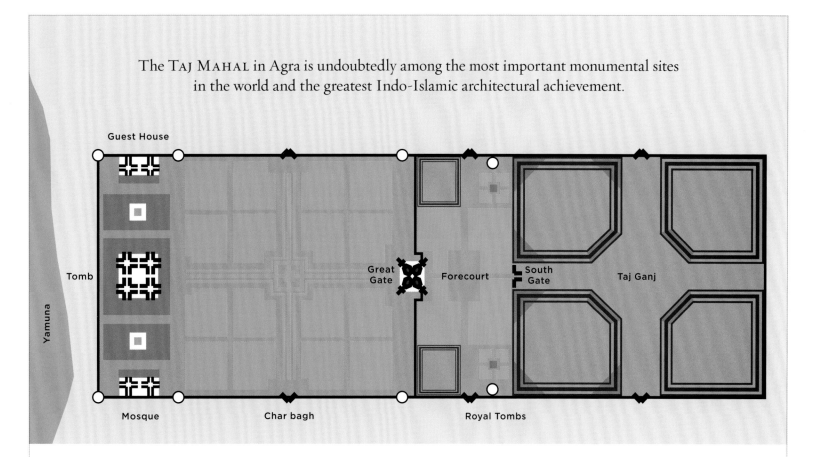

The Taj Mahal in Agra is undoubtedly among the most important monumental sites in the world and the greatest Indo-Islamic architectural achievement.

Guest House

Tomb

Yamuna

Mosque

Char bagh

Great Gate

Forecourt

South Gate

Taj Ganj

Royal Tombs

The city of Agra in Uttar Pradesh remains at the heart of India. Historically at the crossroads of civilization, Agra was described by Emperor Akbar (1542–1605) as 'the emporium of the traffic of the world', when it became the capital of the Mughal Empire. His grandson, Emperor Shah Jahan (1592–1666), was the fifth ruler of the Mughal dynasty. He cherished Mumtaz Mahal (1593–1631) as the favourite of his three wives, the 'Chosen One of the Palace'. After giving birth to the couple's fourteenth child, Mumtaz died. The Taj Mahal was commissioned in 1632 as a mausoleum to commemorate the Emperor's love for her and it took more than two decades to complete.

Unlike many of the royal gardens in this book, this garden is not attached to a royal palace or a castle, but a manmade ecological environment, bound by high walls on three sides and the Yamuna river on the fourth. Seen today, the Taj Mahal complex is exceptional for its monumental scale, stunning gardens, lavish ornamentation, and its overt use of white marble.

THE GARDENS OF AGRA

The gardens that line the banks of the Yamuna are a wonderful insight into the period of the Mughal Empire: the dynasties, their traditions and beliefs. These venerated sites to honour the deceased were created over more than a century and act as places for prayer and respite from the city's heat. They include the Taj Mahal, the Mehtab Bagh (Moonlight Garden), Aram Bagh (Garden of Rest) and Chini ka Rauza (a funerary monument). Historical records, written and pictorial, show that from the time of Emperor Babur (1483–1530) through the reign of Emperor Shah Jahan (r. 1627–58) the riverfront was, according to the World Monuments Fund:

'densely covered by walled enclosures, buildings, pavilions, and lush gardens. Today, more than 40 Mughal gardens survive in ranging states of conservation, all having been significantly changed over time. Four are under the management of the Archaeological Survey of India.'

PREVIOUS PAGES   OPPOSITE

The Taj Mahal   The Mehtab Bagh

MUGHAL LANDSCAPE TRADITIONS

The Taj Mahal's success is more than aesthetic; it also has significant symbolic appeal. The complex and the gardens consist of an apparently symmetrical plan. Stretching in front of the Taj Mahal is a monumental *char bagh* garden, representing the four gardens of paradise mentioned in the Koran. Typically, a *char bagh* was divided into four main quadrants, with a building (such as a pavilion or tomb) along its central axis. In this respect the Taj Mahal deviates from the norm. The mausoleum, when viewed from the main entrance, is not centrally positioned. Instead, it is located at the far end, backed immediately by the river. Never before had this been done in any other garden of the Mughal era.

Constructed in an area of 17 hectares (42 acres), the complex includes several symmetrically positioned buildings, a main gateway and a mausoleum, all designed to create a cohesive whole. Mughal gardens followed Timurid–Persian principles of the walled garden, being quadripartite – divided ideally, but not necessarily, into quarters by raised walkways (*khiyaban*) and canals (*nahr*) which contain a line of fountains (*farwara*). The walls create seclusion and protection. The watercourses, representing the four rivers of life, intersect in the centre of the garden.

One of the oldest references to the 'garden as paradise' is found on an ancient Sumerian cuneiform tablet that dates from 2800 BCE. The word 'paradise' is derived from the Persian *pairidaeza*, which means walled (*pairi*) garden (*daeza*) and the Greek/Latin word *paradeisos*. In the teachings of Islam, paradise is a garden watered by streams. From the palace of Cyrus the Great (600–530 BCE) at Pasargadae in Iran, we learn that the adoption of the cross-axial *char bagh* concept goes back to the sixth century BCE. This garden pattern appeared in the eighth century CE in the Umayyad palaces at Rusafa in Syria and in the ninth century at Balkuwara Palace in Samarra, also in Iran.

A BUILDING TO BE REMEMBERED

Designed and built for longevity, the Taj Mahal was conceived as a building that would be remembered for its magnificence, and the best material and skills were employed. The finest marble came from quarries 400 kilometres (250 miles) away in Makrana, Rajasthan. Twenty thousand workers were employed; Mir Abd Al-Karim was designated lead architect, Abdul Haqq was chosen as the calligrapher and Ustad Ahmad Lahauri was made the supervisor. Shah Jahan ensured that Mughal architectural principles were adhered to throughout the design and construction processes. On its completion, he said that his creation 'made the sun and moon shed tears from their eyes'.

Entry to the complex is through gates in the boundary walls. The Great Gate is huge, towering 30 metres (almost 100 feet), and is highly embellished. Koranic inscriptions invite the visitor into the paradise within. The mausoleum itself is clad in white marble, while subsidiary structures are faced with red sandstone. This contrasting colour hierarchy connects to the Indian traditions where white-coloured stones are assigned to Brahmins, the highest caste in Hindu society, and red stones to *kshatriyas* or the warrior caste. In line with the Great Gate is a long central water channel in the form of a cruciform, and 275 metres (more than 900 feet) from the gateway is the Taj Mahal – its central dome reaching a height of 73 metres (240 feet). The 900-square metre (more than 1,000-square yard) garden is divided into quadrants, again following Timurid–Persian principles, two on either side of the water channel. Each quadrant is further divided into four, creating sixteen sunken parterres. Outside the main garden is a forecourt, the colonnaded Jilau Khana, which provides shade from the heat. At each corner are four smaller courtyards.

The choice of stone also highlights the importance of colour of materials in a garden setting. A central line of fountains hides a network of pipes that take water from the river. Each fountain is fed by a copper pipe that links to a copper pot below ground. Today, the fountains are driven by electric motors; however, originally water from the network of pipes would first reach the copper pipe, fill up and simultaneously go to the fountain heads. Through the use of interconnected water channels the gardens are irrigated while optimizing water resources.

The Mehtab Bagh   A view of the Taj Mahal from the Yamuna River

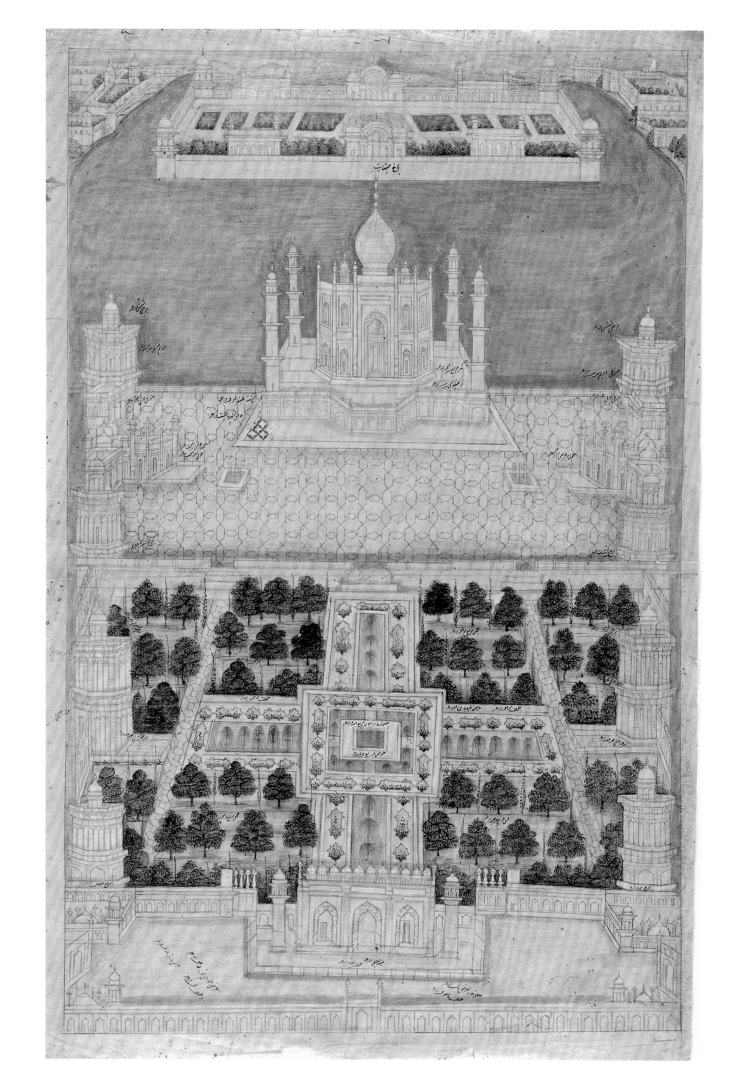

ENGINEERING AND INNOVATIONS

The decision by the garden planners, engineers and architects of Shah Jahan to position the main mausoleum at one end of the quadripartite garden rather than in the centre was a remarkable innovation. It adds depth and perspective to the distant view of the monument from the Great Gate and, viewed from the Mehtab Bagh across the river, the monument appears to be centrally located. By departing from the typical *char bagh*, the centre of the Taj Mahal garden could be used for a pool (*hauz*) with five fountains in a raised marble platform surrounded by marble benches. The corners of the pool are inset with a pattern of organic lobes, waves and volutes, and the reflection of the mausoleum is perfectly captured in its waters.

NINETEENTH AND TWENTIETH CENTURIES

In the early nineteenth century, when the British took over Agra in 1803, the Taj Mahal gardens were overgrown, blocking the view of the mausoleum. A plan made in 1828 by Major General John Anthony Hodgson, Surveyor General from 1826–29, provides some evidence of the planting layout.

After the death of Emperor Aurangzeb (1618–1707) and the subsequent fall of the Mughal Empire the gardens went into decline. A huge quantity of marble inlay (known as *pietra dura*), using jade, crystal, lapis lazuli and amethyst, was stolen or damaged. At the beginning of the nineteenth century the British destroyed many of the structures along the river to create a clear military line of sight. By mid-century photographic evidence shows towering trees and dense thickets obscuring the view of the Taj Mahal.

Lord Curzon (Viceroy of India 1898–1905) brought about major changes to the gardens during the late nineteenth century when he laid out formal European lawns to replace the existing orchards and flower beds. In 1899 a row of cypresses on either side of the central water channel were replanted under Curzon's order. These trees were set into the lawns between intricate inlaid red sandstone patterns.

PLANTS

Mughal gardens were planted with decorative and sweet-smelling flowering trees and aromatic herbs and fruit trees, and the Taj Mahal was no exception. In his memoirs Emperor Babur mentions jasmine, willow, cypress, saffron, almond, apple, apricot, cherry, citron, coconut, date, fig, guava, lemon, lime, mango, melon, mulberry, orange, peach, pear, pineapple, plantain, pomegranate, quince, walnut and watermelon. Peter Mundy, a seventeenth-century British merchant trader, gave details of the garden he saw at Agra:

'The walkways were lined with cypress trees, and the squares of the subdivisions were planted with groves of trees, as apple trees, orange trees, mulberrie trees, etts, Mango, trees, Caco (Cocoanut trees), Figg trees, Plantan trees....In other squares are your (English) flowers, herbes, etts, where of Roses, Marigolds...to bee seene; French Mariegolds aboundance; Poppeas red, carnation and white; and divers other sortes of faire flowers which wee knowe not in our parts, many growing on prettie trees, all watered by hand in tyme of drought, which is 9 monethes in the yeare.'

And Abu Talib Kalim, court poet of Shah Jahan, described:

'bulbun (rose bushes), lala (tulips or red poppies), gul-i-khorshid (sunflowers), nargis (narcissus), gul-I hazara (double poppy), Khiri (gilli flowers), taj-I khorus (cockscombs), gul-I ja'fary (marigolds), keora (fragrant screw-pine, a small tree with fragrant flowers).'

Ground-penetrating radar and archaeobotanical surveys based on pollen analysis are among the techniques now available to provide a complete picture of the Taj Mahal garden, as well as to give insight into which plants to choose, given that water availability is a modern concern. The agencies responsible for the Taj Mahal worked with students from Harvard's Graduate School of Design to identify plant species that once populated the gardens. Although reintroduced plants and trees will need time to fully mature, already there is the scent of jasmine, oleander, hibiscus and cedar, and pomegranate trees are flourishing.

OPPOSITE

Bird's-eye view of the Taj Mahal at Agra, 1790–1810

(pen and ink with watercolour on paper)

TIRTA GANGGA

BALI

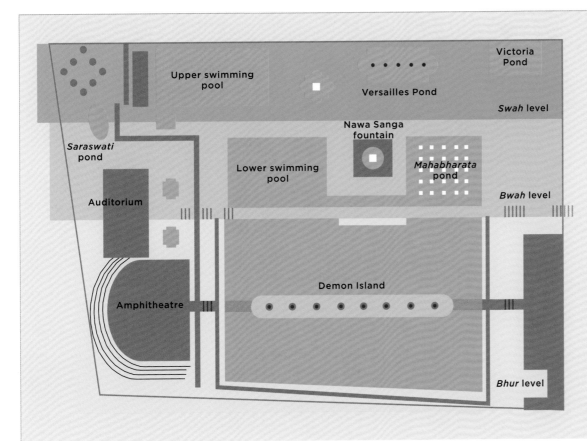

Among the many temples and palaces, nestled in rice fields and around the natural spring of Rejasa, lies the TIRTA GANGGA ROYAL WATER GARDEN concealed beneath towering teak trees (*Tectona grandis*, known locally as *Pohon Jati*).

Tirta Gangga lies just north of Amlapura, the main town of eastern Bali. The Royal Water Garden belongs to the royal family of Karangasem, one of the nine kingdoms of Bali, and forms part of the Puri Agung Karangasem Royal Palace, which includes Taman Ujung Water Palace. The kingdom of Karangasem was formerly subject to the Majapahit Empire, based in Java. It started as a feudal subordinate of the Supreme King of Bali, who became ruler of the largest kingdom in Bali, as well as the neighbouring island of Lombok. These kingdoms flourished between the early tenth and the early twentieth centuries and enriched and shaped the island's culture by establishing the Balinese court culture, combining Hindu influences with Bali's own native spiritual elements and ancient reverence.

Bali's kings built their palaces as centres of power, where they initiated laws, held rituals and received visiting leaders. In the grounds were wild birds and animals, including the now extinct Balinese tiger. Repositories contained sacred manuscripts, *Lontar*, made of dried palm leaves and passed down the generations. Generally written in the old Javanese language *Kawi*, along with ancient Sanskrit written in *Devanagri*, they focussed on health and healing, astrology, astronomy, homeopathy, religious rules and teaching, sacred rituals (*Manusa Yadnya*), holy formulas, magic, ethics and the actual and mythical history of the royal family and Indonesian people.

TAMAN UJUNG

In order to understand Tirta Gangga it is important to take a look at another royal water garden, Taman Ujung, also owned by the Karangesem royal family. Loosely translated as 'the garden on the far end', Taman Ujung has beautiful fishponds surrounding the premises. Taman Ujung Water Palace was built in 1909 on the initiative of the King of Karangasem, I Gusti Bagus Djelantik (1887–1966), also known as Anak Agung Agung Anglurah Ketut Karangasem. Its architects were a Dutchman, Van Den Hentz, and a Chinese man, Loto Ang, although the development also involved the *undagi* (Balinese architect). Standing in the main round pavilion of Taman Ujung panoramic

PREVIOUS PAGES AND OPPOSITE

The *Bwah* level

views open up of Lombok Strait. There is an endless hallway/bridge, which offers perfect symmetry and one-point perspective. Although it looks like one continuous bridge there are in fact two bridges connecting the resting house, called Bale Gili, which is built on an island in the middle of the largest of three ponds within the complex. This is a captivating landscape with a fascinating history.

MAGIC SPELLS AND TORTURED SOULS

There were several palaces during the Karangasem dynasty, of which Tirta Gangga is one. The palace is not a single building but a compound with six large pools of varying depths; the name Tirta Gangga also refers to the surrounding rural area. Visually stunning and tranquil, it is a water garden where magic spells, tortured souls and beauty combine in Balinese folklore, which in turn is integral to every garden detail.

SACRED WATERS

Tirta Gangga is perched on brilliant green hills overlooking the ocean with a view of the sacred Mount Agung, a volcano, in the distance. The water garden was built in 1948 to reinforce the holiness of the place and to create a place of contemplation, rest and joy for all. For all his power, its creator is fondly remembered as a leader who advanced Balinese culture with technology and artistry. A patron of the arts and architecture, the king himself was the architect of the water palace, and he also worked in the mud alongside his labourers, digging out pools and ponds. The sprawling, elegant one-hectare (2.47-acre) complex is remarkably well maintained. The flowers, wildlife and immaculate gardens are testament to the commitment to continue the traditions of the royal family.

One of three water palaces in Bali, the Royal Water Garden is comprised mainly of freshwater pools fed by a daily flow of more than 2 million litres (500,000 gallons) of water from myriad pools and fountains, moats, canals and bridges with various styles of architecture. Tirta Gangga (loosely translated as the 'sacred waters of the Ganges') displays a unique mix of Balinese and Chinese architecture with an eleven-tiered fountain at the centre of the complex. The water is used for prayer rituals in nearby temples.

The garden is on three levels that relate to Balinese cosmology. The highest, northern level, *Swah* (referring to being close to the gods), contains springs under a banyan tree (*Ficus benghalensis*), the upper swimming pool and two decorative ponds, one of which has four fountains and is oddly named the 'Versailles' pond. The other pond contains beautiful sacred lotus (*Nelumbo nucifera*). A smaller *Saraswati* pond (meaning 'the deities, and the divine') completes the upper level waterways. The middle level, *Bwah* (or *Buwah*), which denotes the central body, between heaven and hell, comprises a 10-metre (32-foot) high, eleven-tiered Chinese fountain *Nawa Sanga* (oneness merging into the infinite; *sanagah* also means 'temple') designed to resemble lotus flowers, with a swimming pool to one side and the *Mahabharata* (signifying the greatest spiritual epic of all time) pond with octagonal-shaped stepping stones and Balinese statues on the other side. Eight deity figures encircling the fountain represent the guardians of the cardinal points and are positioned around the powerful central Hindu deity of Siwa or Shiva. Water is pumped through spouts in stone sculptures of animals and mythical creatures such as the legendary bird *garuda*, keeping the pools oxygenated. Crystal-clear waters are inhabited by large koi carp. On the larger lowest level, *Bhur* (hell), is the south pond. This is where 'monsters' reside. The pond contains the provocatively named Demon Island running along the centre, which is reached by a pair of bridges adorned with Balinese dragons. Overlooking the south pond is an amphitheatre.

A reservoir within the grounds receives the spring water, and from it drinking water is delivered via a pipe system to the city of Amlapura. There is a second, underground, pipe system connecting to the upper swimming pool, where it emerges through the mouth of a *raksasa* (demon statue) which stands at a corner of the pool. Here the water overflows into a lower-level pool. From there, it flows into small fish ponds and then into the rice fields that border the gardens.

ABOVE OPPOSITE
The *Bwah* level

BELOW OPPOSITE
The *Bhur* level

DAMAGE AND RESTORATION

In 1963, Mount Agung, dormant for the past century, erupted and damaged most of the garden. Although spared the lava flow, earthquakes and smothering ash devastated the gardens from February to September. Following the eruption, the property was abandoned, and by the time the staff returned its gardens had been looted, the plants and trees were dead and covered in ash. Ten months following the devastation there was no money for rebuilding the ponds and structures and for the next decade and a half, the gardens further declined. With the introduction of the Land Reform Bill the kings, like all other great landowners, had lost their extravagant income. Any restoration could only be done frugally.

Fortunately, the World Bank and Indonesia's government stepped in to sponsor the restoration. An ambitious restoration plan started in 1979 led by the king's son, Anak Agung Made Djelantik (1919–2007), and was continued in 1999 by Ir. Anak Agung Gede Dharma Widoere Djelantik (b. 1953), the king's grandson, who has returned the gardens to their former glory. In fact, what is seen today is purely the design of Widoere Djelantik. A cluster of superb statues created by a master sculptor in Karangasem was placed in the area where the king would spend much of his day composing poetry and meditating. The circle of statues represents the virtuous Balinese man and woman and the dualistic array of spiritual supporters and demonic tempters.

FESTIVAL OF FRIENDSHIP, THE ARTS AND CULTURE

The gardens and waterways form a spectacular backdrop for an annual arts festival that is run by the community to promote friendship and support local artists. The three-day festival celebrates Indonesia's arts culture, featuring dance, poetry, installation art, theatre and landscape painting, echoing the king's commitment to art, architecture, religion and Balinese traditions.

FLORAL DELIGHTS

Bali is truly a botanical feast for the eyes and Tirta Gangga perfectly encapsulates the native flora. It was the Victorian naturalist Alfred Russell Wallace who first observed a striking difference between the flora and fauna of Bali and the island of Lombok, despite the dividing strait being no more than 40 kilometres (25 miles). This division between two of the world's great biogeographic realms, Asia and Australia, became known as Wallace's Line. Bali's – and, in turn, Tirta Gangga's – flora and fauna have stronger connections with the West than with the East. Visually, the experience is thrilling. The water's surface is peppered with large water lily pads and a triumphant display of pink lotus flowers for most of the year. The pools are framed with bursts of red from fuchsias and gold from *Heliconia* spp. (lobster-claw). Splashes of pink from bougainvillea cascade over the edges of the pools. Chinese hibiscus and canna lilies in shades of orange, red and yellow stand proud around the upper pools. Scattered throughout the gardens are old banana trees with large fan-shaped leaves, their bright pink flowers creating a sense of unity with the frangipani, bougainvillea and sacred lotus flowers. Among some of the smaller pools are the long, richly green leaves of *Colocasia* spp. (elephant ear), while the pink-and-green bicolour leaves of *Caladium* spp. (angel wings) pinpoint the garden's shadier corners.

Visiting this royal garden is far more than a visual delight. Pathways are lined with fragrant white or deep pink frangipani, while the scent of *Jasminum sambac* (jasmine) pervades the air. The sound of flowing water and leaves blowing in the breeze is omnipresent and immersive. The lush green lawns add a sensory experience underfoot that contrasts the cool, slightly submerged stepping stones that lead over the pools and waterways. Tirta Gangga is a garden for all the senses, but especially sight, scent and sound. Making the contemplative journey around the garden focuses the mind, enhancing mental wellbeing as well as bringing sensory and spiritual joy.

ABOVE OPPOSITE
The Pavilions at Taman Ujung

BELOW OPPOSITE
The *Bwah* level

TOKYO IMPERIAL PALACE

JAPAN

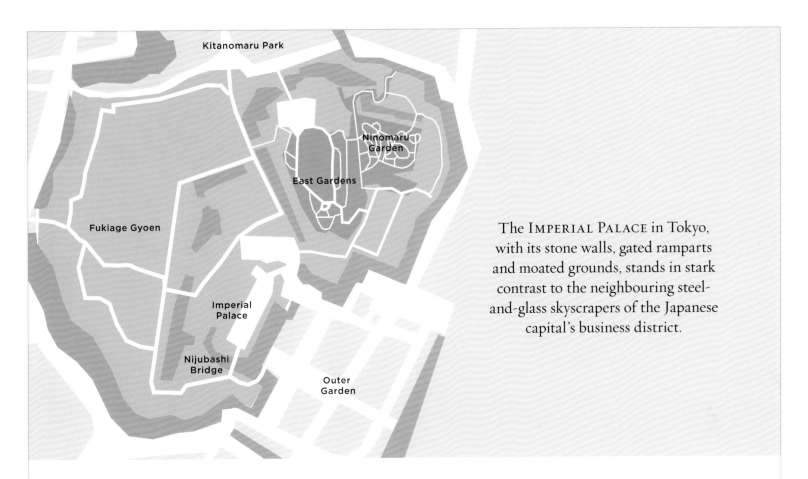

Kitanomaru Park

Ninomaru Garden

East Gardens

Fukiage Gyoen

Imperial Palace

Nijubashi Bridge

Outer Garden

The IMPERIAL PALACE in Tokyo, with its stone walls, gated ramparts and moated grounds, stands in stark contrast to the neighbouring steel-and-glass skyscrapers of the Japanese capital's business district.

It is on the site of the former Edo Castle, dating from 1457 and destroyed by fire in the nineteenth century, in the centre of Chiyoda ward, and is the main private residence of the Emperor of Japan and his family. The grounds – 153 hectares (379 acres) of forest, gardens and public park, roughly a third of the size of New York's Central Park – encompass many buildings, including the Imperial Palace (*Kyuden*) itself. The palace, together with the role of the emperor in Japanese society and a strong sense of tradition, bridge the old and the new.

The original Edo Castle was built from 1456 to 1457 by Ota Dokan, a samurai warrior-poet, tactician and Buddhist monk. For the next 150 years many castles and moats were built; the low-lying city (Shitamachi) needed protection using earth excavated from the moats to level the grounds. Stone for the stronghold was transported some 150 kilometres (almost 100 miles) from the Izu peninsula to the south, as well as lime from Ome, west of Tokyo. For years the Imperial Court was located in Kyoto, but this was changed during the Sengoku Period, beginning with the Onin

War in 1467. Japan, the land of haiku, tea ceremonies and avenues of cherry trees, was to experience during the sixteenth century a war-torn, bloody period in its history as rival *daimyō* (feudal lords) battled for dominance.

THE EDO PERIOD (1603–1868)

Tokugawa Ieyasu (1543–1616) entered Edo Castle in 1590, and in 1603 he became the first Tokugawa Shogun (military dictator); the shogunate went on to govern Japan for more than two and a half centuries until imperial rule was re-established in 1868. Ieyasu's grandson Tokugawa Iemitsu (1604–51) moved to Edo when it was a small town, but the domain or territory of the shogunate was enormous. When he established the central government in Edo he commissioned landscape architect Kobori Enshu to create a garden within the grounds of the Imperial Palace. In 1657 the *donjon* (tower) and its many roofs were damaged by the Great Fire of Meireki and again at various times; each time Edo Castle was rebuilt.

PREVIOUS PAGES

The East Gardens

OPPOSITE

Kitanomaru Park

The complex is built on a fluvial terrace (Musashino) between the Arakawa, Iruma and Tama rivers. There are moats to the north and west, the lowest of which is Shimo-Dokan Moat, remnants of the fifteenth-century watchtowers and the double-span Nijubashi Bridge that traverses the moats from the outer to inner palace grounds. The moats and ramparts once provided a critical defensive function.

When the sixth shogun of the Tokugawa dynasty, Tokugawa Ienobu (1662–1712) was in office from 1709 to 1712 he ordered the *daimyo* to build a 1-hectare (2.47-acre) garden with a large pond (visible today), a waterfall and a river. This became the imperial private garden (Fukiage Gyoen). During the reign of the ninth shogun, Tokugawa Ieshige (1712–61), garden plans were produced; they survive today and were used during the 1960s to reconstruct the garden. Tokugawa Ienari (1773–1841), the eleventh and longest-serving shogun from 1787 to 1837, continued to restore the Fukiage Gyoen, although the later years of the Edo era were fraught with war, famine, rebellions and uprisings, which meant the gardens received scant attention. This turbulent period ended in 1868 when the last shogun Tokugawa Yoshinobu (1837–1913) resigned. He and the inhabitants of Edo Castle were exiled from Edo Castle, and the Emperor was restored.

During the Meiji Restoration, Emperor Meiji (1852–1912) left Kyoto Imperial Palace and relocated to the new Edo Castle, which was renamed Tokei (later Tokyo) Castle or Toyko Imperial Palace. It was destroyed by fire in 1873 and had to be rebuilt. What is seen today, however, is the new Imperial Palace; the palace that replaced Edo Castle was itself destroyed during the Second World War. Reconstruction commenced in the 1960s, this time with the use of a steel frame. It has two visible levels and one underground level.

THE GARDENS TODAY

The palace gardens are divided into four areas, but only three are open to the public, namely the Outer Garden (Kokyogaien), East Gardens and Kitanomaru Park. (The fourth is the imperial private garden,

Fukiage Gyoen, and can only be visited through special tours which depart from the Kukyi-mon gate.) Each garden has its own character. The Outer Garden is considered the most urban with views of towering skyscrapers, a large open plaza with a fountain commemorating the marriage of the Emperor and Empress and a statue of a loyal fourteenth-century samurai, Kusunoki Masashige. There are manicured lawns with 2,000 *Pinus thunbergii* (Japanese black pine), the trees that covered the coastline when the first shogun, Tokugawa Ieyasu, entered the castle in 1590.

The East Gardens contain Ninomaru, the garden originally designed by Kobori Enshu for the third shogun, Tokugawa Iemitsu, and reconstructed in the 1960s. It is a secret garden, its ancient walls containing flowers and 30 species of tree from the 47 prefectures of Japan.

Kitanomaru Park is a public park, but was once a fortified defensive enclosure for the northern area of Edo Castle. Very different in feel, with large modern buildings, such as Nippon Budokan (a martial arts arena) and the Science Museum, nestled among densely planted trees, lawns and pathways edged with black posts – a horticultural feast for garden lovers as the majority of trees are named.

PALACE GROUNDS

Seimon Ishibashi Bridge, commonly known as Nijubashi Bridge, crosses the moat and leads to the main entrance. When crossing this double-span bridge to the palace grounds, the modern city is seen to the left, and to the right are the high stone walls, banks covered in pine trees and perched above is the keep, Fushimi-yagura, with its white facades. The keep once stood in Kyoto, but was dismantled and reconstructed by Tokugawa Iemitsu. When entering the garden, there is a resting pavilion, fronted by the 'Seven Flowers of Autumn', with a path leading further into the garden. These autumn-flowering plants, all native to East Asia, are very popular and can be found in almost every garden in Tokyo. They are: golden valerian (*Patrinia scabiosifolia*), maiden silvergrass (*Miscanthus sinensis*),

balloon flower (*Platycodon grandiflorus*), pinks (*Dianthus* spp.), Japanese joe-pye weed (*Eupatorium fortunei*), kudzu (*Pueraria lobata*) and Japanese clovers (*Lespedeza* spp.).

Between Fushimi-yagura and the Reception Hall and Audience Room of the Imperial Palace lies a reconstructed grove. Previously, this area was laid to lawn with azalea, as in the inner private garden, Fukiage Gyoen, but Emperor Showa (1901–1989), a biologist and nature lover, wanted to create an Edo-period forest, using plants such as oaks (*Quercus serrata* and *Q. acustissima*), maples and hornbeams, as well as Yabutsubaki (*Camellia japonica*), *Pieris japonica* and Japanese red pine (*Pinus densiflora*) from Musashino in the western part of Tokyo. Scattered in this forest are fringed iris (*Iris japonica*) and fairy bells (*Disporum sessile*). Work commenced in 1983 and continued for three years. In 2002, it was extended with the addition of a small brook.

The art of bonsai has been perfected in Japan since the twelfth century and, fittingly, the Imperial Garden contains the Oomichi Garden where about 90 different kinds of bonsai plants are nurtured.

QUINTESSENTIAL JAPANESE FLOWERS

In spring, the Ninomaru in the East Gardens comes into its own when its many iris varieties are in flower. There are three main forms of iris, divided into the areas or prefectures in the Edo area where they were cultivated: Tokyo, Kumamoto and Mie. The famous iris garden in Meiji Jingu (Shibuya ward) provided 84 different cultivars of *Edo hanash bu* irises. In Japan, a zigzag bridge (*yatsuhashi*) is a typical feature of an iris garden, and normally has eight connected bridges which refer to the famous Tales of Ise. In this literary collection eight arms of the Azuma river were connected via eight bridges. In the wilder areas of the Ninomaru there are meadows filled with Japanese iris and ornamental cherry trees, with small brooks edged with either stone or wood. Paths meander around beds of bearded irises, while azaleas and rhododendrons are neatly pruned into sculptural forms. Everything is carefully planned, implemented and maintained. The

canopies of trees, especially the black pines, have been lifted to offer views across the garden. From this area of the East Gardens modern Tokyo can just be seen above the tops of the forest.

After the iris-flowering season ends it is the turn of kerria, azaleas, white and purple wisteria, hydrangeas, day lilies (*Hemerocallis* spp.) and lilies. The lotus, a sacred flower in Buddhism, is also a quintessential flower of Japan, and has long been used in traditional Japanese gardens. During late summer the moat surrounding Tokyo Imperial Palace bursts with lotus flowers.

WATER FEATURES

The pond seen today in the Ninomaru maintains the shape and exact location of the pond that Kobori Enshu originally designed. The pond is intended to represent a typical Japanese coastal landscape – a sand beach – and has elements typical of gardens of the Edo period, including soft banks and a central island with a shore or *suhama*. A special breed of carp, Butterfly Koi (*Hirenaga nishikigoi*), populates the pond.

Aquascaping, known in Japanese as *Sanzon Iwagumi*, is the art of creating a three-pillared rock formation. This is evident in the East Gardens and is clearly visible from the bottom of the waterfall. A bridge on top of the waterfall was built in the Momoyama period, before the establishment of the Tokugawa shogunate. Waterfall building in this manner is recorded in the eleventh-century text *Sakuteiki* (Records of Garden Making) and the same principles are still followed today.

PLANTS

The Imperial Palace has a fascinating biota or ecology, meaning its plant and animal life are a rich and sustainable biodiversity. In a *Japanese Times* article, Tokyo's National Museum of Nature and Science indicated that the number of animal and insect species within the Imperial Palace grounds exceeded 3,600 and plant species numbered 1,366. Additionally, 20 per cent of Tokyo's trees are located in the palace

ABOVE OPPOSITE
Irises in the East Gardens

BELOW OPPOSITE
The Ninomaru Garden

compound. The Emperor Hirohito (1901–89) loved nature. He prohibited the use of pesticides and encouraged staff to create insect habitats on the property. To attract birds to the Imperial Palace he ordered the planting of fruit-bearing trees and shrubs – pyracantha, idesia, marlberry (*Ardisia japonica*), hollies (*Ilex rotunda, I. serrata*) and *Viburnum plicatum* var. *tomentosum*.

Although plant surveys have been carried out throughout the twentieth century, the reports are not generally available to the public. In the East Gardens there are areas for fruit trees, primarily Japanese apricot (*Prunus mume*), including a slope known as *bairin-zaka* (meaning 'hill of the plum trees'). In fact, Ota Dokan is said to have planted the first fruit tree in 1478. However, the private Fukiage Gyoen displays a variety of evergreen and deciduous broad-leaved trees, including mulberry (*Morus nigra*) together with silkworms, holly (*Ilex integra*), Itajii chinkapin (*Castanopsis sieboldii*), Japanese persea (*Machilus thunbergii*), oaks (*Quercus acutissima*), firs (*Abies* spp.), sweet gum (*Liquidamber formosana* 'Hance'), dawn redwoods (*Metasequoia glyptostroboides*) and Japanese zelkova (*Zelkova serrata*).

In 2009 the National Museum of Nature and Science carried out further investigations into lichens at the Imperial Palace, and after collecting sixteen species, 12 of them were discovered to be new macrolichens, among them *Hyperphyscia crocata*, *Parmotrema tinctorum* and *Punctelia borreri*. Later in 2013, the department of botany found two new varieties of bryophyte flora (liverworts, hornworts and mosses).

The gardens and parkland of the Imperial Palace are distinctive and varied with shaded groves, sun-lit spaces of manicured lawns, a series of moats and impressive walls built of smooth-faced massive stones cut and layered using the *kirikomi-hagi* technique. Every tree, shrub and flower has been purposefully placed, sometimes blocking views of modern Tokyo, while others are pruned as 'living art' to open up spaces and vistas. While many parts of the garden complex are public, the private gardens of the Imperial Palace create a sense of mystery and tradition. Walking around the East Gardens, with its carefully crafted trees and shrubs, sinuous borders and water courses, it is easy to assume that it is a modern garden, but on closer inspection the historic design of Kobori Enshu shines through, revealing his deep respect for nature, while being faithful to the Japanese landscape aesthetic in which the use of space and simple sculptural form is finely judged and timeless.

OPPOSITE

The East Gardens

Publications

Sir Harold Acton, *The Bourbons of Naples 1734-1825*, Methuen, 1956

Mea Allan, *The Hookers of Kew, 1785-1911*, Michael Joseph, 1967

Kazuma Anezaki, Mitsuhiko Imamori, Takuya Kanouchi, *Woods in the Palace*, Shinchōsha, 2005

Association of European Royal Residences, *Discovering European Heritage in Royal Residences*, 2011

M. Batey and J. Woudstra, *The Story of the Privy Garden at Hampton Court*, Barn Elms Publishing, 1995

Jaromír Beneša, Věra Čulíkovác, Jitka Kosňovskáa, Jan Frolíkb, Josef Matiášekb, 'New Plants at Prague Castle and Hradčany in the Early Modern Period: a History of Selected Species, Interdisciplinaria Archaeologica', *Natural Sciences in Archaeology*, 2012

Herbert P. Bix, *Hirohito and the Making of Modern Japan*, Harper Collins, 2000

Gerrard Brault, 1985, Hunting and Fowling, Western Europe, *Dictionary of the Middle Ages*, vol. 6, pp 356–363

Jane Brown, *The Garden at Buckingham Palace*, Royal Collection Enterprises Ltd, 2004

Evan Nicole Brown, 'Two Centuries-Old Riverfront Gardens in India Return to Full Bloom', *Atlas Obscura*, 11 January 2019

Sekai Bunkasha, *Biological Study Round* (Buck of Imperial Palace Fukiage Garden, Households of Imperial Palace Fukiage Garden) 2001

Gordon Campbell, *Garden History: a Very Short Introduction*, Oxford University Press, 2019

Yves Carlier, *Histoire du château de Fontainebleau*, Editions Jean-Paul Gisserot, 2010

Brian A. Catlos, *Kingdoms of Faith: A New History of Islamic Spain*, Hurst & Co, 2018

B. Cherry and N. Pevsner, *The Buildings of England: London 2 South*, 1983, pp 481–500

J. Cloake, *Palaces and Parks of Richmond and Kew, Volume II: Richmond Lodge and the Kew Palaces*, 1996

M. Coventry, *Castles of the Clans: the strongholds and seats of 750 Scottish families and clans*. Musselburgh. Page(s): 504,530 RCAHMS Shelf Number: F.5.21.COV, 2008

Janet Cox-Rearick, *The Collection of Francis I: Royal Treasures*, Abrams, 1996

Anthony Cross, 'Russian Gardens, British Gardeners', *Garden History*, Vol. 19, No. 1, Spring 1991

Mikhail Dedinkin and David Jacques, *Capability Brown and Hampton Court*, Fontanka, 2016

Daniel Defoe, *A Tour Through the Whole Island of Great Britain*, 1724-1726; Harmondsworth, 1986

Peter Demetz, *Prague in Black and Gold: The History of a City*, Penguin, 1998

F. Denecourt, *Description generale du château Fontainebleau*, Nouvelle Edition, Fontainebleau, Septembre 1842

Ray Desmond, *The History of the Royal Botanic Gardens Kew*, Second Edition, Kew Publishing, 2007 (First edition Harvill Press, 1995)

Renske Ek, Kurt Almqvist and Susanna Hakelius Popova (eds), *The Royal Garden: Identity, Power and Pleasure*, Axel and Margaret Axson Johanson Foundation, 2016, pp 109-132

Electronic Publication Editorial Department, *It Surrounds the Edo: Tokyo Imperial Palace East Garden walk Edo-jo Castle trace* (Japanese Edition), Kindle Edition

Jonas Eriksson, 'Peterhof and Drottningholm: a comparison of the formal parks' characteristic elements, structures and overall planning', Department of Urban and Rural Development, Uppsala, 2012

H. Fenwick, 'The Castle of Mey', *Scottish Tatler*, July/August.

RCAHMS. (1911b) 'The Royal Commission on the Ancient and Historical Monuments and Constructions of Scotland. Margrethe Floryan, Gardens of the Tsars: a study of the aesthetics, semantics and uses of late eighteenth Century Russian Gardens', Aarhus University Press, 1996

Antoinette Galbraith, 'Merry Months of Mey', *Scottish Field*, 28 May 2014

John Goodall, 'The Castle of Mey: Inside the Queen Mother's Beloved Home in Scotland', *Country Life*, 3 February 2019

John Graefer, *A Descriptive Catalogue of Upwards of Eleven Hundred Species and Varieties of Herbaceous Or Perennial Plants ... exhibiting at one view, the names, magnitude, soil and situation, ... To which is added, a list of hardy ferns ... and the most ornamental annuals, printed, and sold by J. Smeeton. Also sold by J. Sewell*, (London, 1789), reprinted Kessinger, 2009

Gross Max Landscape Architects, Royal Botanic Gardens Kew, Landscape Master Plan, November 2010

Roberto de la Herran, Manuel Casares-Porcel, Francisca Robles and J. Tito, 'The Forgotten Myrtle of the Alhambra Gardens of Granada: Restoring and Authenticating World Heritage', *Journal of Agricultural Science and Technology*, 18: 1975–1983, 2016

'Herrenhausen – Garden Splendour, Culture and Science', Hannover Markerting and Tourism, Maike Scheunemann Grosser Garten Hannover-Herrenhausen, 1998

G. Hersey, *Architecture and Geometry in the Age of the Baroque*, University of Chicago Press, 2003

G. Hersey, *Architecture, Poetry and Number in the Royal Palace at Caserta*, MIT Press, 1983

Ray Desmond Hew, *The History of the Royal Botanic Gardens*, Kew Publishing, 2017

Kathleen M. Higgins, Shakti Maira, Sonia Sikka (eds) *Artistic Visions and the Promise of Beauty: cross-cultural perspectives*, Springer, 2017

Historic Environment Scotland. Castle of Mey, NMRS Number: ND27SE 1.00 (8864), Canmore

Hoikusha, *Biological Laboratory Imperial Household*, Flora

Sedis Imperatoris Japonicae, 1989

Sir William Jackson Hooker, *Curtis's Botanical Magazine, comprising the Royal Gardens of Kew*, Vol. 1, Series 3, Reeve Brothers, 1845

John Dixon Hunt (Ed.), *The Dutch Garden in the Seventeenth Century,* Dumbarton Oaks Trustees for Harvard University, 1990

Lucia Impelluso (Au.), Stephen Sartarelli (Tr.), *Gardens in Art*, Mondadori Electa S.p.A., 2005

David Jacques, 'The Pond Garden at Hampton Court Palace: one of the best-known examples of a sunk garden', *Garden History*, Vol. 33, No. 1, The Gardens Trust, (Summer 2005)

B. Johnson, *Botanic Gardens a living history*, Black Dog Publishing, 2007

Chris Johnstone, 'Maria Theresa: the Empress who left a mixed impression on the Czech Lands', Radio Praha, 6 May 2017

Nigel R. Jones, *Architecture of England, Scotland and Wales*, Greenwood Publishing Group, 2005

Robert A. Kann, *A History of the Habsburg Empire, 1526–1918*, University of California Press, 1980

Andrea Kastens, *Schloss Schönbrunn, Wien*, Westermann, 1983

W. Keane, *The Beauties of Middlesex*, 1850

Christina Keith, *The Romance of Barro Gill Castle: The Queen Mother's New Home: Barrogill Castle is Now Called the Castle of Mey*, Pillans and Wilson Limited, 1954

Hugh Kennedy, *Muslim Spain and Portugal: A Political History of Al-Andalus*, Routledge, 2014

Ebba Koch, *The Complete Taj Mahal and the Riverfront Gardens of Agra*, Thames & Hudson, 2006

Ebba Koch, *Mughal Architecture: An Outline of its History and Development (1526-1858)*, Neues Publishing Company, 1991

Letter from Professor Ebba Koch, dated 2001, University of Vienna, Austria

Marcus Kohler, Joachim Wolschke-Bulmahn (Eds), *Hanover and England – a garden and personal union*, AVM Edition, 2018

Hanae Komachi and Henning Queren, *Royal Gardens of Herrenhausen*, Hinstorff Verlag GmbH, 2014

Pierre Andre Lablaude, *The Gardens at Versailles*, Philip Wilson Publishers, 1995

P.I. Lapin, *Botanical Gardens of the USSR*, Kolos, Moscow, 1984

Ernest Philip Alphonse Law, *The History of Hampton Court Palace*, G. Bell and Sons, 1891

Charles Lecuyer, Marquis of Vandieres, *State of Tree Seedlings, Bowers, Arbutus, Dwarf Boxwood and Wood to Replenish the Gardens of Versailles and Trianon*, National Archive, Paris, 1761

Loelia, Duchess of Westminster, 'From the Archive: The Castle of Mey, the Queen Mother's Scottish retreat', *House and Garden*, 1959

G. London and H. Wise, *The Retir'd Gard'ner*, London, 1706

J.C. Loudon, *An Encyclopaedia of Gardening*, Longman, 1824

Morris Low, *Japan on Display*, Routledge/Asian Studies Association of Australia ASAA East Asian Series, 2012

Therese O'Malley and Joachim Wolschke-Bulmahn (Eds), *John Evelyn's 'Elysium Britannicum' and European Gardening*,

Dumbarton Oaks, 1998

Amina-Aicha Malek (Ed.), *Sourcebook for Garden Archaeology*, Peter Lang AG, 2013

Nicole Martinelli, 'A Pleasure Palace Rises Again', *The New York Times*, 16 December 2007

Maria Master, *Restoration of 18th Century Baroque Parterres in Parks of Peterhof and Strelna*, Thesis

Non Morris, 'Inside the 17th century Versailles vegetable garden', *The Telegraph*, 11 February 2016

Noel Nouet, M. Mills and J. Mills, *Shoguns City: History of Toyko*, Routledge, 1995

Magnus Olausson, 'Lust garden and general plan', In Görel Alm and Rebecka Millhage, *Drottningholm Palace* (Band I), Byggförlaget, Stockholm, 2004

Guillaume Picon, *A Day at Château de Fontainebleau*, Flammarion, 2016

Pliny the Elder, John Bostock, Henry T. Riley (Eds), *The Natural History of Pliny*, Facsimile Publisher, 2015

Progeo La Venaria Reale 1997–2013, I finanziamen per il restauro, Ministero dello Svilluppo Economico, Regione Piemonte, European Fund

Dries Raeymaekers, *One Foot in the Palace: The Habsburg Court of Brussels and the Politics of Access in the Reign of Albert and Isabella, 1598–1621*, Leuven University Press, 2013

Christine Rehberg-Crede, *Theodor Klett: einer der vorzüglichsten Gärtner*, Stadtwirtschaftliche Dienstleistungen Schwerin, 2010

Rekonstruktion, Interpretation. Garten zum Herrenhaus in Grafenort, 1997

Trudy Ring, Noelle Watson, Paul Schellinger (Ed.), *International Dictionary of Historic Places*, Vol. 2, Northern Europe, Routledge, 1995

D. Fairchild Ruggles, *Gardens, Landscape & Vision in the Palaces of Islamic Spain*, The Pennsylvania State University Press, 2000

Rundgang durch das Residenzensemble Schwerin Auf dem Weg zum Weltkulturerbe, Landtag Mecklenburg Vorpommern, produktionsburo TINUS

Robert M. Salkin, *International Dictionary of Historic Places*, Volume 2, Northern Europe, Routledge, 1995

Geoffrey Sanders and David Verey, *Royal Homes in Gloucestershire*, Humanities Press, 1981 International

Vanessa B. Sellers, 'Gardens of Western Europe, 1600-1800', in *Heilbrunn Timeline of Art History*, The Metropolitan Museum of Art

William Shawcross, *Queen Elizabeth the Queen Mother: The Official Biography*, Macmillan, 2009

A.N. Shikov et al, 'Medicinal Plants of the Russian Pharmacopoeia; their history and applications', *Journal of Ethnopharmacology*, Vol. 154, Issue 3, 2014

Dmitry Shvidkovsky, *Russian Architecture and the West*, Yale University Press, 2007

Brendan Simms and Torsten Riotte (eds), *The Hanoverian dimension in British history, 1714–1837*, Cambridge University Press, 2007

Robert Sinclair, *The Sinclairs of Scotland*, AuthorHouse, p. 130, 2013

Didier Stricker, Alain Pagani, Michael Zoellner, 'In-situ visualisation for cultural heritage sites using novel augmented reality technologies', *Virtual Archaeological Review*, Vol. 1, No. 2, May 2010

Roy Strong, *Royal Gardens*, BBC Books/Conran Octopus, 1992

A. Stüler, E. Prosch, H. Willebrand, *The Castle of Schwerin* (Stadtarchiv Schwerin), Berlin, 1869.

John Summerson, *Architecture of the Eighteenth Century* (World of Art), Thames and Hudson Ltd, 1986

1338 Survey of Hampton, The Twickenham Museum

Taj Mahal, Agra – Site Management Plan, Annabel Lopez, Taj Mahal Conservation Collaborative, March, 2003

Elizabeth T. Talbot, *Empress of Russia*, Littlehampton Book Services, 1970

Yasuhisa Tashiro, *Hirohito and golf, A key to the Understanding of the Showa era*, Shufunotom-devas, 2012

Christopher Thacker, *The Genius Gardening: The History of Tardens in England and Ireland*, Weidenfeld and Nicolson, 1994

'The Queen and Her Castle', *The Scotsman*, 16 September 2009

The Trees of Highgrove, *Country Life*, 22 January 2009

Third report and inventory of monuments and constructions in the county of Caithness. London. Pages: 9–11, No. 31 plan RCAHMS Shelf Number: A.1.1.INV(3)

Robin L. Thomas, *From the Library to the Printing Press: Luigi Vanvitelli's Life with Books*, Pennsylvania State University

S. Thurley (ed.), *The King's Privy Garden at Hampton Court Palace 1689–1995*, 1998

Giles Tillotson, *Taj Mahal*, Harvard University Press, 2008

Tom Turner, *English Garden Design, Antique Collector's Club*, 1986

Tom Turner, *Garden History Reference Encyclopedia*, PDF Edition, 2014

Phillip John Usher, *Epic Arts in Renaissance France*, Oxford University Press, 2014

M. Volpianoa, U. Zich, Scientific Monitoring and Documentation of the Venaria Reale Restoration Sites, CIPA 2005 XX International Symposium, 26 September–01 October, 2005, Torino, Italy

Berthold Volz, *Grossherzog Friedrich Franz II Von Mecklenburg-Schwerin: Ein Duetsches Forstenleben*, Wentworth Press, 2019

James Voorheis, 'Fontainebleau', in *Heilbrunn Timeline of Art History*, New York, The Metropolitan Museum of Art, 2000

Christine Waage Rasmussen, *400 Year History of Royal Danish Gardens*, Agency for Culture and Palaces, 2018

Christine Waage Rasmussen, Seminar – 'Restoring Fredensborg Castle Garden', Norway, October, 2018

Christine Waage Rasmussen, 'Common Lime in Historical Plantings: New Knowledge Through DNA Markers Revealed', in Restoration Project in Royal Danish Gardens, ICOMOS/IFLA

Garden Heritage Conference, 21–23 September 2017, Prague, Agency for Culture and Palaces

Kolbjörn Waern, A Short History of Drottningholm's Parks and Gardens, in the English Park near the Chinese Pavilion, conversation

The Prince of Wales and Bunny Guinness, *Highgrove: A Garden Celebrated*, Orion, 2014

Prince of Wales Charles, Charles Clover and Andrew Lawson, *Highgrove: Portrait of an Estate*, Orion, 1993

HRH Charles the Prince of Wales and Candida Lycett Green, *The Garden at Highgrove*, St Martin's Press, 2001

Johann Christoph Wendland, *Hortus Herrenhusanus, seu, Plantae rariores quae in Horto Regio Herrenhusano prope Hannoveram colunturi, Hannoverae, 1798–1801*

Tony Whitten, *Balinese Gardens*, Periplus Editions, 2006

Richard Wilford, *The Great Broad Walk Borders at the Royal Botanic Gardens, Kew*, Kew Publishing, 2016

Peter H. Wilson, *The Holy Roman Empire: A Thousand Years of Europe's History*, Penguin, 2017

Anne Winkel-Kirch (Ed.), Translated by Mic Hale, *The Royal Gardens of Herrenhausen: The Glory of the Garden Art*, Landeshauptstadt Hanover, 2010

Henri Zerner, *Renaissance Art in France: The Invention of Classicism*, Flammarios, 2003

Websites

www.archaeology.co.uk

www.british-history.ac.uk

The Castle of Mey: portal.historicenvironment.scot/designation/GDL00096

Drottningholm Palace: whc.unesco.org/en/list/559

Frederiksborg Palace: dnm.dk/en/frederiksborg-castle/

Highgrove: Google Arts and Culture – The Art of Maintaining the Royal Gardens of Highgrove: head gardener Debs Goodenough discusses her green-fingered work with HRH The Prince of Wales

www.kungahuset.se/

Leading States of the World, Tirta Gangga: www.leadingestates.com

Royal Botanic Gardens, Kew: whc.unesco.org/en/list/1084

Taj Mahal: www.wmf.org/project/mughal-gardens-agra

Abu I-Walid Isma'il, King 126
Adelcrantz, Carl Frederik 171
Adolf Frederick, King 171
Aiton, William 38
Akbar, Emperor 211
Alexandrine, Grand Duchess 72, 79
Alfieri, Benedetto 118
Alhambra 122–31
Asbeck, J. B. Baron van 160
Attenborough, Sir David 41
Augusta, Princess 38, 41

Babelon, Jean-Pierre 101
Babur, Emperor 215
Banks, Sir Joseph 38, 110
Bannerman, Julian and Isabel 31
Barca, Johann Georg 76
Beaumont, Guillaume 20
Bénard, Michel 118
Benson, William 65
Bentinck, Hans William 156, 159
Beyer, Johann Wilhelm 139
Biancourt, Martin 109
Blondel, Jacques-François 136
Bonaparte, Louis 160
Borisov, A. 201, 202
Bořivoj I 145
Braun, Matthias Bernard 146, 150
Braunstein, Johann Friedrich 198, 201, 206
Brewer, J. N. 27
Bridgeman, Charles 20, 37
Brown, Lancelot 'Capability' 19, 20, 37,
    38, 110, 205
Brunow, Ludwig 72, 75
Bruun & Möllers 76
Burn, William 47
Burton, Decimus 37, 38, 41
Buttress, Wolfgang 42

Canning, Viscount Charles John 47
Carl XVI Gustaf, King 172
Casares, Manuel 129
Castle of Mey 44–53
Catherine the Great 205
Catherine Jagiellon, Queen 167
Chambers, Sir William 37, 38, 171
Charbonnier, Martin 57
Charles, Prince of Wales 27–8, 31–2, 51, 149
Charles II 15, 19, 20
Charles IV 145

Charles V 125
Charles VI 135, 136
Charles VII 105–6
Charles XI 167
Charles Emmanuel II, Duke 117, 118, 121
Chaufourier, Jean 101
Christian IV 178, 187, 188
Christian V 177
Christian VI 178, 191
Colbert, Jean-Baptiste 94
Collecini, Francesco 109
Curzon, Lord 215

da Vignola, Giacomo Barozzi 84
della Stella, Paolo 146
Demmler, Georg Adolf 71, 75, 76
Denecourt, Claude-François F. 88
Desmarets, Daniel 156
di Castellamonte, Amedeo 117, 121
di Jacopo, Giovanni Battista 84
Diana, Princess 41
Dienzenhofer, Kilian Ignaz 146
Djelantik, Ir. Anak Agung Gede Dharma
    Widoere 223
Djelantik, Anak Agung Made 223
Djelantik, I Gusti Bagus 219, 223
Dokan, Ota 227, 232
Drottningholm Palace 164–73, 188
du Cerceau, Jean Androuet 87
Dufour, Alexandre 160

Ehrhart, Friedrich 65
Eleonora of Gonzaga 135
Elizabeth, Empress 205
Elizabeth, Queen Mother ...7, 47, 48, 51, 52
Elizabeth II, Queen 31
Emmanuel-Philibert, Duke of Savoy ...117
Enshu, Kobori 227, 228, 231, 232
Ernest Augustus, Duke 57, 65

Falconer, Peter 27
Fairchild Ruggles, D. 126
Ferdinand I 146, 149
Ferdinand II 125, 135
Ferdinand V 146
Fischer von Erlach, Johann Bernhard 135–6
Foerster, Karl 66
Fontainebleau Palace 80–9
Fortrey, Samuel 37
Fouquet, Nicholas 94, 101

Francini, Tommaso and Alessandro 87
Francis I 83, 84, 87, 88
Franz Joseph I 140
Franz Stephan I 136, 139
Fredensborg Palace 174–83
Frederick, Prince of Wales 38
Frederik II 187, 192
Frederik IV 177, 181, 188, 191, 192
Frederik V 178, 181, 182, 191
Frederick VII 188
Frederick Francis II 71, 72, 75
Frederik Hendrik, Prince 156
Frederiksborg Palace 168, 177, 184–93
Fucini, Carlo 121

Gadamer, Hans-Georg 182
Garove, Michelangelo 117, 118, 121
George I 16, 19, 58, 61, 65
George II 37, 58
George III 20, 37, 38, 41
George V 58, 66
George VI 48
Giggus, Michael 61
Goodenough, Debs 32
Graefer, John Andrew 106, 110, 113
Gurzhy, Alexey 198
Gussone, Giovanni 110
Gustaf V 172
Gustav III 168, 171

Hager, Gido 61
Hampton Court Palace 12–23, 178
Hansen, Heinrich 188
Haqq, Abdul 212
Hardouin-Mansart, Jules 16, 94, 97
Harnigflet, Leonardt van 201, 202
Harris, Walter 163
Hartley, James 38
Hatton, Charles 16
Haubo, Dan 172
Havlová, Olga 149
Heathcote, F. G. 47–8
Hedwig Eleonora, Queen 167, 168, 188
Henry IV 84, 87, 88
Henry VIII 15, 19, 20
Hentz, van Den 219
Herrenhausen 19, 54–67
Het Loo Palace 16, 23, 57, 58, 61, 152–63, 191
Hetzendorf von Hohenberg, Johann
    Ferdinand 139

Highgrove 24–33, 51
Hirohito, Emperor 231–2
Hirschfield, Christian Cay Lorenz 65
Hooghe, Romeyn de 156
Hooker, Sir William 37, 38
Hurtault, Maximilien-Joseph 88

Ibn al-Ahmar 125
Iemitsu, Tokugawa 227, 228
Ienari, Tokugawa 228
Ienobu, Tokugawa 228
Ieyasu, Tokugawa 227, 228
Imbert-Terry, Frederic Bouhier 48, 51
Isabella I, Queen of Castile 125

Jacobsen, J. C. 188
Jahan, Emperor Shah 211, 212, 215
James II 20
Jardin, Nicolas-Henri 178, 181
Jiřičná, Eva 149
John Albert I 71
John Frederick, Duke 65
Joseph I 135
Juvarra, Filippo 117, 118, 121

Kalim, Abu Talib 215
Kaňka, František Maxmilián 150
Keck, Anthony 27
Klett, Theodor 72, 75, 76, 79
Kontskaya, Regina 202
Krieger, Johan Cornelius .178, 188, 191, 192

la Fosse, Charles Louis Remy de 62
la Quintinie, Jean Baptiste de 98
Lablaude, Pierre-André 101
Lahauri, Ustad Ahmad 212
Laves, Georg Ludwig Friedrich 58
Le Blond, Jean-Baptiste Alexandre 198,
     201, 202
Le Breton, Gilles 83–4
Le Brun, Charles 94
Le Corbusier 117
Le Geay, Jean Laurent 72, 75
Le Nôtre, André 11, 19, 62, 167
     Fontainebleau Palace 87-8
     pupils of 20, 136, 198
     Versailles 94, 97, 98, 101, 106, 191
Le Vau, Louis 16, 87, 94
Leibniz, Gottfried Wilhelm 58
Lenné, Peter Joseph 72, 75, 76, 79

Leopold I 135, 146
Loelia, Duchess of Westminster 47
London, George 19
Lorenzani, Giovanni Andrea 105
Loto Ang 219
Louis IV 87
Louis IX 83
Louis XIII 94, 97
Louis XIV 11, 58, 125, 202
     Fontainebleau Palace 87, 88
     Versailles 93, 94, 97, 98, 101
Louis XV 87, 98
Louis XVI 98, 101
Louis Philippe I 98, 101
Louise Ulrika, Queen 171
Ludolph, Heinrich 66

Macmillan, Maurice 27
Margrethe II 182, 191
Maria Carolina, Queen 110
Maria Theresa 93, 136, 139, 146, 150
Marie Antoinette 7, 98, 101, 110
Marot, Daniel 16, 156, 159
Mary II, Queen 15, 16, 19, 23, 125, 155, 156, 159
Masson, Francis 42
Masson, Hilaire 93
Matthias, Emperor 135, 149
Maximilian II 135
Mazarin, Cardinal 93
Meader, James 205
Meiji, Emperor 228
Meuer, Karl H. 58
Michetti, Nicola 201, 202
Mir Abd Al-Karim 212
Mollet, André 11, 20
Mollet, Claude 93
Moreno, Francisco Prieto 126
Muhammad III 129
Mumtaz Mahal 211

Napoleon I 83, 88, 125
Napoleon III 88, 98, 101
Navrátil, Josef 149
Nesfield, William Andrews 37, 41
Nugent, Thomas 75

Order of the Knights Hospitaller of St
     John of Jerusalem 15

Paul, John Paul 27

Paul Frederick 72, 79
Permoser, Balthasar 72
Perrault, Charles 98
Perronet, Henri 61
Peter I 98, 197, 198, 201, 202, 205, 206
Peter III 205
Peterhof Palace 65, 194–207
Petersen, Jens 62
Philip, Prince 7, 31
Piloot, Ghert Evert 71
Piper, Frederik Magnus 171
Plečnik, Jože 149
Plukenet, Dr Leonard 16
Prague Castle 142–51, 168
Přemysl Otakar II, King 150
Primaticcio, Francesco 84

Quarenghi, Giacomo 205

Rasmussen, Christine Waage 182
Rastrelli, Bartolomeo Carlo ..198, 201, 205
Rastrelli, Francesco Bartolomeo .198, 202
Rehberg-Credé, Christine 75
Rockefeller, John D. 101
Rothschild, Dame Miriam 28
Royal Botanic Gardens, Kew 34–43, 66
Royal Palace of Caserta 102–13, 117
Rudolf II 146

Saint Phalle, Niki de 61
Salisbury, Lady 28
Salomone, Gaetano 109, 110
Schaumburg, Christian 66
Schinkel, Karl Friedrich 71
Schonbrunn 132–41
Schonck, Philip William 160
Schultz, Stephan 75
Schwerin Castle 68–79
Serlio, Sebastiano 84
Shawcross, William 46
Showa, Emperor 231
Silvia, Queen 172
Sinclair, Alexander Campbell 47
Sinclair, Frederick Granville 48
Sinclair, George 47
Sinclair, Malcolm 188
Sophie, Electress 57-8, 61, 65, 66
Staden, Christiaan Pieter van 160, 163
Stalin, Joseph 205–6
Strong, Sir Roy 11

Stüler, Friedrich August 71
Switzer, Stephen 16

Taj Mahal 208–15
Talman, William 1...............5, 16
Tatarovich, Vladimir 2...............01
Terracciano, Nicola 110, 113
Tessin, Nicodemus the Elder 167–8
Thacker, Christopher 41
Tirta Gangga 216–23
Tokyo Imperial Palace 224–33
Trehet, Jean 1...............36
Trezzini, Domenico 197
Turner, Richard 38, 41
Tuvolkov, Vassily 202

Vanbrugh, Sir John 19
Vanvitelli (Caspar Van Wittel) 105
Vanvitelli, Carlo 109, 110
Vanvitelli, Luigi 105, 106, 109
La Venaria Reale 114–21
Versailles 16, 57, 58, 61, 83, 90–101, 105, 118, 178, 197, 201
Victor Amadeus II 117
Victor Emmanuel II 121
Victoria, Queen 20, 38, 47, 58, 101
Vries, Adriaen de 149, 168, 188

Wallace, Alfred Russell 223
Welf family 57, 65
Wendland, Hermann 66
Wendland, Johann Christoph 66
Wenzel Anton, Prince 136
Wiedewelt, Johannes 181
Wildford, Richard 42
Wilhelmina, Queen 155, 160
William III, King ..15, 16, 19, 20, 23, 125, 155, 156, 159, 160
William V 160
Wilson, Gordon 41, 66
Wise, Henry 19, 20
Wohlmut, Bonifac 146
Wolsey, Cardinal Thomas 15
Wren, Sir Christopher 15, 16, 19, 23

Yatman, William 27
Yoshinobu, Tokugawa 228
Yusuf I, Sultan of Granada 125

Zinner, Johann Anton 136

PICTURE CREDITS

1 Annie Green-Armytage/GAP Photos; 2–3 Robert Harding/Alamy Stock Photo; 5 NoSystem images/iStock; 8 Bridgeman Images; 9 Vera Lebedinskaya/Shutterstock; 10 Marcus Hawkins/Digital Camera Magazine/Future via Getty Images; 12–13, 14 Andy Butler/Historic Royal Palaces; 17a Robert Wyatt/Alamy Stock Photo; 17b Vladislav Zolotov/iStock; 18a Vladislav Zolotov/iStock; 18b Ian Bottle/Alamy Stock Photo; 20 DBPITT/iStock; 21, 22 Andy Butler/Historic Royal Palaces; 23 Chris Harris/Alamy Stock Photo; 24–5, 27 Robert Smith/GAP Photos; 26 Jason Ingram/GAP Photos; 29a Highgrove/Rebecca Bernstein/GAP Photos; 29b Highgrove/GAP Photos. Hollyrood House designed by William Bertram; 30a Highgrove/A. Butler/GAP Photos. Designed by HRH and Mike Miller; 30b Highgrove/Robert Smith/GAP Photos; 32, 33 Highgrove/GAP Photos; 40 Charles Bowman/Alamy Stock Photo; Highgrove photography courtesy Clarence House; 44–5 font83/iStock; 46, 49a & b photo Shirley Farquhar/Castle of Mey; 50a Gabi Secareanu/Shutterstock; 50b, 53 Kenny Lam/VisitScotland; 54–5 velislava-germany/Alamy Stock Photo; 60b Patrice von Collani/Westend61/Alamy Stock Photo; 70 Daniel Rudolf/Alamy Stock Photo; 80–81 Vladislav Zolotov/iStock; 82 Patrick Escudero/hemis/Alamy Stock Photo; 85a Serega Yu/Alamy Stock Photo; 85b baccus7/Pixabay; 86a Beatrice Bibal/Gamma-Rapho via Getty Images; 86b Keith Evans/Flickr; 89 Michael Warwick/Shutterstock; 90–91Angus McComiskey/Alamy Stock Photo; 92 Berthold Steinhilber/LAIF/Camera Press; 95a Philippe Widlling/Design Pics; 95b Peter Stein/Shutterstock; 96a psilosimon/Alamy Stock Photo; 96b Alain Le Toquin/Biosphotos/Garden World Images; 98 Kevin O'Hara/agefotostock/Alamy Stock Photo; 99 Giulia Hetherington; 100 Frederic Reglain/Alamy Stock Photo; 102–3 Ake E:son Lindman; 104 Matyas Rehak/Shutterstock; 107a Salvatore Laporta/Kontrolab/LightRocket via Getty Images; 107b Redmason/Shutterstock; 108a Vittorio Sciosia/Reda & Co srl/Alamy Stock Photo; 108b Ake E:son Lindman; 110 Marbenzu/Dreamstime.com; 111 Sklifas Steven/Alamy Stock Photo; 112 Ake E:son Lindman; 113 De Agostini/Universal Images Group/Alamy Stock Photo; 114–5 Realy Easy Star/Toni Spagone/Alamy Stock Photo; 116 Laura Portinaro/Reda &Co/Cubo Images; 119a Stefano Cavoretto/Alamy Stock Photo; 119b Dmytro Surkov/Alamy Stock Photo; 120a antinoris/iStock; 120b Flavio Vallenari/iStock; 122–3 Paul Williams/Alamy Stock Photo; 124 Luis Dafos/Alamy Stock Photo; 127a kossarev56/Shutterstock; 127b Kiev.Victor/Shutterstock; 128a Insung Choi/123RF; 128b Tomasz Czajkowski/Alamy Stock Photo; 130 Bertrand Gardel/Hemis/Alamy Stock Photo; 131 Mark Bolton/GAP Photos; 132–3 Imre Joo/500px/Getty Images; 134 Have Camera Will Travel Europe/Alamy Stock Photo; 137a Jeremy Graham/dbimages/Alamy Stock Photo; 137b H1N1/Shutterstock; 138a Arxichtu4ki/Dreamstime.com; 138b Maria Wachala/Zoonar/Alamy Stock Photo; 140 Elena Schweitzer/Shutterstock; 141 Karl Allen Lugmayer/Shutterstock; 142–3 arazu/Shutterstock; 144 J. Pie/Alamy Stock Photo; 147a Radomir Rezny/Alamy Stock Photo; 147b Madzia71/iStock; 148a PleskyRoman/iStock; 148b Slawek Staszczuk/Alamy Stock Photo; 151a Ryhor Bruyeu/iStock; 151b Ershov Maks/iStock; 152–3 Paleis Het Loo, Apeldoorn, The Netherlands; 154 Paleis Het Loo. Photo Hans Clauzing; 157 Florian Monheim/Bildarchiv Monheim/Alamy Stock Photo; 158a Paleis Het Loo. Photo Erik Hermerg; 158b Frans Lemmens/Alamy Stock Photo; 161 National Archives, The Hague. Collection of Domestic Maps/Hingman, access 4.VTH, inventory number 1868; 162 Frans Lemmens/Alamy Stock Photo; 164–5, 166 Ake E:son Lindman; 169a The Royal Court, Sweden. Photo Alexis Daflos; 169b Carolina Larsson/Alamy Stock Photo; 170a The Royal Court, Sweden. Photo Raphael Stecksén; 170b Kalin Eftimov/Shutterstock; 173 Ake E:son Lindman; 174–5, 179a Thomas Rahbek/SLKS; 176 Dennis Jacobsen/Shutterstock; 179b BirgerNiss/iStock; 180a Andreas Altenburger/Alamy Stock Photo; 180b André Serensen/Getty Images; 183 wd/iStock; 184–5 Ramon Coloma Mozos/Getty Images; 186 DeadDuck/iStock; 189a Dreamstime.com Stefano Ember; 189b Thomas Rahbek/SLKS; 190a DeSid/iStock; 190b LordRunar/iStock; 192 from Bakkehus og Solbjerg, Volume 1,Troels-Lund Gyldendal, published by Nordisk forlag, 1921; 193 Giovanni Simeone/4Corners Images; 194–5 Artmim/Dreamstime.com; 196 Elena Lysenkova/Shutterstock; 199a katsyka/iStock; 199b Solo122/iStock; 200a Borisb17/iStock; 200b lvinst/iStock; 202 S. Tatiana/Shutterstock; 203 Perry Mastrovito/GAP Photos; 204 Joesboy/iStock; 207 WorldWideImages/iStock; 208–9 meinzahn/123RF; 210 Morganelgd/Shutterstock; 213a Victor Iniesta/ Shutterstock; 213b Pius Lee/123RF; 214 Arthur M. Sackler Gallery, Smithsonian Institution /Bridgeman Images; 216–7, 221a AlexeyPelikh/iStock; 218 Sytilin Pavel/Shutterstock; 221b Martin Moxter/ImageBroker/Alamy Stock Photo; 222a Constantin Stanciu/Dreamstime.com; 222b Alain Bachellier/Getty Images; 224–5 denkei/PIXTA; 226 yaophotograph/iStock; 229a Gwmb2013/Dreamstime.com; 229b Mark Edward Eite/Aflo Co/Alamy Stock; 230a E7551/PIXTA; 230b travelbild-Asia/Alamy Stock Photo; 233 RS Smith Photography/Shutterstock.
Endpapers: front, Urban Road/iStock; back, Karl Johaentges/Alamy Stock Photo

Additional photography on pages 6, 34–5, 36, 39a & b, 43, 56, 59a & b, 60a, 63, 64, 65, 67, 68–9, 73a & b, 74a & b, 76, 77, 78a & b, 79 by Sarah Cuttle for Kyle Books/Octopus Publishing
Maps by Robin Rout

ACKNOWLEDGEMENTS

The Customer Information Team and Media Relations Team, Royal Botanic Gardens Kew
The Royal Parks, London, UK
Royal Communications, London, UK
Royal Collection Trust, London, UK
The Crown Estate, Windsor, UK
English Heritage Press Office, UK
Library Team, Historic Royal Palaces, London, UK
Archive Department, British History Museum, London, UK
Household of the Prince of Wales and The Duchess of Cornwall, London, UK
Debs Goodenough, head gardener, Highgrove, UK
RMN (Réunion des Musées Nationaux), Chateau de Versailles, France
Marc Fernandes, Heymann, Renoult Associées, Paris, France
Schlosshof, Schonbrunn Palace, Austria
Steffen Ejstrup, Kulturministeriet, Copenhagen, Denmark
Christine Waage Rasmussen, Royal Landscape Architect, Center for Slotte og Haver, Agency for Culture and Palaces, Denmark
Seminar: Restoring Fredensborg Castle Garden: Garden History Forum and
School of Landscape Architecture, Norway, October, 2018
The Royal Court, Hofmarskallatet, Det Gule Palae, Copenhagen, Denmark
Paleis Hett Loo, and in particular special thanks to Renske Ek, Conservator, Het Loo Palace, for her insight, editorial comments,
and her chapter 'The Royal Garden. Identity, Power and Pleasure'. The Netherlands
Reggia di Caserta, with special thanks to Dott. Vincenzo Mazzarealla, Area Valorizzazione e Servizi Educativi, Caserta, Italy
Prague Castle Administration, with special thanks to Martin Herda in the archive department and Director Petr Vlk,
Prague, Czech Republic
The Czech Academy of Sciences, Prague, Czech Republic
Jaromír Beneš, University of South Bohemia in České Budějovice, Prague, Czech Republic
Landeshauptstadt Hannover, Fachbereich Herrenhäuser Gärten, and in particular special thanks to Melanie Kuiper-Lehner, Germany
Claudia Schönfeld, Welterbemanagerin der Landeshauptstadt Schwerin, Germany
Jochen Sandner and Dr Josef Wolf, Geschäftsführer, Das Staatliche Museum Schwerin, Germany
The Alhambra Pedagogical and Cultural Association, Granada, Spain
Diputacion de Granada, Spain
General Department, The Peterhof State Museum-Reserve, Russia
Department of Tourism, Government of Uttar Pradesh, Agra, India
Personal discussions with Ebba Koch on Taj Mahal, when Managing Editor at Thames & Hudson
Archaeological Survey of India, Agra, India
Ministry of Tourism, Government of India
Archive Department, The Smithsonian Institution and Museums
Department of Tourism, Taman Tirtagangga, Bali, Indonesia
Biological Laboratory, Imperial Household, Tokyo, Japan

With special thanks to my partner and confidant, Jasen Cavalli, and the initial research support from Georgina Edwards.